PELICAN BOOKS

GUIDE TO THE BRITISH
ECONOMY

Peter Donaldson was born in Manchester in 1934 but left shortly afterwards for Kent, where he went to Gillingham Grammar School and won an open scholarship to Balliol. He read politics, philosophy and economics, and graduated from Oxford in 1956. He then taught very briefly in a secondary modern school and for two years in a college of technology before taking up a university appointment at Leeds. He was a lecturer in the department of economics at Leicester University 1959–62, when he also did a good deal of work for the Leicester and Nottingham University adult education departments and for the Workers' Educational Association.

At the end of 1962, he was one of the first British university teachers to be seconded to key positions in underdeveloped countries under the scheme for Commonwealth Educational Cooperation. He was appointed, for two years, as Visiting Reader in Economics at the Osmania University, Hyderabad, and subsequently extended his stay in India to four years.

In 1967 he returned to England to become Tutor in Economics at Ruskin College, Oxford.

He is married and has three children.

GUIDE TO THE
BRITISH ECONOMY

*

PETER DONALDSON

PENGUIN BOOKS

Penguin Books Ltd, Harmondsworth, Middlesex, England
Penguin Books Inc., 7110 Ambassador Road, Baltimore, Maryland 21207, U.S.A.
Penguin Books Australia Ltd, Ringwood, Victoria, Australia

—

First published 1965
Reprinted 1966
Reprinted with revisions 1967
Reprinted 1969, 1970

—

Copyright © Peter Donaldson, 1965, 1967

—

Made and printed in Great Britain
by Richard Clay (The Chaucer Press) Ltd,
Bungay, Suffolk
Set in Monotype Times

CONTENTS

INTRODUCTION

ECONOMIC affairs have never before had quite the significance which is attached to them today. This is because, although economists have always been concerned with the same basic question of how to make the best use of scarce resources, the sort of answer which they have given has radically changed over the past few decades. *Laissez-faire* thinking of the nineteenth century was optimistically based on the idea that for the nation to prosper and for resources to be used to maximum advantage, all that was required was for individuals to resolutely pursue their own ends. The price mechanism, Adam Smith's 'invisible hand', would then ensure that devotion to private gain would automatically maximize the welfare of the community as a whole. Economics in such circumstances had a limited appeal. The economic mechanism could be described and explained, but then all that remained to be done was to stand back and admire its working. Any tampering would only reduce the benefits which it was geared to produce.

Belief in the necessary correspondence of private and social gain has now been shattered. The thirties, in particular, showed that the invisible hand was not always a benevolent guide, but could beckon the economy into the misery and waste of mass unemployment, stagnation, and restrictionism. A further dimension was added to the economic problem in that human wants could remain unsatisfied, not only because of the inadequacy of resources, but also because some of the means of production were lying idle. Operating freely, the price mechanism led to the paradox of poverty among plenty.

Economics today is more interesting than ever before, because we now realize that the economy is neither an automatic mechanism which can safely be left to chug smoothly along its own optimal path nor governed by blind and unpredictable forces over which we can have no control. Its proper behaviour can only be secured by deliberate manipulation, and developments in economic theory have indicated some of the basic techniques necessary for this purpose. That the economic system requires, and is to some extent amenable to, rational ordering makes it increasingly important that non-economists should be aware of what is implied in economic issues.

This book is intended for the general reader who would like to have some grasp of what economics is about and what makes the economy tick – but who may find the textbook approach a little unpalatably abstract. Economic ideas are, therefore, presented here within the real context of the British economy. The aim is both to give an impression of the working of the different elements in the economy, and to illustrate the extent to which economic analysis can be helpful in solving the problems which face policy-makers.

The fact that the book begins with a chapter on the Stock Exchange and that the whole of the first Part is devoted to matters of finance should not, of course, be taken to imply that the economy revolves around Throgmorton and Lombard Streets. It is just that the stock market is of sufficiently popular interest to be a good starting-point for illustrating certain important trends in the economy, and that non-economists are often particularly perplexed by financial issues (as a consequence of which they tend to exaggerate the importance of monetary factors in the economic system). In both Part II, which deals with the rather more earthy affairs of industry and trade, and Part III, which is concerned with general economic policies, the role of the State in the working of an advanced economy is something which crops up time after time. But although we shall have a good deal to say about the ways in which the government tries to manage the economy, this book is certainly not intended as another of those 'state-of-the-nation' assessments which are currently so much in vogue. All that I have tried to do is to indicate the nature of the issues involved in economic policy decisions, the extent to which economics can be useful in framing policies – and, just as important, the *limitations* of economic analysis.

PART I
FINANCE

CHAPTER 1

THE STOCK EXCHANGE

HE was born in 1900 and at the age of nineteen inherited £3,000 from an aunt of whose existence he had been only dimly aware. After a good deal of thought he divided the legacy into three equal parts. £1,000 he kept in the form of pound notes. Another £1,000 he spent on government bonds (2½% Consols., to be precise). The remaining £1,000 he invested in the ordinary shares of thirty different companies. He decided to reinvest all the income derived from these investments until, at the age of sixty-five, he would retire and enjoy the proceeds of his thrift. This he did at the end of 1965. His £1,000 cash was still £1,000 cash, but in terms of what could be bought with it, its value had fallen by over two-thirds. On the other hand, he was pleased to find that his government bonds were now worth £4,500. But what really staggered him was the fact that his portfolio of ordinary shares now had a market value of £90,000!

Tales such as this have ensured a perennial interest in stock-market activity since the days of the South Sea Bubble. The more equal distribution of wealth and sustained prosperity of the last few decades have greatly widened the appeal of stock-exchange investment, and the rapid growth of unit trusts designed primarily to attract small investors, and of investment clubs pooling savings into sums of investible size, means that dabbling on the stock exchange is no longer confined to a thin crust of heirs and financiers. Although 'playing the market' may perhaps not yet rival the football pools or Bingo as a national sport, it is sufficiently popular for the *Daily Mirror* to run a financial column.

What exactly is the attraction of stocks and shares (together known as 'securities')? Their particular appeal can be seen if we compare them with the other ways in which wealth can be held – material possessions, money, and other types of claim.

Material Possessions

Wealth held in the form of real physical assets generally yields a return or income. If such assets are capital goods – factories and machines – they can be worked to produce a flow of output throughout their life. Similarly, consumer durable goods, things like houses, motor-cars, and television sets, yield satisfaction over a period of time in the form of shelter, journeys, and viewing, which may be thought of as a return on capital comparable to the flow of goods derived from investment in factories and machines.

However, there is a drawback in that the decision to hold wealth in the form of material possessions may not easily be reversible. If it becomes necessary to sell such assets, the problem arises of finding a buyer. For some goods, motor-cars and houses for example, there are highly organized second-hand markets for bringing sellers into contact with buyers. But meeting someone who wants to buy a piece of specialized machinery, or a set of left-handed golf clubs, or a collection of nineteenth-century toasting forks, may present very considerable difficulties.

Finding a buyer is, anyway, only half the problem. Pretty well anything can be sold – at a price. The difficulty is to secure a price which avoids capital loss. Organized markets may serve to bring sellers and buyers together, but the price which prevails depends on *how many* sellers confront *how many* buyers, on the forces of supply and demand in the market at any given time. Thus, satisfaction in my new motor-car is tempered by the knowledge that if I have to resell it tomorrow, its price will almost certainly have fallen. The dealer who exaggerates its unique virtues when selling it to me today will have remembered its defects when buying it back tomorrow.

Money

Holding wealth in the form of money avoids this difficulty of reversing decisions, for the simple reason that to have money implies that no such decisions have been made. Money gives purchasing power over the whole range of goods and services coming onto the market, and the final choice as to which will be bought remains open. This lack of commitment is the great advantage of holding wealth in the form of money. Material possessions also give the owner some purchasing power over other goods, but only indirectly. They must first be sold for cash, and the attendant difficulties add up to what may be called the 'illiquidity' of the asset concerned. Money, on the other hand, is the most liquid form of holding wealth; to have money is to hold wealth in a form which gives *immediate* command over resources.

But, of course, money is useless in itself. It is only useful to buy things with, and the more money we hold and the longer we hold it, the more we are denying ourselves the satisfaction to be derived from spending it. And secondly, although ideally the value of money would remain stable, in practice it behaves less satisfactorily, with changes in its value usually being in the downward direction.

Claims

To put money into a time deposit at a bank is to give up cash in exchange for an IOU from the bank, a promise that it will repay on seven days' notice; similarly with a deposit with a building society or finance house. These are examples of the great variety of claims available in a developed economy, and among them are stock-exchange securities.

Stocks and shares are an attractive half-way house between material possessions and money. Like material possessions, they earn the owner a return in the form of interest and dividends but, at the same time, they are a great deal more liquid than most physical assets. If I buy shares in I.C.I., I am not committed to the fortunes of that firm for ever; nor do my shares represent a title of ownership to some specific part of I.C.I.'s capital, a particular machine or part of a machine which would have to be sold if I wish to withdraw my investment. If investment in an enterprise implied this degree of involvement, relatively few people would be interested in the venture. The great advantage of securities is that they are transferable, and the stock exchange exists as a highly organized market in which such transactions may take place. Investors buying I.C.I. shares do so in the knowledge that they can dispose of them without difficulty – although not necessarily at a satisfactory price.

BUYING STOCKS AND SHARES

Securities may be bought in either the London Stock Exchange or one of the twenty-two provincial exchanges. These are highly exclusive market-places. The general public is now admitted to view the proceedings from a gallery, but is barred from entry to the floor of the House where the right to conduct business is confined to the 3,500 members of the stock exchange and their authorized clerks. Until recently, there were no minimum educational qualifications or professional examinations to be passed. But new members have to purchase a nomination (at present £880) from an existing member, find a proposer and seconder who are already members, and pay 1,000 guineas entrance fee plus an annual subscription of 215 guineas. Members of the stock exchange are of two types, brokers and jobbers, and someone who wishes to make an investment must hire a broker to do his business for him.

A stockbroker makes his living by buying and selling securities for his clients and charging them a commission for his service (his knowledge of the market also puts him in a highly favourable position to make money on his own account as well). He does not hold a supply of shares in readiness to meet his customers' requirements; to obtain shares, or to dispose of them, he goes to the stock exchange and deals with a jobber who performs a wholesaling function in the system.

Jobbers, just over 600 individual members grouped into 57 firms (in 1965), differ from brokers in that they neither deal with the general public directly nor earn a commission from their activities. Their living is derived from the 'jobber's turn' – the selling of shares at a higher price than they paid for them. Jobbers congregate on the floor of the House, each with his price-board like a bookmaker, ready to make a quotation to any broker who approaches. The quotation is always in the form of two prices, e.g. 28s. 30s., and this tells the broker, who will not have revealed whether he wants to buy or sell, that the jobber is willing to buy at 28s. and sell at 30s. The amount of the jobber's turn, the difference between buying and selling prices, depends largely on the amount of activity there is in that class of security. The more that is being bought and sold, the smaller the turn tends to be.

On all purchases of stock-exchange securities (with the exception of its own bonds and new issues) the government imposes a stamp duty which is normally about 1% of the value of the securities but may be nearer 2% for small bargains. When the cost of the broker's commission (which may weigh more heavily on smaller transactions) and the jobber's turn are also taken into account, it is clear that the buyer of shares has to wait until they have risen in price by some 4–5% before he can even recoup his original outlay.

Most dealings on the stock exchange are 'for the Account'. The Account is a period of two working weeks, beginning on a Monday and ending on the Friday of the following week (except at Bank Holidays when it extends to three weeks). The current Account is indicated at the head of a financial column in the Press by three dates, e.g.

25 April   6 May   17 May

This means that the Account opened on 25 April, closes on 6 May and that Settlement Day is 17 May. Settlement Day, as the name implies, is the date by which shares bought during the period of the Account have to be paid for. It always falls on the Tuesday week following the end of the Account, so that an investor buying on the first day of a new Account has three full weeks' credit before payment is due, and even more over Bank Holiday periods.

The generous credit arises because the transfer of a security from one holder to another may be highly complicated. Within a single Account, shares may change hands on a number of occasions, and all the intermediate transactions have to be eliminated before the original seller can be linked up with the ultimate buyer. For the short-term speculator the Account arrangements are invaluable. The price of a share may change considerably during a fortnight, and it may be possible to buy and resell shares within an Account without any capital outlay at all, a process made more attractive by the fact that such transactions do not bear stamp duty. (It is possible, too, for payment to be deferred until the *following* Settlement Day by making a 'contango' arrangement.) Account facilities do not operate for one important class of security – government stock. For these, cash on the nail is the rule, payment being due on the day following the transaction.

TYPES OF SECURITY

'Security' is a general label for the great variety of stocks and shares which are available. Shares represent a title to ownership in a firm. Stocks, on the other hand, are loans, to government or companies, which earn the lender a fixed-interest return.

Gilt-Edged

The most important stocks are found in the gilt-edged market of which the issues of the British government comprise the chief element. These head any list of stock-exchange securities under the title *British Funds*. Among such stocks may be found:

Exchequer	5%	76–78
Funding	5¼%	78–80
Transport	4%	72–77
Treasury	5%	86–89
Treasury	6½%	1976
War Loan	3½%	1952
Consols.	2½%	

The names of the stocks do not mean a great deal. Some, *War Loan* for example, reflect the conditions in which they were issued. *Transport* certainly implies that the loan was floated in connexion with a nationalized industry, but payment of interest on the stock is in no sense dependent on the railways making a profit. As with all other government issues, it is a call on the general exchequer and it is this absolute certainty that interest will be paid, based on the government's power to levy taxes, which makes such stocks 'gilt-edged'. *Treasury* generally indicates that the loan was originally for a long period, while *Exchequer* and *Funding* usually connote short (up to five years) and medium stock (five to ten years). *Consols.* is an abbreviation for 'Consolidated Annuities' and is a collection of smaller stocks dating from the mid eighteenth century.

Government stocks are issued in £100 units, and the figures 2½%, 5%, and so on, refer to the interest payable and are based on the nominal value of the stock. Thus, someone buying an Exchequer 5% stock will receive £5 per annum interest, and it is an important point to bear in mind that he will earn this sum of money whether he purchased the stock in the market for as little as £50, or for its nominal value of £100, or at a market price of £150.

Some of the stocks in the British Funds list have two dates attached, some one date, and others none at all. These dates indicate the period of the loan, and show when the stock will mature and the loan be redeemed or repaid. Most stocks are double-dated, e.g. 86–89, and this means that the government will repay the loan some time between 1 January 1986 and 31 December 1989. Exactly when is up to the government and not the lender. Treasury $6\frac{1}{2}\%$ 1976 has only one date attached, and this loan will be due for redemption, at the government's option, some time in 1976 or at any time after. Finally, there is undated stock like $2\frac{1}{2}\%$ Consols., with no definite repayment commitment. Although all government borrowings are in principle repayable, it is very unlikely in practice that the government will ever redeem its undated stock. War Loan 1952 began life as a single-dated stock, but in most lists the date is now omitted; it is a vast issue and it seems fairly certain that the government will never, in fact, exercise its option to repay the loan.

It may seem strange that there are people foolish enough to invest money in a loan which will never be repaid. But we have to remember that holders continue to receive interest of the stated amount; and secondly, that although the owners of such bonds can never force the government to repay them, or expect it to do so of its own accord, they *can* always dispose of them in the stock exchange, where they have a definite market value based on the stream of interest payments which they will yield. The extreme case of undated stock illustrates the point which we made earlier – that the stock exchange, by providing a highly organized market for securities, greatly increases the liquidity of such assets. Without a stock market, irredeemable stock would be a highly illiquid and unattractive way of holding wealth.

Company Securities

Private firms issue stocks similar to government bonds which are known as *debentures*. If I buy a debenture stock, I am merely making a loan to a company. I have no say in how the firm should be run, and my income, a fixed-interest payment, does not automatically increase with the firm's profits. But the return on debentures is at least relatively certain, because the firm has to meet its fixed-interest obligations before any other claims.

Next call on a company's profits comes from the preference shareholders. Preference shares carry only limited rights of participation in the running of the firm (voting rights when dividends are in arrears, for example), and they yield only a fixed or limited dividend; but cumulative preference shares imply that if the company is unable to meet its obligations in any year, the arrears of dividend become payable in the following year.

After debenture stockholders and preference shareholders have been satisfied, some part of the remaining profits may be ploughed back into the business. The left-overs, if there are any, are distributed as dividends to the ordinary (or equity) shareholders. But although the ordinary shareholders are thus last in the queue, they are the owners of the company, and, in theory at least, elect a Board of Directors to carry out their policy in running the firm. In practice, the passivity of many shareholders (it is not only trade unionists who can be accused of inertia in exercising their democratic privileges) means that many Boards are no more than self-perpetuating oligarchies; the practice, indeed, has recently developed of issuing *non-voting* ordinary shares.

Since dividends depend on prior claims being met, and also on the Board's decision about the proportion of profits which should be ploughed back, ordinary shares are in many ways very much riskier investments than other types of security. The equity-holder may get no return at all on his capital. On the other hand, since dividends are related to profits, he also stands to gain a good deal more in prosperous years. An example will make this clear.

Let us suppose that a firm has a nominal capital of £3 million made up of one million 5% debentures, one million 6% preference shares, and one million ordinary shares, all in £1 units, and that over a three-year period it is able to distribute an increasing amount of profit – £80,000 in the first year, £140,000 in the second, and £250,000 in the third. Profits will then be divided between the three classes of stock- and share-holders in the following way:

	Year 1 £	Year 2 £	Year 3 £
Distributed profits	80,000	140,000	250,000
1 million 5% debenture holders	50,000	50,000	50,000
1 million 6% preference shareholders	30,000	90,000	60,000
1 million ordinary shareholders	Nil	Nil	140,000

In the first year, the company hands out £80,000 profit.

Debenture stockholders get their 5% fixed interest amounting to £50,000, and the remaining £30,000 goes to the cumulative preference shareholders (but is insufficient to meet their 6% fixed dividend in full). Ordinary shareholders receive nothing.

Distributed profits increase in the following year to £140,000. Debenture interest of £50,000 is paid first, and in this year, the remaining £90,000 is just sufficient to cover the firm's commitments to preference shareholders, who receive £60,000 for this year *plus* the £30,000 arrears of dividend which the firm was unable to pay in the previous year. Ordinary shareholders again earn nothing.

Dramatic progress is made in Year 3. The amount of profit which the firm distributes increases from £140,000 to £250,000. Interest on debenture stock and dividends on preference shares are paid in full, £50,000 and £60,000 respectively. Ordinary shareholders are relieved to find that there is at last some residual profit accruing to them. £140,000 is paid out on the million ordinary shares, giving a rate of return of 14%. Having taken the rap in the lean years, the equity-holders receive a much higher yield in the good year than the prior claimants, a reward which is related to the greater prosperity of the company.

The relative attractiveness of the different types of company security in general depends on two factors:

(i) the 'gearing' of the firm's capital structure, i.e. the ratio of the company's ordinary share capital to that provided by prior claimants. The greater the proportion of ordinary to other capital, the lower geared the firm's capital structure is said to be; and

(ii) the ratio of good years to bad, whether profits are rising or falling.

We can illustrate this by considering two firms, X and Y, each having a capital of £1 million, but that of X being lower geared than that of Y.

	Company X	Company Y
Ordinary capital	£800,000	£500,000
Debenture stock 5%	£200,000	£500,000

If profits increase in each firm from £50,000 in the first year to

£100,000 in the second year, equity-holders in Company Y, with the higher-geared structure, receive a much larger increase in dividends than ordinary shareholders in company X.

	Ordinary capital	*Amount paid to the ordinary shareholders*	
Company X		*Year 1*	*Year 2*
	£800,000	£40,000	£90,000
	(i.e. an increase from 5 to $11\frac{1}{4}\%$)		
Company Y			
	£500,000	£25,000	£75,000
	(i.e. an increase from 5 to 15%)		

We can draw the very general conclusion that if profits are rising, ordinary dividends tend to increase more in companies with a higher capital gearing (because the increasing residual element in profits is being spread over relatively few ordinary shares) than in those with low gearing (where the increasing profits are diluted in the larger equity). The opposite applies if profits are falling.

PRICE OF SECURITIES

In a single year on the stock exchange the number of bargains or transactions which are officially recorded reaches around the four million figure, and the actual number of deals which take place is certainly much greater. Every day, thousands of bargains are struck, each one involving the bringing together of a buyer and a seller. How is it that Mr Jones of Leicester can order 500 Penguin shares from his broker, and *know* that they will be forthcoming – that individuals whom he has never met and institutions of which he may not even have heard, will be selling just that quantity of Penguin shares on just that day? What is it that ensures that the flow of securities on to the market is precisely balanced by the demand for them, so that no orders are left unfulfilled, and no stocks of unwanted securities build up? We can find the answer by watching the activities of a jobber.

If nothing unsettling has happened since the market closed the previous evening, the jobber opens the day's business by quoting yesterday's closing prices, say, 28s. 29s. The first customer of the day is a broker who offers for sale 1,000 shares which the jobber buys at 28s. each. The jobber's 'book' of shares has now increased by 1,000. To make his turn, he has to 'undo' this bargain by selling those shares at a slightly higher price. Supposing, however, that no brokers offer to buy from him, but that a number come to him to sell. The jobber finds that he is accumulating a considerable book of unwanted shares, of bargains which he cannot undo. He may be quite content to see his book extended in this way if he thinks the selling pressure in the market is a purely temporary phenomenon so that he will have no difficulty in disposing of the shares later.

If, on the other hand, he agrees with the market view that the shares are relatively unattractive and are likely to remain so, he must in some way act to prevent any further increase in his holding. This he does by altering the prices at which he is prepared to buy and sell. His new quotation may be 27s. 6d. 28s. 6d., with the hope that these lower prices will put off some potential sellers and attract some additional buyers.

If, even at the lower price, he still finds that he is buying more shares than he is selling, a further drop in price is called for. But following the market down in this way, adjusting his prices *after* his book becomes unmanageable, is unlikely to be a very profitable business. He will soon find himself selling shares at a lower price than he has paid for them. To be successful, he must try to *anticipate* market feelings. Given an overnight announcement of revolution in Bolivia, no jobber in tin shares would open business at yesterday's closing prices and wait for the certain flood of selling before reducing his prices. By the time the market opened, prices would already have been marked down in an attempt to deter such unloadings.

The jobber is a specialist in his particular type of security. His knowledge of the market may lead him to act as a buffer, buying when others are selling, because he thinks that demand will later pick up again. But his major function is performed as he tries to balance his book, because, in doing this, he is fixing a price which ensures that the day-by-day demand for securities is matched by the supply available. If, for example, we suppose that over a range of possible prices, say from 22s. to 25s., investors' *plans* would be as follows:

Price of securities	Amount which would be bought	Amount which would be sold
25s.	1,000	5,000
24s.	2,000	4,000
23s.	3,000	3,000
22s.	4,000	2,000

Then, if the actual market price was 25s., the amount of securities which would be offered for sale would greatly exceed the amount which buyers demanded. At price 22s., the opposite state of affairs would exist, with demand for securities much greater than the supply forthcoming at that price. Plans to buy and plans to sell are incompatible at all prices except 23s. Only at that one price is the demand for securities just matched by the amount offered for sale.

In very general terms, then, security prices fluctuate in a way which brings about a balance between the plans of thousands of separate buyers and sellers acting from a great variety of motives and without knowledge of each others' operations. We will now consider what determines the supply and demand of particular classes of security, and the relation of their prices to each other.

Gilt-Edged Prices

(a) *Supply of Gilt-Edged Stock*. The securities listed under British Funds have a total nominal value of over £18,000 million, a measure of the extent to which the British government has found it necessary to raise loans on the stock exchange in order to finance its activities. What have these vast sums been used for? Isn't it rather reprehensible that a government should be reduced to touting for loans in order to meet its obligations?

The twentieth century has seen a vast extension of the sphere of government activity. In particular, Britain has been involved in two world wars in which it became necessary, if sufficient resources were to be released for war production, to effect a great transfer of purchasing power from private into government hands. In broad terms, this could be achieved by either taxation or borrowing, but although they both have the same aim – the shift of spending power from the private to the public sector of the economy – these two methods have very different incidental implications. Quite apart from its political unpopularity, taxation beyond a certain limit may have serious disincentive effects. These need not arise, on the other hand, if people can be induced to voluntarily lend to the government (although, of course, the government can only borrow if it offers sufficiently attractive interest rates and these payments, in turn, can only be met by taxation or further borrowing).

The National Debt is the sum total of government borrowing which remains outstanding, and it has shown a colossal rise over the past fifty years:

	£m.
1913	656
1919	7,435
1939	7,131
1945	21,366
1960	27,000

These figures confirm that government borrowing has taken place chiefly during the two war periods. But what is most interesting is the difference which emerges between the periods 1919–39, and 1945–60. Whereas in the inter-war years, the National Debt was cut by some £304 million as State activities dwindled again to their peace-time scope, the debt has actually *increased* since 1945 by nearly £6,000 million. The British government has, for the first time, become a net borrower in time of peace.

It is not hard to see why. The level of arms expenditure has continued to be astronomical: in this day and age, keeping the peace seems as expensive a business as waging war. Moreover, since 1945, the State has been far more active in the working of the economy than ever before. The provision of a wide range of welfare facilities, the taking over of several major industries into public control, the creation of new towns – all imply expenditure by the government which had been previously undertaken (or, sometimes, neglected) by private individuals or firms. The vast scale of government borrowing since the war is a reflection of the shift of spending power from the private sector necessitated by all these new calls on public resources.

To attract different types of lender, the government offers a great variety of claims on itself. These range from the 'Floating Debt' in the form of three-months Treasury Bills appealing to the banks and discount houses, to National Savings Certificates issued in low denominations and aiming at small savers. Government bonds on the stock exchange account for over half the total National Debt. The supply of gilt-edged securities has enormously increased and there seems little reason to expect any great reduction in the future. A reduction will only occur if the government either finances its activities by other methods – increasing taxation, or borrowing through channels other than the stock market – or if government expenditure is itself curtailed. But taxation is already at a high level, to increase the Floating Debt would lead to repercussions in the banking system which will be discussed in the next chapter, and small savings have already been substantially increased over the last decade.

Reduction of the National Debt therefore seems to imply cutting government expenditure – a policy which certainly commends itself to many popular critics. However, its advocates are often those who make the most indignant complaints about the consequences. The vital question is, how *can* government expenditure be reduced? One possibility is elimination of extravagance, a streamlining of existing services to provide better value for money. No one would dispute that this should be, and often is not, an important aim of every government. But we cannot reasonably hope that 'economies' of this kind could make more than a marginal contribution. And apart from this, lower outlay by the public sector implies the provision of *fewer* services, or services of lower quality. Which, then, should suffer? Should we make cuts in the defence programme, or education, or public health? Both main political parties are, in fact, committed to developments which must imply very much *higher* levels of spending – on transport, on towns, on all types of education. We have to accept that the State no longer provides services just because many of the community are too poor to fend for themselves; a large part of public investment is now the concomitant of affluence, complementary to and induced by a high level of prosperity in the private sector. More leisure implies the need for more educational and cultural facilities, more private cars increase the pressure on the authorities to build better roads.

Perhaps we have said enough for the time being about the difficulties of cutting government expenditure to suggest that it is at least extremely unlikely that the supply of gilt-edged, which is what we were originally considering, will be reduced in the foreseeable future.

(*b*) *Demand for Gilt-Edged Stock*. The prime attraction of gilt-edged stock is the certainty that interest will be paid regularly, a certainty which arises because such payments are a call on national revenues. However, a glance at a list of British Funds shows that rates of interest vary considerably from stock to stock – from 2½% on some Consols. to 6¾% on Treasury 95–98. The different rates payable on these stocks arise from the varied conditions in which they were originally issued. To sell a new issue, the government has to offer inducements comparable to those found elsewhere, and the fact that some bonds carry high interest, and others low interest, merely reflects the general levels of interest at the time the stocks were first issued. Low-interest bonds were therefore bought in the first place because no more could be earned on alternative investments of a similar degree of risk. But this does not account for the fact that people continue to buy them second-hand at a time when interest rates have generally risen. Why should any investors *today* buy 2½% Consols. when they could earn 6¾% on new, and equally safe, bonds? To understand this puzzle, we have to distinguish between interest and 'yield'. On the 2½% Consols., interest is the £2 10s. 0d. per annum which will be paid to the owner of £100 nominal value of stock, regardless of how much he paid for it. Yield, on the other hand, is interest expressed as a rate of return on *market price*. There would be buyers for a 2½% stock if it could be bought in the market for about £37 because, at that price, the £2 10s. 0d. interest would represent a *yield* equivalent to the £5 15s. 0d. interest payable on the new stock (with a nominal *and* market value of £100), and pressures of supply and demand operate on yields in just this way. When interest rates in general rise, existing low-interest stocks become relatively unattractive; those who wish to sell can only do so if prices fall to the level at which the *yields* on the old and new stocks are thought by investors to be comparable.

The yield which we have so far been discussing is more strictly termed 'flat yield'. The 'yield' on stocks which is generally referred to in the financial press is a rather more complicated concept – 'gross redemption yield'. Suppose that a 3% stock, due for redemption in thirty years' time, is priced in the market at £60. The flat yield is £3 interest/£60 price, or 5%. However, there is another source of gain to take into account. An investor buying the stock at £60 and holding it for thirty years to maturity will receive from the government its nominal value of £100. This capital gain of roughly 1% per annum is added to the flat yield to give a gross redemption yield of 6%.

The type of investors who are most likely to be attracted to gilt-edged are those who are primarily interested in a sure and guaranteed income, and those who expect to hold the bonds to maturity and enjoy a certain and calculable capital gain (in money terms, at least). It is not therefore surprising that estimates suggest that only about a quarter of identified private holdings of gilt-edged are in the hands of private individuals. The major lenders are the financial institutions whose activities basically consist of the investment of their clients' money, large portfolios of gilt-edged providing them with a safe and solid base for more risky investments. Again, the commitments of, for example, insurance companies and pension funds, are themselves long term, which enables such institutions to ignore short-term fluctuations in the price of gilt-edged in the knowledge that they will be ultimately redeemed at their full nominal value.

Equity Prices

(a) *Supply of Equities*. The total market value of all company securities quoted on the stock exchange in March 1965 amounted to some £34,000 million – about 70% of the total market value of all quoted securities. Equities account for nine-tenths of this sum.

The stock exchange is by no means the only source of company finance. A firm may also borrow through the banks, finance houses, trade credit, etc., or finance itself by ploughing back profits rather than distributing them to shareholders. However, investigation of the balance sheets of 2,500 quoted companies over the years 1949–53 revealed that while retained profits provided the most important source of financing the growth of firms, companies remained very dependent on new issues of stocks and shares. Nearly a third of the companies resorted to the stock exchange during these years, and new issues accounted for 27% of the capital needed for expansion. This is an average figure for all the companies, and a more detailed analysis showed that the more rapidly a firm was growing, the more dependent it was on the new issue market.

New shares may be issued in any of three ways:

1. Public issue by prospectus. This is an offer direct to the public by the company itself. Regulations require that a detailed prospectus of the company's record and future intentions should be advertised in at least two national newspapers, and the combined cost of this and the use of the technical services of banks and brokers is very considerable. Since these expenses are to some extent indivisible, they weigh more heavily on smaller issues. As a result, a sum of about £250,000 is the smallest which it is economic to raise by a new issue.

2. Offer for sale. By this method the company sells the whole issue to a specialist Issuing House which then undertakes to dispose of the issue to the public – at a higher price in order to cover its costs and remuneration for saving the company the trouble and risk involved.

If the company misjudges the type and price of share which appeals to the investing public, difficulty may arise in getting rid of the whole issue. Both types of issues which we have just described are therefore generally 'underwritten' or insured against this possibility. An underwriter agrees to take up any part of an issue which is not subscribed by the public, and is paid a commission per share up to the amount which he agrees to cover. If the issue proves to be successful, he will be 'relieved', i.e. not in fact called upon to take up any shares, in which case the commission is clear profit. On the other hand, he may be stuck with shares which he has to hold for some time before they can be disposed of at an economic price. Insurance companies have been the most important underwriters during the post-war period.

3. Rights issues are a popular way of eliminating many of the expenses involved in the other methods. Under this system, existing shareholders are given the right to take up a new issue in proportion to their existing holding. For example, a company

may offer a two to five rights issue which entitles shareholders to buy two shares of the new issue for every five which they already hold. Rights are renounceable and saleable in the market.

Rights issues should not be confused with 'free scrip' issues. The mechanism is similar in that existing shareholders get new shares in proportion to their present holdings, but no new money is raised in the process. The aim of a free scrip issue may be to lighten 'heavy' shares. For example, a firm may, some years ago, have issued shares of £1 par or nominal value which have since risen, as a result of the success of the firm and general economic conditions, to a market value of £5. A scrip issue of 4:1 may now reduce the market value closer to the original par – the purpose perhaps being to attract the smaller investors who sometimes prefer to buy lower-priced shares. Scrip issues may also be used to distribute to shareholders ploughed-back profits which have been retained in liquid form.

(*b*) *Demand for Equities.* Roughly one-third of the total stock of equities is held by institutional investors (insurance companies, pension funds, investment trusts, etc.), with the remainder in the hands of private individuals. We have already seen that there is a good deal of income uncertainty attached to equities. Dividends depend on total profits of the firm, on the amount due to prior claimants, and on the company policy with regard to self-financing; the yield of a share (dividend as a percentage of market value) is primarily determined by the riskiness of the investment. Investors will not buy shares in South African gold-mining companies when 'blue chip' (highly dependable) home securities are available unless the price of the former is such that the dividends paid give a correspondingly higher yield. Similarly, the shares of firms which seem certain to expand rapidly and earn a higher return on capital will carry a low yield. This may seem incongruous at first until it is remembered that it is because high *dividends* are being paid or expected in the future that the demand for such shares has pushed up their price and reduced the current yield.

During the post-war years, investors have been increasingly interested in the capital attractions of ordinary shares resulting from a rise in their market value. Since capital gains have not until recently been subject to taxation, £1 derived from a rise in the price of his shares has been the equivalent of £3 dividend earnings for an investor paying tax at the standard rate. How do capital gains arise? First, share prices may rise in sympathy with movements in the general price level. If the prices of goods and services are generally increasing in money terms, then the profits of the firms providing them will also be rising – provided, as is probable, that producers are able to increase their prices sufficiently to cover inflated costs of production. The money value of firms' assets also increases, and since equities are titles to ownership of these assets, they may be considered a good 'hedge' against inflation. Figures for the post-war period show that, in general, this has been the case, although over a good deal of the period even the rise in share prices lagged somewhat behind the increased cost of living. Certainly, equities are a far better method of maintaining the real value of wealth in an inflationary period than fixed-interest securities. More genuine capital gains – over and above merely maintaining the real value of an investment – arise with 'growth stocks'. These are the shares of companies which are expected, as a result of higher productivity, to be able to increase the return on their assets above present levels.

Relative Yields of Gilt-Edged and Equities

We have seen that government stock is in some ways a safe investment, whereas ordinary shares involve the holder in considerable risks. The safeness of gilt-edged lies both in the guaranteed income, and, with double-dated stock, the added certainty of repayment at par. The income of ordinary shareholders, on the other hand, is threatened from within and without. There is the spectre of general trade depression slashing profits throughout the economy; there is the possibility that a government will be elected which is unsympathetic to private business. And even when the economy is generally prosperous, particular firms may fail or their shareholders be burdened by boards with over-cautious policies.

The risklessness of gilt-edged as compared with the hazards of equity holding would suggest that investors would only be induced to hold equities if the yield were sufficiently higher to compensate them for the additional risks involved. Until recently, this was indeed the case. However, since 1959, a 'reverse gap' has developed with the yield on gilt-edged *exceeding* that on equities. Holders of government bonds now apparently have the best of both worlds – a safe income *and* a higher one. This makes sense only if we widen our notion of the riskiness of alternative investments to include *capital* as well as income considerations. We have already noted that gilt-edged prices change with the general level of interest rates; when interest rates are rising, the market value of existing stocks is pushed down so that their *yield* is increased into line with the interest payable on newly issued bonds. During the post-war period, fluctuations of bond prices have been considerable. Government policy immediately after the war aimed at establishing extremely low interest rates, and reversion to dearer money by the fifties led to a substantial fall in gilt-edged prices – to the cost of those investors who had bought bonds during the 'cheap money' phase. At the same time, the fact that governments since the war have accepted responsibility for maintaining a high and stable level of employment has moderated the risk of general trade depression which was previously involved in holding equities. And finally, gilt-edged compare unfavourably with ordinary shares when the inflation risk is taken into account. Given a rising general price level, the fixed money interest and fixed capital repayment due on maturity of government stock both fall in *real* value, while equities offer some sort of hedge against inflation as profits, values of the company's assets, and, therefore, share prices, tend to follow movements in the general price level.

Furthermore, the government's responsibilities now extend beyond merely stabilizing the economy. Since 1956 it has also been pledged 'to foster conditions in which the nation can realize its full potentialities for *growth* in terms of production and living standards'. Ignoring for the time being the delicate question of whether it has succeeded in fulfilling this promise, investors in equities have come to anticipate an expanding economy in which profits and the market values of equity investments will rise. These expectations themselves have the effect of increasing equity prices and reducing yields, even though such discounting of future gains will only, in fact, be justified if the rate of return on capital increases (if growth takes place just because *more* capital is used, there will be a corresponding dilution of profits). However, to the extent that genuine 'growth stocks' exist, the attraction of equities is justifiably enhanced, and even if investors merely confuse expansion of profits with an increasing *rate* of profit, equity prices will still tend to rise even though this discounting of future yields may later prove to have been mistaken. What has been said of businessmen applies equally to investors, that they 'play a mixed game of skill and chance, the average results of which to the players are not known by those who take a hand'.

Thus the different economic background of the post-war years has led to an increased appetite for equities. It has brought about a reassessment of the relative attractions of different securities by even the staidest of the institutional investors, and the development of new institutions to facilitate the channelling of small savings into outlets which might still be too risky for small investors acting independently. The equity holding of insurance companies has risen from 10% of their assets in 1939 to over 21%, a considerable increase when it is remembered that the total invested funds of insurance companies amount to some £9,000 million. Other corporate investors as diverse as the Church Commissioners and the National Coal Board have similarly found equities an increasingly attractive proposition. Much of the vast increase which has taken place in the amount of private pension funds has reached the equity market, and the Labour Party once produced a scheme for national superannuation which provided for the investment of accumulated funds in private industry. Finally, there is the post-war growth of unit trusts which offer to the small investor the benefit of a spread of investments and an expertise which he could not afford on his own.

To sum up, the great expansion of the gilt-edged market has taken place during a period when there has been a marked shift in taste in favour of equity investment. In view of the change in the relative attractiveness of gilt-edged and equities in conditions of full employment, inflation and growth, and the consequent movement of new funds into company shares, the fact that good-class equities give a lower yield than gilt-edged is of little surprise. Given the continuation of the present economic environment, we may well come to regard the 'reverse gap' as normal.

Finance

EXPECTATIONS AND SPECULATIONS

No account of the stock market would be complete without some emphasis on the importance of the expectations of the investor in the determination of security prices, and of the role of the speculator.

The price of a security is ultimately determined by what investors think it will be. Take the case of a stock priced in the market now at £80. If most investors *think* that the price of this stock will fall in the future, then fall it will. Investors will act in such a way that their expectations will be justified. No one will want to buy a stock which is generally expected to fall in price, and there will be a scramble on the part of those holding the stock to unload. Equilibrium between supply and demand can be maintained only if the price falls. The market will have proved itself right, and this will be so whether the original reasons for expecting the price to decline were good ones – for example, an anticipation that a new and more attractive issue was about to be made – or whether they were completely irrational – a feeling that a recent sunspot augured ill for the stock market!

Since market expectations are self-justifying regardless of their basis, the way is open for a further type of stock-exchange activity – speculation. It is difficult to draw a hard-and-fast distinction between speculation and other investment, but generally the speculator can be reckoned to concern himself not so much with the long-term prospects of the security in question as with the psychology of other operators. What he tries to assess is not what the market value of the security will be in, say, two years' time, but rather what the average investor *thinks* its price will be. And since other investors may be working along the same lines, the problem is complicated. The successful speculator must try to determine what other investors think the security will be fetching! Lord Keynes nicely compared professional investment to a newspaper competition

in which the competitors have to pick out the six prettiest faces from a hundred photographs, the prize being awarded to the competitor whose choice most nearly corresponds to the average preferences of the competitors as a whole; so that each competitor has to pick, not those faces which he himself finds prettiest, but those which he thinks likeliest to catch the fancy of the other competitors, all of whom are looking at the problem from the same point of view. It is not a case of choosing those which, to the best of one's judgement, are really the prettiest, nor even those which average opinion genuinely thinks are the prettiest. We have reached the third degree where we devote our intelligence to anticipating what average opinion expects average opinion to be. And there are some, I believe, who practise the fourth, fifth and even higher degrees.

(*General Theory of Employment, Interest and Money*, p. 156.)

Taking advantage of the credit facilities which we have already mentioned (to which should be added the option market which gives the investor, for a charge, the option of buying or selling shares at some future date at a price fixed now) are the members of the well-known stock market menagerie. 'Bulls' buy securities in the expectation that their price will rise, and 'bears' sell in the hope that they will later be able to buy them back at a lower price. Both aim at being one step ahead of the rest of the market. 'Stags', the most parasitic of the speculators, subscribe to new issues in the knowledge that, to be successful, a new issue must be floated at a price which is slightly more attractive than that of a comparable second-hand security, and that its price will almost certainly rise shortly after the issue has been made. The ultimate in zoological activity came recently when stags (who are really a form of bull) profited handsomely from an issue of Penguins.

It may be argued that the speculator performs a useful function in the market. By trying to be one step ahead of other investors, he may help to stabilize prices – by bullish buying when others are selling, and bearish selling when others are still inclined to buy. But although this may be what happens in relatively quiet market conditions, more serious price movements are likely to be reinforced or initiated by speculators acting in concert.

We have to remember, too, that the function of the stock exchange is not only to increase the liquidity of existing claims on the government and firms. It also serves to channel *new* savings into the most economic uses. Prices of their own and similar shares on the stock exchange indicate to potential borrowers their chances of success in increasing their capital by a new issue. But market prices will only reflect the most efficient uses of new savings if they are the result of rational estimation by investors of the long-run prospects of different companies. If they are more the result of speculative assessments of market psychology they will be poor guides to the most efficient use of resources.

To give Lord Keynes the last word

Speculators may do no harm as bubbles on a steady stream of enterprise. But the position is serious when enterprise becomes the bubble on a whirlpool of speculation. When the capital development of a country becomes a by-product of the activity of a casino, the job is likely to be ill-done.

(*General Theory of Employment, Interest and Money*, p. 159.)

Keynes was writing in the mid thirties following the 'great crash' of the stock market boom in 1929. During the post-war period, high income taxation made speculation for tax-free capital gains more attractive than ever. On the other hand, the redistribution of private wealth and the increasing importance of institutional investors have probably, nevertheless, led to a reduction in the *amount* of speculative activity – even before the introduction of capital gains taxation in the Finance Acts of 1962 and 1965.

CHAPTER 2

MONEY, BANKING, AND LIQUIDITY

THE nature and functioning of money is a prolific source of confusion in understanding the working of the economy. The government itself, after reverting in 1951 to reliance on 'traditional' monetary weapons to control the economy, finally admitted its doubts about just what it was doing by setting up the Radcliffe Committee in 1957 to examine how the monetary system worked and the extent to which it could be controlled. Particularly misunderstood (*vide* Mr Thorneycroft in 1957) is the relationship of money and monetary policy to the problem of inflation. However, we shall tackle the question of inflation later, and confine this chapter to a consideration of the financial institutions which are responsible for creating and handling 'money' and 'near-money'.

The fundamental importance of money in a developed economy hardly requires emphasis. Economic development implies specialization, and the consequent interdependence of economic units necessitates the use of money – to lubricate the exchange of surpluses as the division of labour becomes more sophisticated, and to facilitate the process of saving and capital accumulation necessary for the break-through to higher living standards.

Money acts as a link. It is a link between goods *now*, a common denominator in terms of which a vast variety of output can be expressed, and a medium through which exchange transactions can be effected. It is also a link between goods now and goods in the future, allowing comparisons to be made of the value of present consumption and consumption later, and extending the time horizon for economic decisions by the introduction of money-contracts relating to income and loans.

What is Money?

This simple question can be answered simply, if rather unhelpfully, by the adage 'money is what money does'. In other words, anything qualifies as money which performs the functions of a medium of exchange and a store of value. But what do salt, silver, goats, cigarettes, gold, and paper – which have all at times served these purposes – have in common which fits them for the role of money?

First of all, money obviously has to possess certain convenience qualities – portability, durability, divisibility, and so on (which suggests that goats may not have proved very satisfactory!). It must also be relatively scarce, and this scarcity may be either natural as in the case of precious metals, or man-made as when the printing of bank-notes is concentrated in the hands of State authorities. But what above all entitles something to be called money is that it is *acceptable* as money. It must be widely regarded as a means of settling debts and making future contracts. Money is what people think of as money. Unless they do regard it as money, then no legal sanction can *make* it money, and similarly, a money can operate perfectly well without being labelled legal tender.

We have so far implied that money must at least be something which can be touched or carried about or built up in piles. But, in fact, money need not be tangible at all. It can take the form of transferable book debts. Suppose Mr X owes Mr Y the sum of £10. This debt may be recorded by both X and Y making entries in their accounts. If Y now himself incurs a debt of £10 with Z, and Z is prepared to accept as payment of the debt a claim on X, then these book entries are serving as money. In principle it would be possible to rely exclusively on a non-physical money of this kind, but in practice the difficulty would arise of having to establish credit-worthiness in each individual case before such claims could be accepted as settlement of debts. If Mr Z does not know Mr X and cannot quickly assess his integrity and resources to meet the claim against him, he will clearly not be happy about regarding such a claim as part of his assets.

Money in the U.K.

So much for money in general. What counts as money in the British economy? Notes and coins is the answer which most people would give to this question. These are legal tender up to legislatively stipulated amounts and are generally accepted as a means of payment (a small limitation is the occasional difficulty in persuading an English trader to accept a Scottish bank-note). The basis of this acceptability is the fact that they are issued nationally with uniform denominations and physical characteristics by an institution in which there is the highest public confidence – the Bank of England.

This concentration of notes and coinage issue in the hands of a single institution (Scottish banks continue to issue their own notes, but only to the extent that they are backed by Bank of England notes) is a relatively recent phenomenon. The process of monopolization which began with the Bank Charter Act of 1844 and which replaced a system of different paper monies of only limited regional acceptability, was not completed until some seventy years later.

Parallel with this concentration has been the establishment of a purely paper currency unbacked by precious metals or any similar commodity of alternative value. The 1844 Act limited the quantity of currency which the Bank of England could issue to the value of its stock of gold – into which bank-notes would be freely transferable. Paper money was thus used merely as a more convenient method of effecting transactions than the specie which it represented. But the Act also allowed the Bank to issue £14 million of notes unbacked by gold, the so-called 'fiduciary issue'. After this initial breach, the fiduciary element was consistently increased until the break from gold was completed in 1939 with the transfer of the Bank's gold holding to the Exchange Equalization Account, for use only in international payments.

The *I promise to pay the bearer on demand the sum of* . . . which rather regrettably continues to be printed on Bank of England notes, has therefore no significance whatsoever. There cannot be many optimists who think that taking such notes to the Bank and demanding payment would yield anything more than an equivalent amount of identical currency, but a surprising number of people still seem to cherish the belief that the currency is in some way ultimately backed by gold. The fact is, however, that the Bank of England and its nominal master, the Treasury, are legally empowered to issue any amount of currency they see fit, with the limitation only of *post hoc* approval by parliament – which is always forthcoming. The acceptability of a paper currency of no intrinsic value ultimately rests on confidence in the monetary authorities' ability to ensure that the system functions soundly and smoothly.

A large proportion of the transactions taking place in the economy do not involve any use of currency at all. The practice of payment by cheque, first popularized during the late nineteenth century, has enormously increased in the present century, and is likely to continue to do so as more and more people keep bank accounts. The question therefore arises as to whether cheques should also be included as part of the money supply. However, it is quite clear that they should not. Cheques do not have general acceptability as a means of payment, the reason obviously being that although an individual may be rich in cheques he may be poor in the means of honouring them. Cheques are only instruments for drawing on bank accounts and in themselves cannot be classed as money. The bank accounts on which the cheques are drawn *are* money, and the limited acceptability of cheques among friends or businesses or in particular localities arises from the knowledge that the drawer of the cheque is in a position to honour his pledge.

But since bank accounts are created by customers going to the banks and depositing notes and coins, receiving in exchange IOUs from the bank, will it not be double counting if we include *both* bank deposits and notes and coins in the total money supply? That it would be a great deal more than mere double counting becomes clear on comparison of the totals. In April 1966, for example, the deposits of all U.K. banks amounted to over £10,000 million. The amount of paper and metal money in existence was very much less:

	(*£m.*)
Notes and coin outstanding	3,296
held by public	2,632
held by banks	664

We can see that only a small proportion of the total notes and coins in circulation is held by the banks, the remainder already being in the hands of the public. Moreover, bank deposits vastly exceed the amount of notes and coins which the banks hold against them and amount to roughly three times the *total* currency in circulation. It looks from these statistics as though banknotes as well as coins have become the small change of the system, and that it is bank deposits which are far and away the most important element in the money supply.

The U.K. money supply thus consists primarily of bank deposits only fractionally backed by currency, and a currency which is itself 'backed' by nothing at all. This is a sobering thought for those who still cling to the superstition that the value of a money depends on its connexion with precious metals, but perhaps they may take some reassurance from the following account of just how this state of affairs has come about.

The Process of Credit Creation

The discrepancy between total bank deposits and the amount of currency which the banks hold against them certainly suggests that banking business is being conducted on rather reprehensible lines. What would happen if all bank depositors suddenly took it into their heads to go along to their banks and demand encashment of their deposits in notes and coins? Before we go on to discuss the British banking system in particular, it may be helpful to see in general, by use of a simple model, how bank deposits can come to exceed cash reserves.

Let us suppose that the public initially holds wealth in two forms, currency and government bonds:

Stage I

Public
£500 currency
£2,000 bonds

If people now feel that keeping such large amounts of currency or cash is both unprofitable and unsafe, they may decide to keep no more than £400 under the bed and up the chimney, and to deposit £100 with a bank for safe keeping. A bank, like any other enterprise, can draw up a balance-sheet of matching assets and liabilities. Its assets are now the £100 of currency, and its corresponding liability is £100 of bank deposits (which to depositors are assets withdrawable at any time).

Stage II

Bank		Public
Assets	*Liabilities*	
£100 currency	£100 deposits	£400 currency
		£2,000 bonds
		£100 deposits

Nothing very significant has happened by Stage II. The public have merely exchanged £100 cash for £100 bank deposits (which they regard as being as good as currency), and bank deposits are still backed 100% by currency.

However, that is by no means the end of the story. Through experience, the banker realizes that the cash deposited with him by and large remains idle. Although deposits are constantly being withdrawn, they are replenished by fresh deposits from those firms and individuals who receive payments as a result of the original withdrawals. Inflows roughly match outflows, and the banker discovers that only a small proportion of his cash reserves are, in fact, ever needed to meet any excess of withdrawals over deposits. He may find, for example, that 10% of his cash holdings are all that he needs to keep in his till to meet day-to-day demands, and that the remaining 90% continuously lies idle in the bank vaults.

By his next move, the banker evolves from mere 'cloakroom banking' by investing that idle £90 in assets which he thinks will be easily resaleable should there ever be a 'run on the bank' by depositors. If he buys £90 of government bonds (from the public), then Stage III will look like this:

Stage III

	Bank		Public
Assets	*Liabilities*		
£10 currency	£100 deposits		£490 currency
£90 bonds			£1,910 bonds
			£100 deposits

Bank deposits still stand at £100, but only 10% are now backed by cash reserves, government bonds being held against the remainder. But Stage III is not likely to be a position of equilibrium. It was assumed in the first place that the bank began operations because the public did not like holding more than £400 in cash. If this feeling still persists, then the public, which now finds its cash holdings inflated by the sale of bonds, will redeposit £90 with the banks.

The bank which in Stage III released its unused cash resources by buying bonds, finds in Stage IV that the public has redeposited the excess of £90 cash which it does not wish to hold.

Stage IV

	Bank		Public
Assets	*Liabilities*		
£100 currency	£190 deposits		£400 currency
£90 bonds			£1,910 bonds
			£190 deposits

The bank is thus in a similar position to before. It now has to deal with day-to-day business on a larger volume of deposits, but if we continue to assume that a 10% cash reserve figure is sufficient, then £19 currency will be all that is needed in the till and £81 (£100 less £19) will still be lying idle. Once again, as a profit-maker, the banker invests this sum in bonds.

Stage V

	Bank		Public
Assets	*Liabilities*		
£19 currency	£190 deposits		£481 currency
£171 bonds			£1,829 bonds
			£190 deposits

And once again the public finds that it has excess cash holdings, which it duly redeposits with the bank (£81):

Stage VI

	Bank		Public
Assets	*Liabilities*		
£100 currency	£271 deposits		£400 currency
£171 bonds			£1,829 bonds
			£271 deposits

The banker has £100 currency again! Since only £27·1 is needed to service deposits now totalling £271, he still has £72·9 surplus cash available for further investment in bonds.

And so it goes on. We can omit further stages, not just because the arithmetic is getting complicated, but because, on the assumptions given, the final outcome becomes predictable. Although the banker continues to invest his surplus cash in bonds and the public continues to redeposit the cash proceeds with the bank, at each stage the bank finds it necessary to retain a larger absolute amount of cash (although the same proportion) as a reserve against withdrawals.

The final stage will thus be reached when the whole of the bank's cash holding is active in that it is required for servicing deposits. And since the public are insisting that £100 cash be held with the bank, the pyramid of deposits which can ultimately be supported on this cash base must be ten times £100, i.e. £1,000. The final balance sheet of the banks and public when the process has fully worked itself out will, therefore, look like this:

Final stage

	Bank		*Public*
Assets	*Liabilities*		
£100 currency	£1,000 deposits		£400 currency
£900 bonds			£1,100 bonds
			£1,000 deposits

We should emphasize that the activities of the bank have led to no increase in the total *wealth* of the community. The public still own only £2,500 assets – which is what they started with – but they now hold that wealth in a different form. The bank certainly has assets of £1,000 which it did not have at the outset, but it has liabilities of just the same amount. All that has happened is that the bank has been prepared to make the wealth held by the public more *liquid* by accepting immediate claims against itself in exchange for less liquid bonds. However, although the bank has not added to total wealth in the process, it has most definitely created more *money* by its operations. The exchange of bank deposits for bonds is just as much the creation of money as the issue of bank-notes by a central authority.

Clearly, too, there are limits to the extent to which the banks can create money of this type. These limitations largely correspond to the assumptions which were made in the model. We first assumed that the public demand for cash balances remained constant at £400. To the extent that people felt inclined to hold more cash as their bank deposits increased and bond holdings were reduced, the amount redeposited with the bank and the consequent credit multiplier would have been correspondingly less. Another 'leakage' might occur if the sellers of bonds or the recipients of the proceeds were not clients of the bank and did not, therefore, redeposit the currency which came into their hands. If, for example, such proceeds were used to finance payments to the government sector, this would – unless the taxes were paid out in equivalent benefits – amount to a destruction of money.

The really crucial assumption underlying the process of credit creation is, however, the fact that the banker is able to operate safely on a fractional cash reserve basis. If there was doubt or suspicion in customers' minds about the security of their deposits and the bank's ability to encash those deposits on demand, then the possibility of the public testing the bank's soundness by frequent 'runs' would imply that the bank would have to maintain a high reserve–deposit ratio in readiness to prove itself. It is the fact that there is a high degree of public confidence in the banks' ability to meet their obligations that makes low cash ratios possible.

The essence of banking is thus to conceal or minimize the difference between currency and bank deposits. So long as the public has sufficient trust in bank soundness, they will not bother to distinguish between cash and deposits. Banking turns out to be a highly sophisticated confidence trick.

BRITISH COMMERCIAL BANKING

Like much of industry, British banking now has an oligopolistic structure as a result of integration during the past century. Competition is between the few, with something like 86% of English banking business now performed by the 'Big Five' – Barclays, Midland, Lloyds, Westminster, and National Provincial, all with branches extending throughout the country. A further 8% is in the hands of the District and Martins banks, and most of the remainder falls to four smaller businesses – Williams Deacon's, Glyn, Mills & Co., Coutts & Co., and the National Bank. These eleven are together known as the 'London Clearing Banks', indicating that they are members of the scheme which originated in the late eighteenth century for the clearing of inter-bank transactions and limitation of inter-bank payments to the net deficits arising from a day's business.

A commercial, or joint-stock bank, has a dual responsibility. It is a private institution, with its capital subscribed by stockholders and shareholders who expect profits to be made. On the other hand, the bank has a responsibility to its customers to safeguard their deposits. In the long run these responsibilities can hardly conflict, but it is perhaps worth stressing that the commercial banks are part of the private sector. Their concern with the public interest must necessarily be incidental. 'We are bankers not statesmen,' said the chairman of one of the banks before the Radcliffe Committee, with the implication that the banks would consider it fair game to find and exploit any loopholes in government restrictions which might conflict with their profit-maximizing activities.

Commercial banks function very much along the lines already described in our model by creating a pyramid of credit greatly in excess of the amount of currency which they hold. Bankers, however, have sometimes been at pains to dispute this. 'We do not create new money. All we do,' they say, 'is to lend what has been deposited with us.' Obviously, with bank deposits totalling over £10,000 million and the total cash holding by the banks less than £700 million, the first part of this statement is easily refutable. But that they only re-lend what is deposited with them does appear to be true from the point of view of a single banker.

If, for example, Barclays receive additional deposits of £100, they certainly do not create £1,000 of fresh deposits on that basis at once (assuming a 10% cash ratio). They will, however, feel able to lend some £90, and that, as far as they are concerned, may be that. But when the loans are used to make payments, the recipients will probably also be depositors at some bank or other, and the £90 will therefore mostly flow back into the banking system. To the extent that some returns to Barclays, it will be indistinguishable from any other deposit of cash and will be used for yet further creation of deposits. Thus any fresh deposit of cash with a bank is shunted round time after time until deposits have increased to the point where the cash is all needed by the banks as part of their reserves. The banking system as a whole will have created deposits; any *one* bank will merely have re-lent what was originally deposited with it.

The balance sheet of a commercial bank is rather more complicated than that presented in the model. In April 1966, for example, the aggregate assets and liabilities of the London Clearing Banks were as follows:

Assets	(£m.)	Liabilities		(£m.)
Cash:	786	Gross Deposits:		9,363
in tills	504	in current		
in Bank of		accounts	5,058	
England	282	in deposit		
Money at call and		accounts	3,460	
short notice	966	in other		
Bills discounted	1,098	accounts	844	
Investments	1,096			
Advances	4,902			

The fact that total liabilities and assets do not exactly match is due to the omission of certain minor items.

The deposit liabilities mainly consist of current account deposits and deposit account deposits (the American title 'time deposits' is both less clumsy and more explanatory). The distinction lies in the fact that whereas deposits on current account are immediately withdrawable, time deposits can be withdrawn only after a period of notice, but earn depositors interest, normally at Bank Rate minus 2%.

The assets side of the balance sheet shows what sort of 'backing' there is for the deposits. The first three items – cash, money at call and short notice, and bills discounted – comprise the banks' 'liquid assets'.

Liquid Assets

Cash consists of notes and coin held in the banks' own offices and deposits held by the banks with their own banker – the Bank of England. The latter are regarded by the banks as the equivalent of ready cash, since they can at any time be exchanged for notes. The ratio of cash to total deposits held by the banks stands at the remarkably low figure of 8% – a proportion observed as both a minimum and a maximum. Money at call and short notice is lent primarily to the 'discount market' (which will be dealt with shortly), and, as the name implies, such loans are repayable either on demand, or at most in a matter of days. 'Bills discounted' requires a little more explanation.

A commercial bill of exchange is an instrument of short-term credit, generally for three months. If the seller is agreeable, the financing of a transaction can be postponed by the creditor 'drawing' a bill of exchange on the debtor, who 'accepts' the bill by signing it (the amount of the debt including an interest payment for the loan). If the creditor wants cash now rather than in three months time, he can take the bill to a specialist institution known as a discount house, which discounts the bill by paying its cash value less an interest charge for the inconvenience of holding the bill to maturity (when it will receive payment from the original debtor whose name is on the bill).

The commercial bill of exchange was particularly popular in financing international trade transactions around the turn of the century, but has now largely fallen into disuse with the development of more convenient credit instruments like the bank overdraft. Its decline has, however, been accompanied by an increasing volume of Treasury Bills which are issued by the British government. The 'Floating Debt', as the Treasury Bill issue is known, is chiefly used to finance the short-term gap between government revenue and outlay which periodically appears. Bills are issued every week for periods generally of ninety-one days. They are offered for tender, bids coming from the Discount Market syndicate and also from 'outside' institutions like foreign banks and industrial firms with cash to spare.

The discount market (largely financed by money at call and short notice from the commercial banks) buys the bills in the first place and holds them during the early part of their life while they are least liquid. The 'bills discounted' element in the commercial banks' assets are parcels of bills which the discount market has sold to the banks as they approach maturity, and thus give the banks a constant flow of cash which may either be re-invested in the bills or switched to some more profitable use.

Earning Assets

The final two items in the banks' balance sheets – investments and advances – are known as 'earning assets'. 'Investments' refers to holdings of gilt-edged securities, Evidence before the Radcliffe Committee showed that in recent years the banks have held only bonds with ten years or less to maturity, and that their portfolios are arranged to give a steady flow of maturities year by year. 'Advances and loans', the financing of trade, industry, professional and personal expenditure, is the most lucrative of banking business, carrying interest at Bank Rate plus 1% (with a minimum of 5%), and also calls for the greatest acumen and judgement.

Advances are a far more common form of lending than loans. Whereas a loan implies that the client's account is credited with a specific sum, the overdraft system operates by allowing the borrower to draw on his account in excess of his current balance, his account being debited correspondingly. From the borrower's point of view this is obviously the cheaper method, since interest is charged only to the extent that the customer has *availed* himself of overdraft facilities and not on the overdraft limit which the bank has imposed.

British banks have a traditional preference for financing working rather than fixed capital expenditure. Their ideal remains the self-liquidating 'seed-time to harvest' type of lending – for the payment of running costs or purchases of raw materials rather than for investment in machinery and plant. Industrial banking of the latter type, common in the U.S.A. and Germany, has always been regarded with suspicion by British bankers as implying too much involvement in the activities of particular firms, and although there have been recent innovations such as term loans for the building of tankers, there is no indication that the banks are interested in venturing further into this sort of business.

Liquidity and Profitability

The distribution of bank assets among these alternatives is the result of conflicting pulls. From their clients' point of view, banks must aim at maximum *liquidity* – keeping assets in a form which enables them to meet all possible withdrawals by customers. But banks are also profit-makers, and considerations of *profitability* imply a concentration on less liquid assets. Generally, the more liquid an asset, the less profitable it is for the banks. Distribution of bank resources is therefore a compromise between the competing ends of profitability and liquidity. Thus, cash is perfectly liquid, money at call almost so, since it consists of immediately repayable loans, and bills discounted will be due to mature very shortly. None of these yield a high interest return, but the banks nevertheless cover themselves against possible withdrawals by depositors by maintaining liquid assets at a minimum of 28% (recently reduced from 30%) of their deposits – the 'liquidity ratio'. The 'earning assets', investment and advances, are both more profitable, but relatively illiquid. Investments are perfectly marketable – the stock exchange ensures that they can always be sold – but perhaps only at prices which involve capital loss. For advances, on the other hand, marketability exists only if the bank has insisted on collateral security which can be disposed of if necessary. However, since most advances are in fact unsecured, they will be self-liquidating only if the banker has correctly judged the creditworthiness of the borrower.

During the post-war period, when the banks were restricted from increasing advances to the level which they considered 'normal', investments came to be regarded as a residual outlet for their resources. The extent to which the banks considered themselves under-lent during those years is shown by the massive switch to advances which the London Clearing Banks made as restrictions were removed:

	(% of total deposits)	
	Investments	*Advances*
1952	32·6	30·3
1964	14·3	52·7
1966 (March)	12·0	54·0

MONEY AND LIQUIDITY

The 'quantity of money' sounds a definite enough concept, and we have so far treated it as comprising bank-notes, coins, and bank deposits. However, limitation of the definition to just these assets is not entirely satisfactory and may lead to inappropriate policy conclusions.

On the one hand, it could be argued that if money is money because it performs the twin functions of a medium of exchange and a store of value, then not *all* bank deposits should be included. A medium of exchange gives *immediate* command over resources; time deposits, requiring a period of pre-withdrawal notice, do not strictly satisfy this criterion. If, on the other hand, this is regarded as quibbling and time deposits are included, then, for the same reason, so also should a number of other assets such as Post Office and Trustee savings accounts, and deposits with finance houses and building societies, which can similarly be turned into cash after a short period of notice. The case for their inclusion is strengthened by the fact that some such deposits are officially withdrawable on demand up to stipulated amounts; others are immediately withdrawable in practice, even when the rules require a notice period.

There are thus difficulties in drawing a rigid distinction between two groups of assets – money and non-money. If we define money in terms of certain qualities which it should possess and which enable it to perform monetary functions, we have to admit that 'moneyness' or 'liquidity' is an attribute which may be found in a much wider variety of assets than coin, notes, and bank deposits. Perhaps it is therefore better, instead of distinguishing two clearly defined *quantities*, money and non-money, to think in terms of a range of assets possessing 'moneyness' to different degrees, and of the place which the same asset holds in the liquidity spectrum also varying according to time, economic conditions, and ownership. Thus, a Treasury Bill due to mature today is clearly a good deal more liquid than one issued today; government bonds are less liquid today than they were during 1947 when the government was supporting very low interest rates and effectively 'monetizing' such assets; bills held by the discount market are more liquid than those held by outsiders, since the discount house is entitled to encash them at the Bank of England (a privilege which we will explain in a later section). It is this sort of reasoning which dominated the Report of the Radcliffe Committee and led to a shift of emphasis from the quantity of money to 'the whole state of liquidity in the economy' as a major variable for analysis and control.

Banks and Non-Banks

Apart from the banks, there also exist in a developed economy a large number of non-banking financial intermediaries – insurance companies, investment trusts, savings institutions, finance companies, and building societies. These have traditionally been sharply distinguished from the commercial banks on the grounds that they merely function as brokers, acting as intermediaries between borrowers and lenders of loanable funds; only the banks actually create something, that something being the medium of exchange in which all payments must finally be made.

However, the basis on which some of the non-banking financial intermediaries work is, in fact, very similar to that of the banks. Take, for example, the activities of building societies. Individual X deposits £1,000 with a building society which then re-lends that sum to individual Y for the purpose of house purchase. Y, in receipt of £1,000 cash, is clearly more liquid, has more immediate purchasing power, than previously. The important point to note, however, is that his increase in liquidity is not necessarily at the expense of X. X, now holding a building society deposit rather than a bank balance, may *feel* no less liquid than before; this is because it is a common practice among building societies to allow depositors the right of immediate withdrawal. What has happened, therefore, is that the building society has done more than act as a mere broker between lender and borrower; in the course of bringing lenders and borrowers together, it has actually increased overall liquidity. The parallel with the process of credit creation is obvious, and the ability of the building society to increase liquidity rests on precisely the same basis as that of the banks to create money. The success of both operations depends on the assumption that not all depositors will avail themselves of withdrawal rights at *the same time*. However, there is an important difference of degree in the 'pyramiding' element of the two processes. The banks, when creating deposits, can be fairly sure that a large proportion of the proceeds will be redeposited in the banking system to provide the basis for a further round of credit creation; the proportion of the receipts of house sellers which is redeposited with building societies will be very much smaller. It is interesting in this connexion to see the rapid development of branch offices by building societies which is currently taking place – the prime motive being, presumably, not so much to facilitate repayments by borrowers as to attract new lenders. Moreover, perhaps a breach is even being made in the banks' monopoly of the medium of exchange in which all payments must ultimately be made. Sometimes, particularly in the North of England, wages are paid directly into building society accounts; it may only be a short step to the situation in which building societies then settle members' accounts with shops and local authorities. Hire purchase companies already frequently provide full banking facilities, including overdrafts, for some of their major clients such as motor traders.

Thus a rigid demarcation between money and non-money, and between the activities of banks and 'non-banks', does not seem altogether justifiable. Closer to reality is the Radcliffe Committee's view that there is rather 'a single market for credit', in which the banks and non-banking financial intermediaries create assets and offer facilities which are frequently quite close substitutes. Some of the policy implications of this view are spelled out later in the chapter.

THE BANK OF ENGLAND

In its youth, the Bank of England was just a particularly large and rather privileged commercial bank competing vigorously for deposits. It now stands aloof at the apex of the banking system and confines itself, apart from an insignificant residue of private business, to handling the accounts of a few, highly important customers – the government, other banks, and the discount houses.

As the government's banker, it looks after the Exchequer accounts, and has the further responsibility of seeing that its client is always in a position to meet its commitments. If government expenditure exceeds income from taxation, the shortfall must be made good by borrowing. Direct loans from the Bank itself are traditionally limited to overnight Ways and Means advances to cover temporary miscalculations, but it is the job of the Bank of England to organize the government's major borrowing operations – from the banking system through the issue of Treasury Bills, or from the long-term market by the sale of bonds.

The commercial banks, as we have already seen, each keep part of their cash reserves in the form of a deposit at the Bank of England, such accounts being highly convenient in facilitating payments between themselves, or between the private and public sectors of the economy. However, the Bank does not act as bankers' banker to the extent of giving them overdrafts: as a result of a historical reluctance to seem dependent on a fellow banker, British banks have never borrowed from the central bank directly. Instead, they have dealt with shortages of cash in a more roundabout way, through the agency of the discount market.

The discount market (or 'money market' as it is frequently known) chiefly consists of the twelve major houses which are members of the London Discount Market Association, the body responsible for putting in a syndicated bid for the Treasury Bill issue each Friday. The L.D.M.A. houses are highly privileged customers of the Bank of England, having access to its Discount Office. We have already seen that the business of the discount houses is to purchase bills with money borrowed 'at call and short notice' from the banks; if, in order to meet a cash shortage, the commercial banks withdraw those loans, the discount houses are consequently in some financial embarrassment. The only course open to them is to go along, cap in hand, to the Bank of England, and this they can do in the *certainty* that they will be fully accommodated. The Bank will either rediscount some of the discount houses' bills, or take them as security for an advance. The Bank of England's acceptance of responsibility for meeting the cash needs of the banking system, which is what this amounts to, evolved very gradually during the nineteenth century. After a series of painful and disruptive 'confidence crises' in the then fragmented banking system, the Bank came to see that it could not just stand by and watch the structure collapse, and its obligation to 'lend without stint in times of crisis', articulated by Walter Bagehot in the 1870s, was a vital element in the evolution of low cash ratios. In acting as 'lender in the last resort', the Bank of England underwrites the liquidity of the banking system and eliminates the possibility of cumulative runs on the banks arising from loss of confidence by depositors.

MECHANICS OF MONETARY CONTROL

The basic function of a central bank is to implement the monetary policy of the government, a responsibility generally assumed by the Bank of England long before its position was formalized by nationalization in 1946. The enabling Act gives the Bank and

Treasury combined almost complete coercive authority over the banking system, with the Bank (which can itself be directed by the Treasury) empowered to make requests or give directions to the commercial banks. In practice, however, the Bank has mostly continued to rely on more traditional technical and persuasive pressures, and we shall spend the rest of this chapter in looking briefly at some of the techniques by which the Bank of England can make its influence felt on the rest of the financial system: 1. Bank Rate; 2. open-market operations; 3. funding and special deposits; and 4. credit squeezing.

1. Bank Rate

We have already explained that the discount market, linking the central and commercial banks, can always get help from the Bank of England when pressed for cash. There is, however, a qualification to this generosity. The Bank will always meet the market's requirements, but *at its own price*, the price usually being Bank Rate. Bank Rate is thus a highly esoteric rate of interest, the price which the Bank of England will pay when re-discounting first-class bills of exchange. It has no intrinsic significance for anyone in the economy except the discount houses, which, since Bank Rate is usually penally set above the market rate of discount, incur capital losses on the bills which they rediscount. The fact that we all nevertheless feel involved on an announcement of a change in Bank Rate is chiefly because a number of other rates are more or less tied to it.

The discount houses naturally keep the rate which *they* charge, the market rate of discount, very close to the rate which they themselves have to pay in times of stringency; the commercial banks, as profit-makers, will adjust the charge they make for money at call to the yields which they see the discount houses earning on bills bought with such funds; the rates which the banks pay on time deposits and charge for advances are both related to Bank Rate by traditional formulae; when these rates change, the competitors of the banks, particularly building societies and finance houses, gradually have to bring their rates into line; when short-term rates of interest are being generally pushed up, there may be some tendency for long-term rates to rise in sympathy as selling pressure develops in the market for bonds from holders tempted to switch into the now more attractive short-term market.

Changing a single, and quite special, short-term rate of interest can thus start a considerable chain of repercussions throughout the monetary system. However, these effects can only be expected if the discount houses believe that there is a real likelihood that they will have to borrow at Bank Rate. It is in the process of making Bank Rate effective, of letting the money market feel its sting, that the second of the Bank's weapons comes into play.

2. Open-Market Operations

By means of this device, the Bank can artificially induce a desired degree of stringency in the money market. The mechanism hinges on the fact, which we have already noted, that the commercial banks all maintain accounts at the Bank of England and regard these 'bankers' deposits' as part of their minimal cash reserves.

All that is meant by 'open-market operations' is that the authorities make net sales or purchases of securities – bills or bonds – in the open market. By this means, the Banks can manipulate the level of 'bankers' deposits'. Let us suppose, for example, that the Bank makes net sales of securities. They are paid for, by institutions or members of the public, by cheques drawn on the commercial banks. These cheques will be cleared and result in a debit item owed by the banks to the Bank of England which will be settled by a reduction in 'bankers' deposits'. Since such deposits are regarded by the commercial banks as part of their cash reserves, the banks will find that their cash ratios have fallen below the strictly observed minimum. To restore their position, they will therefore call in part of their short loans to the discount market, which will be 'forced into the Bank', i.e. have to ask the Bank of England for assistance, Bank Rate will have been made effective.

In the days when the discount houses dealt chiefly with commercial bills of exchange, operations of this kind could be expected to provide an additional secondary pressure on interest rates. A rise in Bank Rate would, in such circumstances, have the dual effect of making London an expensive source of finance for international trade transactions, and a relatively attractive place in which to deploy short-term funds. As a result, the discount houses would ultimately find themselves holding a smaller proportion of a reduced volume of business. This, in turn, would react on the commercial banks. As the discount market failed to renew maturing bills, payments would be due from their clients (holding deposits at the commercial banks) which would enable the discount houses to repay any borrowing which they had been forced to incur with the Bank of England. The outcome would be that cash would be withdrawn from the banks, and this, together with pressure on their liquidity ratios because of a depletion in the 'bills discounted' item, might force them into a multiple contraction of deposits in order to restore their normal asset structure. Increasing Bank Rate and making it effective by open market operations would thus have the secondary impact of reducing the total *money* supply; a reduction in the proportion of wealth taking the form of money could be expected to have some effect in pushing up the price at which people could be induced to part with money, i.e. raise interest rates.

When, in 1951, the Conservative government tried to revert to the traditional orthodoxy of monetary control, the conditions which we have just described no longer existed. The money market now dealt almost exclusively in Treasury Bills the supply of which, unlike commercial bills, is unlikely to be sensitive to interest changes. The issue of Treasury Bills depends on the gap which exists week by week between government expenditure and receipts; it can be reduced, when short-term borrowing becomes more expensive, only if the necessary funds can be raised from alternative sources. This, as we shall see below, may not be easy.

3. Funding and Special Deposits

In the typical post-war situation where the banks have had ample liquid assets, attempts by the authorities to squeeze the banks through their cash reserves by means of Bank Rate and open-market operations have been thwarted by the ability of the banks to squeeze them back; the commercial banks have been able to replenish their cash reserves via the discount market without risking a fall in their liquidity ratios below what they regard as the minimum level. The history of monetary policy in the fifties is largely of attempts by the authorities to reduce the commercial banks' liquidity ratios to the minimal levels at which they would again become responsive to orthodox techniques of control. But how can the main item in the supply of liquid assets, the Treasury Bill issue, be reduced? Assuming that taxation is not increased, the remaining alternative is to expand sales of long-term government bonds. However, 'funding', the process of lengthening the average maturity of the National Debt, involves considerable difficulties in present conditions. In Chapter 1, we saw that the vast increase in the National Debt has reduced the prices of gilt-edged securities (i.e. increased yields). At times, from the point of view of monetary policy, still further increases in the long-term rate of interest might be desirable, but this aim conflicts with the requirements of National Debt policy; the problem here is that it is not easy to sell stock on a falling market. It is true that for most *goods* there tends to be a greater demand at lower prices; with bonds, on the other hand, falling prices may induce expectations of further falls, so that demand may actually be reduced.

Limited in their ability to work through market forces, the authorities finally turned, in July 1958, to the type of *direct* control which is such anathema to British bankers. The authorities were empowered to order the commercial banks to make 'special deposits' with the Bank of England; these deposits, although earning interest, would be effectively frozen in that they were not to be regarded as part of the banks' cash or liquidity reserves. This system amounts to the power to vary the real cash or liquidity ratios observed by the commercial banks. The scheme was not put into operation until 1960–61 when three calls of 1% each were made on the banks' deposits. The purpose of these calls (later released) was to permit an increase in government borrowing without giving the banks a basis for further expansion of deposits, and the device was used again in 1965.

4. Credit Squeezing

As well as influencing the level and structure of interest rates in the economy, monetary policy may be directed at restricting the availability of finance at *given* interest rates. In this respect, the authorities have made efforts throughout much of the post-war period to regulate, in particular, bank advances. They have tried to bring about a situation in which the demand for finance, from applicants whom lenders would consider credit-worthy, has exceeded the supply at current rates of interest. Up to 1955 the commercial banks were requested to limit advances to 'essential' purposes. In July 1955 the emphasis switched to quantitative control with a request by the Chancellor for 'a positive and significant reduction in advances' over the next few months, a request that was echoed in a number of similar exhortations and 'requirements' (slightly stronger than requests?) during the next few years. In July 1958, with the introduction of the Special Deposits scheme, the ceiling on bank lending was removed for the first time during the post-war years. But the spectacular rise in advances which followed led the authorities to hurriedly revert to control during 1961–2, and since that time the banks have generally been operating under official restraint of one degree or another.

A policy of credit squeezing suffers from two serious drawbacks which were hammered home by the Radcliffe Committee. There is, first of all, the time lag between a request for a contraction of bank advances and its implementation. How *can* a bank reduce its loans? It can hardly insist on immediate repayment of existing advances and ignore the embarrassment which it would thereby cause its clients. All that can be done is to reduce the volume of new lending below the total of maturing loans, and to cut down on unused overdraft *limits*. But this takes time.

A second and more serious line of criticism can be directed at the policy of concentrating exclusively on the banks. We have stressed, earlier in this chapter, that the banks are only one element in a credit market providing many substitutes (though perhaps more expensive and less convenient) for bank advances. 'The main effect of restriction of bank credit was to drive frustrated borrowers to other sources of credit,' concluded the Radcliffe Committee. To squeeze only the banks merely caused a spill-over into the uncontrolled sectors of the credit market, with borrowers turning to alternative sources of finance like hire purchase companies, bills of exchange, and trade credit.

However, we are now moving into the realm of assessment, whereas the purpose of the present chapter was mainly to show

how the monetary system works and to explain the methods by which the authorities attempt to control it. *Why* they should do so, whether monetary policy is an effective regulator of the economy, and how it compares with other weapons for achieving the ends of economic policy – these are all matters to which we shall return in Part III.

CHAPTER 3

INTERNATIONAL PAYMENTS

THE British economy during the post-war period has been characterized by recurrent balance of payments crises, and we have become accustomed to the exhortations or self-congratulations of politicians at each announcement of the current trading figures. The balance of payments has been presented as a restraint on the rate of growth which the economy can achieve and as the most important reason for controlling the rise in money incomes and prices. The 'strength of the pound sterling' seems to have been a major end of government policy, and each indicator of our international reserve position is met with relief or dismay. We shall, however, again postpone discussion of policy to a later chapter, and concentrate in the following sections on simply explaining how international payments arise, how they are made, and why they should cause more concern than domestic payments.

The Nature of International Trade

Exporting is not an end in itself. Basically, we export in order to pay for imports, and the justification of an export drive lies in the need to import. It is, therefore, as well at the outset to see why it is sometimes preferable to obtain goods in a roundabout fashion via exports instead of diverting resources from export industries to produce the required goods at home.

The major reason for international trade is *not* that it enables us to obtain goods which we just cannot produce ourselves. There are, in fact, relatively few goods falling into this category – in particular, natural minerals and fuels, deposits of which are spread unevenly throughout the world. Most other things, e.g. tropical foodstuffs like bananas or cocoa, *could* be produced anywhere although the cost of doing so, of artificially simulating the necessary climatic conditions, would be enormously high. And so the second and much more important reason for participating in international trade is that by doing so we are able to achieve savings in scarce resources. Britain is superior in the production of certain goods; other economies, with their different supplies of labour, capital, and natural endowments, have the advantage over us in other lines. Specialization and trade may thus lead to savings in resources for both parties.

All this is very commonsensical and obvious. However, there is a third reason for international trade, based on rather more uncommon sense. Trade may be of benefit to two countries even in the case where one of them can produce *all* the goods which it requires more cheaply than the other. Even in these circumstances it may pay the more efficient producer to concentrate on those lines of output in which its superiority is the most marked and to satisfy its needs for other goods by importing them. The businessman who can type better than his secretary still finds it economic to employ her because this leaves him free to devote his energy to taking decisions – at which, it is to be hoped, his superiority over his secretary is even greater.

The gains from international trade are thus similar to the benefits which arise from specialization and exchange between individuals. The justification for international trade is that it leads to a more economic utilization of resources – although whether specialization will, in fact, be pushed to the level suggested by economic reasoning depends also on the strength of political and strategic considerations.

BALANCE OF PAYMENTS

The balance of payments is simply an account of the credits and debits arising from the transactions of members of an economy with non-members. However, the term is frequently used rather loosely. To sort out its various connotations we shall concentrate in this chapter on the British balance of payments for the year 1965 which is presented in the table on page 61 in a schematic form.

The first distinction to be made is between the 'balance of trade' and the 'balance of payments on current account'. The balance of trade is limited to purchases and sales of *merchandise*. About a quarter of the goods consumed in Britain come from abroad, and the table shows that we were not able to export sufficient merchandise to foot the bill. There was therefore a 'trade gap' of £265 million – 1965 was not a good year but even this deficit only amounted to some 5% of the total import bill – vast improvement on, say, 1938, when our merchandise exports only paid for about 64% of our merchandise imports.

U.K. Balance of Payments 1965

	(£m.)
Imports	5,044
Exports and re-exports	4,779
Balance of Trade	**−265**
Net invisibles	+129
Current balance	**−136**
Net outflow of long-term capital	−218
Basic balance	**−354**
Reduction in short-term debts	4
Gain to reserves	246
Total to be financed	**604**
Drawing from I.M.F.	499
Balancing item	+105

It would be a remarkable coincidence if the balance of trade actually happened to *balance*. Export and import operations are generally undertaken by quite different elements in the economy acting in independent ignorance of what the others are doing. Imports could be *made* to just equal exports if a complex and comprehensive licensing system kept continuous track of items on both sides, but in any free system, a surplus or deficit is almost bound to arise.

We have been expressing imports and exports in terms of millions of pounds, and their total *value* is obviously equal to Volume × Price. Consequently, the balance of trade can change as a result of movements in either of these variables. Between 1950 and 1960, for example, the volume of British exports increased by 21%, while import volume rose during the same period by 38%. Nevertheless, the trade gap in 1960 was substantially smaller than in 1950. The explanation for this lies in the fact that import *prices* did not rise so rapidly as export prices, so that a larger volume of imports could be earned for any given volume of exports. Changes in the relative prices of imports and exports are known as movements in the terms of trade, and can be of the greatest importance.

Adding certain items to the balance of trade gives the 'balance of payments on current account' – the most general connotation of the term 'balance of payments'. The balance of payments on current account includes, not just imports and exports of merchandise, but also 'invisible' imports and exports. These are invisible in the sense that although no transfer of goods is involved, certain transactions have the same end result, namely, the creation of credits and debits between economies.

Thus, for example, both the government (in maintaining embassies and consulates, and military bases) and individuals (as tourists or members of the armed forces) spend considerable sums of money on goods and services bought in foreign countries. Despite the fact that such expenditure takes place abroad, it involves payments from u.k. residents to non-residents and is, therefore, equivalent to importing merchandise into Britain. Expenditure by foreign governments and tourists in Britain is classed, on the same basis, as 'invisible exports'. Other invisible exports arise from the sale of services to foreigners when they use British shipping, insurance, banking, and commercial facilities. Exports may also be invisible when, instead of producing goods in the u.k. and then shipping them abroad for sale, British-owned firms actually produce the goods overseas in foreign-based subsidiaries. To the extent that such activities lead to profits, interest, and dividend payments to the British owners, additions must be made to the export side of the balance of payments accounts. Similarly, payments to foreign owners of British-based firms are invisible imports.

In 1965, as has always been the case, invisible exports earned more than we spent on invisible imports. Frequently, gains from invisible trade have been sufficient to offset an adverse balance of trade. However, this was not the case in 1965 when net invisibles amounted to only £129 million; the balance of payments on current account was thus unfavourable to the extent of £136 million. The major net invisible credits came from the provision of commercial services and receipts of profits, interest, and dividends; however, a large part of these earnings were swallowed up in the heavy net debit resulting from government activities.

International Payments

As with the balance of trade, there is no automatic process whereby the balance of payments on current account actually balances; once again, it would be remarkable if in any year it did happen to do so. But a deficit on current account, an excess of visible and invisible imports over exports, certainly does not mean that we are getting something for nothing. All that it implies is that export earnings alone are insufficient to meet the import bill. So far, however, we have only been dealing with *current* transactions. When we also take into account the impact of *capital* flows and net monetary movements, there is a sense in which the balance of payments does have to *balance*. But before going on to discuss these aspects of the international payments mechanisms, we shall first say something about the means.

EXCHANGE RATES

One of the features which distinguish international from domestic transactions (though by no means the fundamental one) is that participants in international trade generally have different currencies. An American exporter to Britain wants to be paid for his goods in dollars, which he can then spend in his own economy; pounds sterling are no good to him at all. International payments must, therefore, be made in some medium which is acceptable because it is convertible into the required currency.

Traditionally, it is gold which has performed this function. Dating from the era when domestic currencies were also either of gold coinage, or at least of paper exchangeable for gold, it remains fully acceptable as a means of settling international debts. It has the major drawback, however, of being in relatively inelastic supply; the amount of gold available for international payments does not necessarily bear any relation to the amount which is needed. At present it is quite inadequate to support the volume of trade which is taking place.

Gold has therefore come to be supplemented by a second means of settling international debts – the use of certain domestic currencies. Although pounds sterling are of no value to the American who wants to buy goods and services in his own country, they *are* required by the American *importer* of goods from Britain, who will be prepared to purchase sterling for dollars in order to settle his British debts in an acceptable form. Since 1938, there has been a very considerable expansion in the use of national currencies as a means of making international payments. But since gold, dollars, and pounds are quite different units of exchange, the question arises of how they can be reduced to a comparable basis. What determines the value of each in terms of the others?

Flexible Exchange Rates

One possibility would be to allow the external value of national currencies to find their own level in free markets. Unimpeded by any intervention from the authorities, the rate at which one currency exchanged for another would then depend on supply and demand, the major element in which would come from import and export transactions. The demand for pounds in the market would chiefly be from foreigners who had bought British exports and required sterling in order to pay for them; a supply of pounds would similarly be coming on to the market from British importers demanding foreign exchange. A deficit in the balance of payments on current account would mean that the supply of pounds in the foreign exchange market exceeded the demand. Equilibrium would be achieved by a fall in the external value of the pound, i.e. a depreciation in the rate at which sterling was exchanged for other currencies.

However, current payments and receipts are not the only elements in the market for a currency. Demand and supply may also be affected by capital movements. To the extent, for example, that u.s. investors wish to set up factories in the u.k. or merely lend money at what they consider to be attractive rates of interest, they will have to exchange their dollars and thereby create an additional demand for pounds. A deficit on current account can therefore exist *without* a depreciation in the exchange rate – if capital movements sufficiently supplement the demand for the currency arising from trade.

A system of flexible or 'floating' exchange rates suffers from a number of defects. Exchange rates which are liable to alter at any time would be a source of inconvenience and uncertainty for traders engaged in international transactions, and expose them to the risk of losses when their assumptions about the future of the exchange rate proved wrong. This is a serious problem only to the extent that free exchange rates imply frequently *fluctuating* rates. Unfortunately, this is only too likely to be the case because of the increased likelihood, in free exchange markets, of speculative pressures.

The fact that exchange rates can alter freely enhances the importance of guessing the future course of the exchange rate. If the pound does depreciate, those holding sterling will be able to obtain less foreign exchange than previously. Those who predict such a depreciation will therefore sell pounds now in the hope of rebuying them more cheaply later; failure to have foreseen the fall in the value of the pound will cause capital losses for foreigners who continue to hold sterling. Similar possibilities of gain exist if the currency is expected to appreciate.

It is true that, to some extent, fluctuations in exchange rates may actually be moderated by the activities of speculators, who sometimes oppose general market opinion, buying when others are selling and vice versa. The danger, however, is that any consensus of opinion about the future of the exchange rate will be self-justifying. If, because of signs of weakness in the balance of payments, it is thought that the pound is likely to depreciate, holders of sterling will be anxious to rid themselves of it and by so doing will *cause* the depreciation which they fear. Demand for pounds will be reduced, supply will increase, and the value of the pound will fall in terms of other currencies. The possibility always exists, with a flexible exchange-rate system, of cumulative downward movements which may ultimately destroy confidence in the external value of the currency.

Speculation is not only undertaken by professional financiers shunting 'hot money' from one centre to another. It also arises out of the normal process of trade. A foreign importer of British goods, anticipating a fall in the value of the pound, will naturally attempt to delay payment for as long as possible in the hope that he will get his pounds more cheaply. Similarly, payments by U.K. importers will be accelerated in order to benefit from the higher exchange value of the pound at present prevailing. The overall effect of these 'leads and lags' is to reduce the demand for sterling in the foreign exchange market and increase its supply. The significance of leads and lags is indicated by the Radcliffe

Committee's estimate that in the third quarter of 1957 such activities led to an outflow from the U.K. of £100 million.

The advantage of a free exchange-rate system is that the brunt of adjusting payments imbalance is thrown on to the foreign exchange market rather than the domestic economy. However, the disadvantages – that the volume of trade may be reduced because of uncertainty, and disturbed by distortions in exchange rates due to speculative operations – seem to outweigh the benefits. Those who today advocate that sterling should be allowed to 'float' therefore usually propose only *some* flexibility – within limits pegged by official intervention and coupled with measures to control purely speculative movements of capital.

Fixed Exchange Rates

These difficulties led to a ready agreement by members of the International Monetary Fund (which we will deal with more fully in a moment) to introduce stable exchange rates for the post-war period. The Fund initially determined the value of each of the member's currencies in terms of gold, and it then became the responsibility of each country to intervene in its foreign exchange markets to ensure that the agreed parity of its currency was maintained within very narrow limits.

Thus, if, at the agreed parity, the supply of a currency exceeds the demand for it in the foreign exchange market, it is up to the authorities to prevent the fall in exchange rate which would otherwise take place by itself supplementing the demand; similarly, the authorities must be prepared to provide additional supplies of a currency in circumstances where excess demand would lead to appreciation of the currency. Such operations in Britain are conducted by the Exchange Equalization Account and its ability to maintain the existing sterling rate clearly depends on its having sufficient gold and foreign exchange to meet demands.

The immediate impact of balance of payments adjustment in such a system thus falls on reserves. This has been a particular problem for the U.K. since the war, since at no time has it been felt that the level of gold and foreign exchange reserves has been adequate in relation to the potential drains upon them. In 1938 U.K. international reserves stood at £605 million. During recent years they have fluctuated around the £1,000 million mark. But although reserves have been approximately double the pre-war level, we have to remember firstly, that since that time the general price level has trebled, so that the real value of the reserves is now substantially less; secondly, that there has been a very considerable rise in the volume of trade which the reserves have to service; and finally, that during the same period the potential drain on reserves additional to normal trade swings has been increased by the colossal rise in sterling balances – liquid holdings of sterling which can be drawn on immediately by foreign owners and which make the present reserve position particularly precarious. These short-term liabilities amounted to £476 million in 1938, rose sharply as Britain accumulated debts during the war, and today stand at some £3,500 million. Just how troublesome sterling balances are, and whether it is reasonable to treat the reserves: sterling balances ratio as an index of the precariousness of the pound – are questions which will be discussed in Chapter 12.

Devaluation

Exchange rates are not fixed for all time under the I.M.F. rules. Provision is made in the Articles of the Fund for changes, after prior consultation, in the case of a 'fundamental disequilibrium' in the balance of payments. Such occasional adjustments may be termed 'devaluation' or 'revaluation' to distinguish them from the less exceptional 'depreciation' or 'appreciation' under a flexible system.

What, in general, can be hoped for from a devaluation like the 1949 U.K. adjustment from £1:$4 to £1:$2·8? The first effect is on import and export prices. A £600 car produced in the U.K. and sold in the U.S. which would previously have fetched $2,400 will now sell at $1,680 ($2·8 × 600). A car produced in the U.S. for $4,000 which would, before devaluation, have sold in the U.K. for £1,000, will now cost a British buyer £1,428 10s.

The possibility of gain from devaluation lies chiefly in the effects of these relative price changes. Lower export prices will lead to increased sales; higher import prices should reduce the volume of imports. However, whether the balance of payments consequently improves depends on by *how much* import and export volumes change as a result of their new prices.

So far as imports are concerned, the position is quite straightforward. *Any* reduction in the volume of imports will save foreign exchange (we have to remember that although a British consumer will have to pay a higher *sterling* price for an imported good, its foreign exchange cost remains the same as before). Unfortunately, it is not similarly true to say that *any* increase in the volume of exports will result in increased earnings of foreign exchange. If, for example, the decline in the export price of cars from $2,400 to $1,680 leads to an increase in the number of British cars sold in the u.s. only from 1,000 to 1,200, the effect of devaluation is to actually reduce, rather than increase, the total revenue earned.

1,000 cars sold before devaluation at $2,400	.	$2,400,000
1,200 ,, ,, after ,, ,, $1,680	.	$2,016,000

For an improvement in the balance of payments, it is necessary that the net effect of the increased export volume and the decreased import volume is sufficient to *outweigh* the lower unit price of exports.

Part of the benefit of the change in relative prices may also be lost if the success of devaluation in cutting import spending reduces foreign incomes and therefore has repercussions on export sales. Finally, the fall in export prices may be limited by increases in costs resulting from the devaluation. This is possible if exports have a high import-content, or if workers in the export industries demand higher wages to compensate for increased import prices, or if export producers have to bid resources away from domestic uses in order to exploit the new situation.

It is not possible to be precise about how these various factors would operate if Britain were to devalue. (The case study which might have been available in the 1949 devaluation is unfortunately obscured by other events of the time, particularly the outbreak of the Korean War.) Certainly the bulk of British imports are of foodstuffs and raw materials and the demand for such necessities is probably unresponsive to price changes. But there would surely be scope for substituting home-produced goods for certain of the manufactured and semi-manufactured imports which have recently been running at 40% of the total. The key question, however, is what difference lower prices would make to the volume of British exports. Admittedly, they are sold in competition with a few major rivals who are hardly likely to stand aside and watch their sales being whittled away without retaliation. On the other hand, the degree of price sensitivity necessary to make devaluation successful is not all that great and the evidence now seems on the whole to suggest that the net effect on foreign exchange earnings would be favourable.

If this is *not* so, if price is not an important consideration in determining the level of exports, then it is important to remember that it would not just be devaluation which would have to be discounted as a means of solving the balance of payments problem. Similar objections would have to be brought against such alternatives as tariffs or incomes policy which also rely on adjustment of relative prices as the means of bringing about an improvement in our foreign trading position.

INTERNATIONAL BORROWING

Apart from drawing on reserves or altering the exchange rate, a payments deficit may be met by borrowing operations. If foreigners, instead of insisting on payment now in their own currencies, are prepared instead to hold their credits in the form of sterling balances, they are in effect lending to Britain. Generally, such balances are invested in liquid assets. They can be withdrawn at any time by either exchanging them for foreign currencies (drawing on U.K. reserves) or by using them to finance unrequited imports from Britain. A balance of payments deficit may also be financed by long-term flows of capital if foreigners invest the proceeds of export sales in British industries. The opposite case also holds good. If a country has a balance of payments surplus, this *means* that either its reserves are increasing, that it is lending abroad or repaying past debts.

The basic way to attract foreign capital is by offering high interest rates, and it is in this connexion that Bank Rate changes have their greatest significance. Internationally, a rise in Bank Rate still carries the implication that the British authorities are keeping a tight rein on the economy; apart from this psychological impact, we have already seen that increased Bank Rate causes a general increase in short-term interest rates, and foreign funds may flow to Britain if a differential is thereby created over interest rates in the other major financial centres. Certainly, this seems to have been a powerful mechanism under the Gold Standard conditions of pre-1931, when the pound was apparently immutably tied to gold with no likelihood of a change in the exchange rate. However, its effectiveness has been seriously reduced by the present widespread use of domestic currencies for financing international trade. Relative interest rates are no longer the only factor which those with surplus funds have to consider; they also have to bear in mind the possibility of devaluation and of official restrictions being imposed on withdrawal of funds. Today, in circumstances of reasonable doubt about the future of the pound and other major currencies, speculators can insure themselves against the risk of capital loss through currency depreciation by operating in the forward exchange market, where contracts can be made to buy or sell foreign exchange at some *future* date. The rate at which this is possible diverges from the 'spot', or current rate, according to expectations about the future of the official exchange rate. Thus, for example, if it was felt likely that sterling was going to appreciate in terms of other currencies, the pound would stand at a premium, with the 'forward' rate exceeding the spot rate; fear of devaluation, on the other hand, would be reflected in the pound selling at a discount in the forward market.

Therefore, if the short-term rate of interest is 4% in New York and 5% in London, the differential will not necessarily lead to a flow of funds to the U.K. If the pound is at a discount in the forward market, the cost of forward cover will have to be set against the interest gain, and may make the shift of funds unprofitable. Since the forward exchange rate is essentially an expression of market confidence or doubt in a currency, interest rates are likely to be least effective in causing capital movements when funds are most needed; at such times, confidence will be at its lowest and the cost of forward cover correspondingly high. Moreover, even if a policy of high interest rates is successful in attracting foreign capital, the operation may prove expensive. The higher interest has to be paid, not only on new funds which have flowed in, but also on existing liabilities. This cost is substantial in the case of Britain and represents an additional burden to the balance of payments which has to be weighed against the temporary relief afforded by an inflow of foreign capital.

A second source of international borrowing is the International Monetary Fund, which we have already mentioned with regard to the fixing of exchange rates. The I.M.F. began operations in 1947, and essentially acts as an economizer of international liquidity. Each of the member-states was initially set a quota which was to be paid in to the Fund, 25% in the form of gold and 75% in its own currency. The Fund thus acquired substantial stocks of both gold and a variety of foreign exchange. Each member has purchasing rights on these resources – automatic if the amount is less than 25% of its own quota, and up to 200% of its quota at the discretion of the managers of the Fund. The basic criterion of eligibility to buy foreign exchange is that the funds should be employed only to finance trade imbalances arising from current transactions. The Fund may also attach other conditions to borrowing, including advice on what remedial action should be taken to remove the imbalance. Clearly, given its limited resources, the Fund can only continue to fulfil its functions if its stock of foreign exchange is replenished by borrowers later buying back their own currencies. The Fund's operations are therefore confined to temporary assistance. The balance of payments problems of the immediately post-war period were not judged to qualify according to this criterion; it has been said that 'during this long period the Fund seemed content to sit on its considerable hoard of specie and exchange waiting for the golden age when the world would be fit for it to operate in.' During the fifties there was considerable liberalization of the Fund's eligibility criteria with the result that extensive use was at last made of its resources. A particularly useful innovation during this period was the system whereby the Fund offered stand-by credits to members who felt that there was a possibility of their requiring assistance during the near future. The mere existence of such stand-by arrangements was frequently sufficient to restore confidence in a currency and obviate the need of actual purchases.

In recent years the resources of the Fund have been supplemented by the Paris Club agreement – between Britain, the United States, Japan, Sweden, Canada, West Germany, Italy, France, Belgium, and Holland – to create a secondary pool of

$6 billion available on a stand-by basis and with the particular function of offsetting speculative movements; borrowing rights are limited to the ten contributing members. An additional element of quasi-official cooperation has developed in the practice of 'currency swaps' – informal arrangements between the authorities in the major financial centres to supply each other with scarce currencies on a short-term basis and avoid adding to private pressures in the foreign exchange markets. The extent to which official assistance could be augmented by inter-bank action was further revealed by the £1,000 million short-term loan rapidly contributed by eleven central banks to 'save sterling' during the crisis of late 1964.

CAPITAL AND MONETARY MOVEMENTS IN 1965

Under a system of pegged exchange rates, failure of the balance of payments on current account to actually balance means that the gap between imports and exports is filled by either (*a*) capital flows, i.e. international borrowing or lending, or (*b*) changes in a country's reserves of gold and foreign exchange. Another look at the table on page 61 will show how these capital and reserve movements worked out in 1965.

We interrupted our analysis of the balance of payments for that year at the point where visible and invisible transactions had yielded a current account deficit of £136 million. This was the amount by which our export earnings fell short of the foreign exchange required to pay for imports. Since foreigners had no intention of *giving* us goods, how was it to be found?

An individual spending more than his income can sometimes meet his bills by disposing of some of his assets. So can the nation as a whole, and overseas investments could have been sold off to bring in the necessary foreign exchange. This was certainly not the course which was followed in 1965: in fact, British overseas investment (by the government, private individuals and firms) *exceeded* long-term investment in Britain by non-residents, so that there was a net *outflow* of long-term capital amounting to £218 million. Despite the fact that there was a current account deficit, Britain continued to build up its stock of factories and share portfolios abroad.

Together, the current and the long-term capital balances are known as the 'basic balance of payments'. We now have to explain how it was possible to run a basic deficit to the tune of £354 million. The answer is not the obvious one that gold and foreign exchange reserves fell by that amount; astonishingly enough, they *increased* by £246 million during 1965. Add that (and a £4 million fall in overseas liabilities) to the basic deficit and there is a grand £604 million to be accounted for! How could Britain import more than it exported *and* invest large sums abroad *and* reduce certain overseas liabilities *and* increase its gold and foreign currency reserves? In 1965 it was nearly all made possible by massive use of our drawing rights at the I.M.F. £499 million came from that source – a short-term expedient in that it would have to be repaid during the near future.

There was also help, on paper at least, from the mysterious 'balancing item'; in 1965 this was £105 million. Its origin lies in the inaccuracies of the process of tracing the trade and capital transactions which comprise the balance of payments accounts. Errors and omissions can arise because traders buy and sell goods at prices different from those at which they are officially invoiced, because transactions may be completed in a different period from that in which the goods were moved (here, 'leads and lags' are of considerable importance), because movements in long-term capital are estimated by surveys and sample inquiries which are known not to give full and accurate coverage, or because foreign short-term capital may find its way into British financial institutions like hire purchase companies to which the authorities have not yet extended their system of official returns.

The balancing item is the discrepancy between what the current trade and long-term capital accounts suggest the balance of monetary movements *will* be, and what is *actually* recorded under this heading. By definition it consists of unknowns, and it is therefore very difficult to interpret. Thus we cannot conclude, just because the balancing item in 1965 was a *positive* £105 million, that earnings on current account must therefore have been underestimated or expenditure overestimated. It is also possible that the positive item resulted from a failure to fully record an increase in U.K. liabilities or a running down of our assets.

So long as the balancing item is fairly small, its existence is no real impediment to policy making. But if it is large, as in

1960, when it rose to no less than £364 million, very considerable difficulty arises in interpreting balance of payments figures to give a basis for future policy. Unreliability of the statistics is just one of the factors which makes it hard to decide when we ought to *worry* about the balance of payments.

WHEN IS THE BALANCE OF PAYMENTS A PROBLEM?

We have so far assumed that a deficit in the balance of payments on current account implies the need for action, and balance of payments terminology has strong persuasive overtones of this kind. To say that the balance of payments is 'adverse' is to suggest in the same breath that something should be done about it, while a 'favourable' balance of payments sounds very much like a matter for congratulation. In fact, however, interpretation of balance of payments statistics requires a much more sophisticated approach than this. We have just been stressing the complexity of balance of payments accounts. There is a variety of meanings which can be given to the notion of 'balance of payments' itself; changes can take place in the composition of the accounts even when the totals remain constant; statistical difficulties may bedevil the task of deciding even what *is* happening. *Evaluating* the situation, assessing whether a given payments position is satisfactory or not, involves still more basic considerations.

A balance of payments deficit on current account is not a problem in itself. The discrepancy between imports and exports does not necessarily mean that exports failed to reach the planned level or that imports were unwarrantably high; it may also reflect a quite deliberate policy of facilitating a larger volume of imports than can be paid for currently. Filling the gap by long-term borrowing from abroad makes good sense so long as exporting potential is meanwhile or consequently increased at least enough to meet the flow of profits, interest and dividends which will become due to foreign creditors.

On the other hand, it is possible for a country to run a surplus on current account and still claim to have a balance of payments problem – because the actual surplus is less than the desired surplus required for achieving a particular level of overseas investment, building up reserves or reducing liabilities. (It should be remembered, however, that although all countries may *desire* current surpluses, they can't all succeed; any surpluses must be matched by corresponding deficits somewhere in the system.)

Our conclusion is that the balance of payments is a problem when it is *thought* to be a problem. A so-called 'adverse' account may in certain circumstances be of no concern at all while a 'favourable' account may call for urgent remedial measures. In the light of this discussion it is not difficult to see why, in Britain, the balance of payments in recent years has been causing increasing official anxiety.

Policy has aimed at earning a substantial surplus on current account. What has actually happened, on the other hand, is that in 'good' years the surplus has been well below the target level and that there have been more and more 'bad' years in which the current account has slipped into serious deficit. The strains of such deficits (augmented by a sustained net outflow of long-term capital) cannot be borne by gold and foreign exchange reserves already only precariously adequate to maintain sterling as an international currency; resort has therefore been made to short-term borrowing to fill the gap. Given the government's reluctance to devalue, the brunt of the necessary adjustment has fallen on the domestic economy. A payments crisis has meant cutting the import bill by reducing the level of demand and activity – the 'stop' phase of the notorious 'stop–go' system.

It is clear that such a situation demands a fundamental re-orientation – either of the economy so that it achieves the objectives which it has been set, or of the objectives themselves. These are matters we shall return to in Part III.

DOMESTIC AND INTERNATIONAL PAYMENTS

A lot of fuss is made about international payments, and it may still not be clear from this brief account of international financial problems quite what it is which distinguishes them from imbalances in payments between parts of the *same* country. After all, internal balance of payments problems *do* arise between, say, counties, although we may call them something different. Depressed regions probably import more from other parts of the country than they manage to export to them and the immediate implications are exactly the same as in international trade – that the deficit is financed either by drawing on reserves (past savings) or by borrowing (increased credit, or raising funds on the stock exchange).

Domestic payments do not reach the international degree of 'crisis' for two reasons. First, there is a much greater mobility of resources within one country. It is a good deal easier for people and capital to move in and out of depressed regions in response to market pressures. However, as the history of depressed areas in Britain amply illustrates, we cannot altogether rely on disparities being evened out by market forces alone. There may be *more* mobility inside a country than between countries, but still not enough to ensure that necessary changes in the economic structure are achieved rapidly and painlessly. The second difference between domestic and international payments difficulties is one of attitudes. When we recognize that free play of the market is unlikely to resolve the 'balance of payments' problems of our own depressed regions, we at the same time accept the need for a deliberate state policy of encouraging capital to move in and labour to move out. It is, therefore, not just their greater intractability which distinguishes international from domestic balance of payments problems. Equally important is that we consciously try to deal with chronic payments deficits when they affect members of our own economy; we are not so concerned at the plight of other members of the international economy.

PART II

INDUSTRY AND TRADE

CHAPTER 4

PRIVATE MANUFACTURING INDUSTRY

IT is frequently said of the British economy that it lacks the flexibility which is so necessary in a world of rapidly changing techniques and tastes. But although it may be true that there is insufficient flexibility, the degree to which the economy *has* altered and adapted itself to new conditions during the last few decades is none the less remarkable. By the outbreak of the First World War, British industry had certainly settled into a fossilized pattern from which adjustment was only painfully begun during the inter-war period; the extent to which the process has been completed under the stimulus of the Second World War, technological developments, and growing world trade can be seen if we compare the present pattern of industrial output with that of the pre-1914 period.

It was during this earlier period that Britain enjoyed the fruits of a head-start in the Industrial Revolution. About a third of world industrial exports then came from this country, of which some 70% were coal, iron and steel, or textile products. The prosperity of the economy rested heavily on these three great staple industries, which employed a quarter of the labour force and produced nearly half of British industrial output.

However, being first in the field has its disadvantages, not least of which is the danger of complacency at past progress and a consequent lack of interest in continued innovation. As other nations industrialized, they not only initially concentrated on producing, generally by more up-to-date methods, the basic products with which Britain had previously supplied them; they leapt ahead in the production of new products by new techniques which, although sometimes invented in the u.k., had been largely neglected there. The extent to which the world had passed Britain by was revealed in the dreadful decline of the staple industries in the inter-war period.

Today, employment, out of a much expanded labour force, has fallen substantially in the case of coal-mining and drastically in the textile industry. The other old staple, iron and steel, although relatively less important, has recovered under the stimulus of demand from the new industries which have since developed. Nearly a quarter of manufacturing workers are now employed in engineering, electrical goods, and shipbuilding industries, with their highly variegated output of products which fifty years ago were largely unheard of. A further 10% find employment in the production of vehicles, which, in their greater homogeneity, have the only real claim to being a new staple industry. However, simple comparison of the industrial pattern now with that of earlier periods is hampered by the breakdown of traditional classification of 'industries', which has resulted from the far-reaching technological changes of the past few decades. The developments of petro-chemical products, synthetic fibres, and plastics have all served to blur previous lines of demarcation.

Parallel with these changes in the occupational and output pattern of industry has been a reversal of its earlier geographical distribution. Location was originally heavily concentrated on the coalfields, and it was the development of a new source of energy, electricity, which first released industries to locations closer to the final consumer markets – in particular the London and south-eastern areas. The ties to particular locations have since been loosened further by the immense expansion in the use of oil since 1938, the post-war development of nuclear energy, and the increased use of man-manufactured 'raw materials'.

STRUCTURE OF INDUSTRY

Industrial Concentration

The majority of British manufacturing establishments still operate on a relatively small scale, employing few more workers than Mr William Lever's Bolton grocery business in the 1880s. But far more significant today are the Unilevers which have developed from such humble origins. Concentration of industrial power has been an outstanding feature of the British economy during the present century. The process of integration has for the most part been quietly unspectacular, only spasmodically exciting public attention as the giants ponderously perform their

cannibalistic take-over rites. Sometimes it takes the form of a
simple union of enterprises producing the same product, who
emerge with a single identity. Frequently, however, it is thought
prudent to allow old identities to continue in order to retain
traditional loyalties of customers and within the firms themselves.
It is difficult to remember, as Omo and Surf flash their competing
signals across the television screen, that they are both made by
the same firm – together, among others, with Sunlight, Lux,
Lifebuoy, Vim, Rinso, Pears, Vinolia, Knight's Castile, Persil,
Domestos, Sqezy, Stork, Echo, Summer County, Blue Band,
Spry, Gibbs, Signal, Pepsodent, Mentasol, Erasmic, Pin-up,
Twink, Icilma, Sunsilk, Atkinsons English Lavender, Walls,
Batchelors, Birds-Eye, and Macfisheries products.

A great deal of industrial concentration took place even
before the First World War, with a further spurt in face of the
intensive foreign competition in the depressed inter-war years.
Indeed, it is doubtful whether the average degree of integration
has much increased since that time. In a classic survey based on
the 1935 Census of Production, two investigators, Leake and
Maizels, tried to measure the degree of concentration in certain
'trade groups' by calculating the percentage of the total workers
occupied in each group who were employed in the three largest
business units:

Percentage of total workers occupied in fifteen trade groups
employed by the three largest business units

Chemicals	48	Textiles	23
Miscellaneous	47	Paper and Printing	22
Public utilities	44	Clay and Building	
Engineering and		materials	22
Vehicles	43	Leather	15
Iron and Steel	39	Clothing	13
Food, Drink, and		Mining and Quarrying	10
Tobacco	32	Timber	10
Non-ferrous metals	26	Building	4

The average degree of concentration was 26%. However, we
have to treat the conclusions of this and other similar inquiries
with a certain amount of caution. If the largest firms in an
industry are highly automated, the use of only labour as a yardstick of importance may be very misleading. The firm's assets

or turnover as a guide to size might give quite different results. Then again, there are difficulties in the definition of 'business unit'. The Leake and Maizels survey almost certainly underestimated the real degree of concentration by not taking into account the significance of minority shareholdings or interlocking directorships.

The results of a further survey for the period 1954–60 are shown below. This time the yardstick for concentration was the percentage of the total *net assets* of trade groups held by the largest *ten* firms:

Percentage of concentration of the net assets of trade groups in the ten largest firms in each group

	1954	1960		1954	1960
Food	61	64	Bricks	54	55
Drink	54	64	Paper and Printing	60	67
Chemicals	81	82	Leather and Timber	63	65
Metal manufacture			Construction	33	33
excluding Steel	46	58	Wholesalers	40	43
Engineering	56	59	Entertainment	74	74
Vehicles	58	65	Transport	57	58
Textiles	62	71			

The figures for 1960 show how the 1954 assets would have been distributed had the 1960 degree of concentration already been attained; we can see that over these years there was increased integration in all of these groups except Construction and Entertainment.

Looking at individual industries or broader trade groups in this way ignores the fact that many enterprises extend their activities across such boundaries. A marked feature of recent decades has been the development, under the stimulus partly of the petro-chemical and other technological advances, and also of the search for security, of multi-product or joint enterprise firms cutting across the traditional industry demarcations. The example of Unilever has already been quoted. Another is Monsanto Chemicals producing specialist chemical products for the following industries – adhesives, agriculture, aircraft, dental goods, disinfectants, dyestuffs, electrical engineering, food, glass, iron, leather, motors, packaging, paint, paper, perfumery and cosmetics, petrol, pharmaceuticals, plastics, printing and ink, rubber, soaps, textiles, and timber. Joint enterprises, on the other hand, arise where firms from different industries combine resources to exploit new products or processes, e.g. I.C.I. and Courtaulds in the development of nylon (British Nylon Spinners).

At the apex of the industrial structure are the 340 largest manufacturing establishments, which accounted in 1949 for no less than 20% of the total U.K. labour force. The hundred largest firms accounted for 51% of the net assets of all quoted companies in 1957, a proportion which had increased to 54% by the end of 1960.

The ten biggest of all, as measured by capital employed in 1966, were:

		£m.
1.	Shell	1,375
2.	I.C.I.	1,059
3.	B.P.	1,034
4.	Unilever	491
5.	British-American Tobacco	431
6.	Courtaulds	300
7.	Imperial Tobacco	284
8.	Esso	269
9.	Guest Keen & Nettlefold	266
10.	P. & O.	232

Economies of Large-Scale Production

In much of this chapter we will be discussing the need for and the difficulties in controlling these concentrations of economic power. At the same time it must be stressed that a major motive behind the process of industrial integration has been the quest for increased efficiency. In many lines of production, the large manufacturing unit enjoys enormous advantages over its smaller competitors which enable it to achieve substantial reductions in costs of production.

Many of these economies arise from the sheer technological superiority of the large firms. This is most obvious when a very high level of output is necessary for the most efficient machines to be used at all, e.g. the automatic loom in the cotton industry which for really economic working requires continuous shift-work. However, even if the best machines can be produced in either large or small versions, the small firm, while able to enjoy the same quality of input as its larger rival, may find that the cost of producing and maintaining the smaller version is proportionately higher. A ten-ton lorry, for example, both costs relatively less than a five-tonner and requires only the same number of men to operate it. Again, only the large firm may have sufficient demand for its product to be able to afford to *combine* its inputs optimally. Consider, for example, a new entrant to an industry who estimates that his daily sales will be 500 units of a product which is produced by performing three successive manufacturing processes – X, Y, and Z. From the manufacturers, he learns that the best machines available for these three processes have the following capacity:

in process X	300 units per day
in process Y	400 units per day
in process Z	500 units per day

His estimated demand of 500 per day is large enough for him to put in the most efficient machines. But it falls below the level at which he could use them in the most efficient *combination*. Manufacturing 500 units per day, the two machines necessary for the X and Y processes would have surplus capacity of 100 and 300 units per day respectively. Only machine Z would be fully employed. It is not difficult to see that the minimum output which would allow him to work at full capacity would be 6,000 units per day, employing twenty machines in process X, fifteen in Y, and twelve in Z.

So far we have considered large-firm superiority in static terms. In a context of rapid technological progress, of quickly changing consumer preferences, and restriction of many other forms of competition, further benefits accrue to the firms which can successfully undertake research and development of new products and processes. Once again, God seems to favour the big battalions. It may be that the small firm devotes the same proportion of its resources to research activities as its larger rival. But research being primarily a hit-or-miss affair, what tends to count more is the *absolute* level of expenditure. The large firm will enjoy a similar advantage at the stage of translating research into commercial terms. Operating pilot schemes to test commercial viability may be a very expensive business indeed.

The large firm is also likely to be more efficient in its deployment of labour. Adam Smith's famous dictum that 'the division of labour is limited by the extent of the market' sums the position up nicely. The opportunities for labour, on the factory floor or in the board-room, to increase in efficiency through specialization, are clearly enhanced in a firm producing for a mass market. The use of labour in occupations best suited to individual talents, increased dexterity arising from repetition of the same task, saving in time and tools involved in moving from one job to another – these simple and obvious economies are exemplified on the factory floor by the assembly line fitter and also have their counterpart in the board-room.

The application of these superior techniques may be made possible either by integrating or disintegrating the process of manufacture. Sometimes, economies depend on *bringing together* different processes within the same plant, so that substantial savings can be made, for example, in transport and fuel costs. In other lines of production, increased efficiency may chiefly arise from a *separation* of the individual processes to enable specialist plants to deploy standardized, mass-production techniques.

The business of manufacturing industry consists of more than transforming raw materials into final products. The materials have to be purchased, the customers wooed and the products sold, and capital must be found to make it all possible. In all these commercial activities the large firm enjoys further advantages, and for similar reasons to those already discussed. National Press or television advertising, market research and extensive after-sales service, the raising of capital on the stock exchange – are all examples of facilities which, because they are in some sense indivisible, are not economic for the small firm. And even when the same quality of inputs are available to large and small alike, the big firm may still find that the cost of using them may be relatively less. A million-pound issue on the stock market does not cost twice as much to float as an issue of £500,000; nor need a salesman necessarily take twice as long to take an order twice as large. Moreover, its size may enable a large firm to cut out many of the extra costs involved in passing a product through a number of middlemen; concentration of the whole business of manufacture within a single enterprise may reduce both the level of stocks of semi-finished goods which is required and uncertainty about what that level should be; when manufacturers are large enough to do their own selling, either direct to the public or through their own chain of retail outlets, they can minimize commercial risks by being closely in touch with consumer requirements.

We can conclude, then, that large firms are very frequently able to make considerable economies in production costs. However, these economies of scale do not exist to the same degree in all industries. In some lines of production, the advantages lie more with the smaller units. The benefits of mass production arise primarily from standardization of the product, and, where flexibility, personal service, and a variety of lines is demanded, it may be the small firm which is most suited. Indeed, the very existence of large firms creates the need for smaller enterprises to meet the demand for deviations from their standardized output.

Prices, Profits, and Diseconomies of Scale

The argument so far is just that large firms can often cut their average *costs*. For this to be of social as well as private benefit depends on whether the economies are passed on to consumers in the form of lower *prices*. However, firms do not grow only in order to become more efficient; size also gives greater control over the market. Thus, from the point of view of maximizing profits, the output produced by a monopolist may be below that which would be produced by a number of competing producers; a degree of monopolistic control may enable a firm to restrict output and reap exceptional profits – always providing that new entrants to the industry can be kept out. Control over raw materials, or tied markets, the setting up of special 'fighting companies' to eliminate new entrants, and size in itself are among the ways in which potential competition can be stifled. But the fact that the 'new entrant' may not be some puny, inexperienced newcomer, but another industrial giant anxious to extend its empire, or even the State itself, sometimes checks exploitation. So also does ignorance of the precise level of profits which would induce such a response.

The two impulses to integration which we have so far mentioned – the possibilities of reducing costs and increasing prices – both involve the not unreasonable assumption that the firm is interested in making profits. We should beware, however, of generalizing this into the quite different assumption that *entrepreneurs* are *only* concerned with the *maximization* of profits. With site values at present levels, a sole preoccupation with maximizing profits would probably mean that a large number of the smaller firms now operating in the London area would sell out at once. Their directors or proprietors could live happily ever after in Cannes were it not for the fact that in addition to making *some* profits, they also enjoy being businessmen. Similarly, it would be wrong to conclude that large-scale enterprises have developed only because integration was dictated by profit maximization. Security of profits, or the wish for a relatively quiet life, also enter into the picture. But perhaps most significant, with the separation of nominal ownership of the firm from the actual control of its operation by what are often self-perpetuating and internally impregnable Boards, is the possibility that growth of the firm may come to be regarded as an end in itself.

This is not, of course, to argue that firms ignore the effects on profits when deciding whether to expand; however, other considerations may also be thought important and lead to growth of firms which increases total profits but does not *maximize* them. We have shown that integration *can* bring about substantial economies, but it is not true to say that it always does so. First, there are limits to the reductions in costs which can be achieved by increased size. After a certain stage, which will differ from industry to industry, the firm becomes unwieldy and 'diseconomies' may begin to become significant. As the firm becomes bigger so also do the problems of running it effectively. The process of decision-taking becomes more complex as the scope of the firm's activities is extended, and the gap between policy making and execution increases. Bureaucratic delays and waste, the difficulty of achieving just the right delegation of authority – these are functions of size, and as much problems for large private enterprises as for the government departments with which they are more generally associated.

Again, much of the concentration of economic power which has taken place has taken the form of diversification – firms branching out into quite different activities, pharmacists manufacturing jam, beverage producers making pharmaceutical goods or air sweeteners, brewers fishing, and so on. Sometimes such diversification can be justified in terms of commercial if not technical economies. And from the point of view of the firm itself, diversification can nearly always be defended in terms of risk-spreading in volatile market conditions. But it is probable that much integration of this type yields no positive *social* gain. The economies of bulk buying or selling, for example, may be only at the expense of some other intermediary between producer and consumer, the latter enjoying none of the consequent benefits; the spreading of risks is a useful insurance for the firm, but it might be the customer who pays the premium in the form of higher prices to cover the increased management costs. It is difficult to see, for example, precisely where the social economic benefits would have arisen in the proposed merger of I.C.I. and Courtaulds – firms producing different products on the whole, and already engaged in a joint enterprise where their activities genuinely overlapped and could be expected to yield economies.

THE STATE AND BIG BUSINESS

Before the Second World War, the official attitude towards industrial integration was one of guarded approval. To secure the advantages of 'rationalization' in an increasingly competitive world seemed far more important than avoiding the dangers which went with it, and government policy was primarily directed at encouraging rather than controlling concentration. The problems of directing a war economy, the need for viable units with which government departments could communicate and cooperate, reinforced this tendency. But towards the end of the war, with sights set more optimistically on the creation of an economy in which the pre-war evils of unemployment and economic fluctuations would be eliminated, it became clear that many of the restrictive practices which were defensible in conditions of depression would be quite unjustifiable in a sellers' market.

And so, in 1948, very late in the day of industrial integration, and following a number of *ad hoc* inquiries into particular industries, the government took its first tentative steps in the direction of curbing monopolistic power. The Monopolies Commission was established, empowered to investigate industries to which it was referred by the Board of Trade, industries in which 'one-third of the final output or the processing or export of a good is in the hands of a single firm or two or more firms being interconnected bodies corporate . . . or where firms within the industry are acting in such a way as to prevent or restrict competition'; these were very wide terms of reference which must have covered the greater part of British industry. Once it had been referred to an industry, the Commission would undertake an investigation of its monopolistic tendencies and their consequences. When its inquiry was completed, it could submit either a purely factual report or one including recommendations for the removal of practices which it considered contrary to the public interest.

This at first sight seems fairly strong medicine. However, as an instrument for controlling restrictive practices in industry the Commission must be judged an almost total failure. Its progress was agonizingly slow. By 1956, when its terms of reference were altered, it had investigated only twenty-one cases. The reasons for its dilatoriness were obvious. Its maximum membership was ten (increased in 1953 to twenty-five), supported by a small staff, and working on an annual budget which never exceeded £70,000. Moreover, there was a serious internal bottleneck in that although in later years the Commission was allowed to divide itself into sub-commissions simultaneously investigating more than one case, reports even then had to be the product of the Commission sitting as a whole.

A second reason for its ineffectiveness was that if the Commission concluded that a certain practice was contrary to the public interest in, say, the dental goods industry, its conclusions and recommendations were limited to that industry alone. It was not entitled to make general recommendations until it had built up a body of case studies. This case-by-case approach meant that restrictive practices in British industry were probably increasing at a more rapid rate than the Commission's attempts to control them.

Thirdly, the Commission singularly failed to provide industry with any self-rectifying incentive. There was no tendency, as there is in certain other countries, for the mere threat of investigation to induce British manufacturers to put their own houses in order. The real power behind the threat of inquiry is, of course, the public attention which is drawn to the industry on the publication of a report, and one of the most damning criticisms of the Commission's activities was the failure to arouse any real public interest. The real culprit in this respect was the Board of Trade which was responsible for selecting the subjects of the Commission's inquiries. They showed a somewhat staggering lack of imagination in choosing such industries as dental goods, rainwater goods, or electric cable manufacture; exposure of even the most outrageous malpractices in such industries could hardly be calculated to arouse public notice, let alone indignation. Moreover, the threat of investigation was substantially lessened for manufacturers when they realized the improbability of the Commission's recommendations being enforced. Enforcement was the responsibility, not of the Commission itself, but of the government department most closely connected with the industry investigated; despite the fact that the Commission found practices contrary to the public interest in all but three of its investigations, in only one case was an order for their abandonment made – in the dental goods industry, which, to all intents and purposes, then effectively disregarded it.

Why, having created the Commission in the first place, were the authorities so reluctant to enforce its proposals? Cynics might argue that this was precisely what had been intended – to make a nominal show of controlling big business without going to the extreme of making such control effective. It might, on the other hand, be thought unfair to penalize those firms which were unlucky enough to have been investigated when similar practices were known to be continuing elsewhere. But it is a weak argument that activities contrary to the public interest in one industry should be condoned until all such practices in all industries had been exposed.

Despite all this, the Monopolies Commission did perform a useful function. If it failed to regulate restrictive practices, it at least proved the need for such regulation by a number of excellent case studies. The real criticism of this seven-year concession to pragmatism was that it could have been doing more at the same time. However, in 1955, its first general report was published – on the practice of Collective Price Maintenance – and was the basis of Part I of the 1956 Restrictive Practices Act which outlawed the practice of manufacturers jointly enforcing the retail prices of their products (this is a matter to which we will return in Chapter 7). Part II of the Act dealt with agreements between two or more parties which limited freedom in respect of prices, sales, or production. All such agreements were to be registered with a newly created office, that of the Registrar of Restrictive Practices. Penalties could be imposed for failure to register, and, by January 1957, the register held some 2,300 agreements. At the initiative of the Registrar, selected agreements are brought before the Restrictive Practices Court, consisting of five judges and up to ten lay members. It is then up to the parties to an agreement to demonstrate to the Court that the agreement is positively in the public interest, and that it results in public benefits which would be foregone if it was discontinued.

Attempts were made in the Act to give that utterly vague concept 'the public interest' some specific content by creating a legal framework within which cases before the Court were to be argued. Parties to agreements are thus expected to prove that their agreement yields benefits under one or more of seven headings. Of the seven 'gateways', as these have become known, two are concerned with the protection of consumers, either against the possibility of physical injuries or because the removal of the agreement would deny to purchasers or users some 'specific and substantial benefit'. There are three more which cover agreements necessary to ensure fair competition between producers, e.g. agreements which give firms collective bargaining strength against a monopolist or parties to another agreement which has been allowed by the Court. A sixth gateway refers to the case where abandonment of the agreement might lead, in 'current conditions or conditions reasonably foreseeable', to 'serious and persistent adverse effects on the general level of employment in an area'. And finally, it can be argued by defendants of an agreement that its removal would lead to a reduction in exports which 'is substantial in relation to the whole business of the industry'.

The onus falls on defendants to prove that their agreement

falls into one or more of these classes. The procedure followed is very similar to that of an ordinary court of law, with each side producing expert witnesses who are then subject to cross-examination by opposing counsel. In the court's assessment of the case there are three stages. First, it has to determine whether or not the parties have succeeded in proving that public benefit stems from the existence of the agreement. Second, it must consider whether the Registrar has shown that any 'detriments' arise from its operation. And, finally, there is the 'tail-piece' – a balancing of the benefits and detriments and an evaluation as to whether, on the whole, the agreement is in the public interest.

So much for the formal procedure. How has it worked in practice? By the end of 1960 only some fourteen cases had been defended before the Court, and, although about twice that number had been undefended and there were a large number in the course of preparation, it might nevertheless be thought that the new procedure suffered from the same defect as the Monopolies Commission – of dealing with restrictive practices at a slower rate than they were developing. However, the Registrar adopted the policy in deciding which agreements should be put into Court, of selecting those which are typical of many other such arrangements, so that a decision in a single case could have widespread repercussions.

Thus, by the end of 1959, after only nine cases had been defended in Court, the Registrar estimated that some 770 agreements had been abandoned or modified. With a further three cases dealt with, the number of abandoned agreements rose to 1,030 and by 1966 more than two-thirds of the agreements which had been on the register had been terminated.

Of the fourteen agreements defended by the middle of 1961, only three passed the scrutiny of the Court. It therefore seemed, particularly in the early hearings, as though it would be very difficult to persuade the Court of the overall public benefit conferred by a restrictive agreement. Certainly, the wording of the gateways is not generous to defendants. It is not sufficient to prove that an agreement confers *some* public benefit; the benefit must be 'specific and substantial' – something which can be definitely indicated and articulately assessed. Again, it is not enough to argue that unemployment would occur as a result of abandoning an agreement: the unemployment must be 'serious and persistent', and is only considered relevant if the industry provides a substantial proportion of the total employment within an area. Similarly, a fall in exports is only to be taken into account if it represents a sizeable part of the whole business of the industry.

Although agreements have now been defended at all of the seven gateways, the most popular defence has been under the hold-all 'specific and substantial benefit' clause and those relating to employment and exports. The failure of the Cotton Yarn Spinners Agreement to be proved in the public interest was a cold douche for those who thought that the Court might adopt a more lenient attitude towards industries which were in decline. The Association succeeded in showing that without the agreement there would be persistent and adverse unemployment, but, in the tail-piece of its judgment, the Court concluded that the detriments arising from the price-fixing arrangements outweighed the benefits.

Although a large number of other agreements were abandoned as a result of this judgement, the approach remains pragmatic. That price-fixing was held contrary to the public interest in this particular case does not imply a condemnation of the practice in general. It is still open to respondents to justify similar arrangements in other circumstances, and, indeed, in the strange case of the Black Bolt and Nuts Agreement, the Court decided that price-fixing *did* confer a specific and substantial benefit on the public. Black bolts and nuts are steel fastenings used in a host of constructional activities, their cost generally being negligible in relation to the price of the final product. They are produced in about three thousand different shapes and sizes, mostly by the forty-four members of the Black Bolt and Nuts Association. The agreement of the association which was brought before the Restrictive Practices Court took the form of a uniform Price List being issued for all the standard specifications. The Court concluded that the substantial and specific benefit which the public enjoyed as a result of these arrangements was that without a fixed price agreement, prices would vary from one manufacturer to another, and that buyers would have to incur the expense and trouble of 'shopping around'.

This is a very odd conclusion. If buyers *were* sufficiently interested to shop around, then the probable effect would be a lowering of prices, but not necessarily greater variability. Competition would tend to impose its own uniformity, the keenness of buyers to purchase at the lowest price ensuring that prices held together and eliminating the need for much shopping around. If, on the other hand, customers were not anyway much concerned with the prices they had to pay for their black bolts and nuts, then there would be no shopping around for them to be saved if their inertia led to varying prices on abandonment of the agreement.

On the whole, ostensibly the Restrictive Practices Act has been highly effective. Judged by the number of existing agreements which have been abandoned and the discipline imposed on new agreements by past decisions of the Court, the Act seems to be a forceful curb on the development of restrictive practices in the British economy. However, for important reasons which have been stressed by the Registrar himself, it must be doubted whether the system has really worked satisfactorily.

A large number of the arrangements which the Court has or would have judged restrictive have been replaced by apparently innocuous 'open-price agreements'. Instead of specifically colluding in fixing prices and disturbing markets, members of an association may merely agree to circulate information about what prices they are charging and where they are selling. The danger is, of course, that an exchange of information coupled with a *tacitly* restrictive outlook may effectively amount to an agreement contrary to the public interest while falling outside the scope of the Registrar. When restriction has reached the point where written arrangements are unnecessary, how can 'gentlemen's agreements' be controlled?

Then again, the Act dealt with agreements between a number of parties. This emphasis against associations could well encourage *mergers* in order to escape the surveillance of the Court. Admittedly, the single-firm monopolies resulting from integration might have to bear the scrutiny of the reconstituted Monopolies Commission, but its even more ponderous progress in its new role since 1956 and the apparent lack of intention to implement its recommendations hardly seemed likely to act as a disincentive to such tendencies.

Recent Moves

Government awareness of these shortcomings was shown by the passing of the Monopolies and Mergers Act in 1965. Yet again the Monopolies Commission was reorganized; this time it was restored to its pre-1956 strength of twenty-five members and empowered to conduct a number of inquiries simultaneously. Coupled with this effort to speed up its work was a measure to ensure that its recommendations, if accepted, could be implemented. The powers of the Board of Trade were increased to the point that they can even dissolve a monopoly by requiring a company to divest itself of part of its interests. Finally, the Commission can now look at two further types of case: where services (as opposed to goods) are produced in monopolistic conditions, and at mergers, either actual or proposed, where the assets involved amount to more than £5 million.

The Commission has been commendably active in its new role. Particularly encouraging is the way in which public attention has been attracted by its reports: there was widespread interest, for example, in its investigation of Kodak (which forced the firm to accept substantial cuts in prices and profits), and into detergent prices which it considered 20% too high partly as a result of wasteful advertising expenditure. With respect to mergers, the Commission has maintained its pragmatic approach – giving the go-ahead, for example, to B.M.C. and Pressed Steel (on condition that existing customers would continue to be supplied) while recommending that the proposed merger between the Ross Group and Associated Fisheries would be contrary to the public interest. Threat of investigation seems to have loomed large in the decision by Imperial Tobacco to abandon its attempt to take over Smith's Crisps.

Meanwhile, the Registrar of Restrictive Practices has made a valiant start in tracking cases where an abandoned restrictive agreement has been replaced by an information arrangement and tacit price collusion. Substantial fines have been imposed when firms have been caught out – £80,000 in the case of Dunlop, Goodyear, Michelin, and five other tyre manufacturers detected in 1966.

Rationalization

At the same time that it has been trying to control the abuses of industrial concentration, the government has been pursuing an active policy of *encouraging* the formation of larger enterprises in certain circumstances. There is nothing necessarily inconsistent about this. The aim of monopoly policy is to *regulate* large firms; to break them down into small independent units would generally imply throwing out the baby with the bath-water. We have already seen that very large scale production is frequently necessary if firms are to compete successfully with their giant counterparts in the U.S.A. and Europe, and it seems likely that costs in many British industries could be substantially reduced by an even greater degree of industrial concentration than now exists. It therefore makes good sense for the government to try to stimulate re-grouping of firms where such rationalization is slow in developing naturally.

Until recently, the government has concentrated most of its efforts in this direction on industries suffering from particularly intense foreign competition. The cotton industry, in long-term decline because of competition from newly developed countries, has been encouraged by financial assistance since 1959 to become more compact and better-equipped. The aircraft industry, where technology dictates very large production units indeed, has similarly been subject to government-inspired reconstruction. And the Geddes committee, set up in 1964 to inquire into the plight of the shipbuilding industry, reported in 1966 that a fundamental reorganization was called for, including a merging of the most important yards into five regional groupings. Although each of these industries is in a state of decline or potential decline, policy has been hastening the establishment of a viable size and structure rather than propping them up at an artificially high level of output.

The system was generalized in 1966 with the creation of the Industrial Reorganization Corporation. Its function is to detect situations where rationalization would be beneficial and then to overcome obstacles to mergers by providing financial and other assistance. In practice, its £150 million initial capital may well prove less significant than its researching and prodding – accelerating the operation of market forces which, when they work at all, can sometimes work painfully slowly. When it was first mooted, the I.R.C. was attacked from the right as an agent of back-door nationalization and from the left as a channel of public money for augmenting private wealth. Whether it can make a positive contribution to increasing the efficiency of the private manufacturing sector remains to be seen.

Conclusion

In this section we have been examining certain techniques by which the government tries to regulate private industry. The extent of its involvement is, however, very much wider than is suggested by these few examples. It can modify the basis of private business by company legislation; it determines the level of aggregate demand for the output of private industry; it operates directly on profits and prices through taxation, hire purchase controls and other means; it is the main sponsor of research and development work; it influences the location of industry through regional policy; and even more detailed consideration of the private sector is implied by the development of national planning and a national incomes policy.

We shall be returning later, particularly in Part III, to some of these ways in which State action impinges on private industry. Immediately, however, we shall take a look at *the* most direct form of government participation in the productive process – where the State has itself taken over private enterprises and made them part of the public sector.

CHAPTER 5

NATIONALIZED INDUSTRIES

PERHAPS nationalization is now a rather less dirty word than it used to be. Proposals for further extension of public ownership still arouse violent reactions, but there are not very many people who would seriously support denationalization of the present public industries. But if there has been a lowering of emotional temperatures since the stormy days of 1945–50, it can hardly be attributed to increased understanding of the aims and nature of nationalization, of the difficulties and the real achievements and failures of the nationalized sector. This, indeed, is one of the major shortcomings of the public enterprises – that they have done too little too late in the way of explaining to their owners just what they were trying to do, whether they were succeeding, or why they were failing.

Nationalized industries are very big business indeed. They include the largest employers in the U.K. and provide jobs for over 1½ million people. The assets of the largest public enterprises are greater than those of the private enterprise giants, and nationalized industry investment has been running at about 17% of the national total.

Their financial record has been mixed. Electricity and gas have both regularly achieved surpluses. Coal and the airlines have sometimes made profits and sometimes losses: the deficits have outweighed the surpluses. Railways have been the major money-losers – although even they made a small profit in one year, 1952. Critics regard the making of losses as almost axiomatic of nationalized industries, the inevitable concomitant of bureaucratic inefficiency. To some advocates of nationalization, on the other hand, it is one of the advantages of public enterprise that they *can* be permitted to incur financial deficits on their operations.

What is not always made clear is the precise nature of these 'losses' or the reasons why they arise. In the following section we shall try to clarify these points by particular reference to the largest of the loss-makers, the railways. Only when the nature and causes of deficits are understood is it possible to turn to the question – are they justified? What, in other words, are the objectives of nationalization? But first, the railway problem, which, in one way or another, affects us all.

Railway Losses

The accounting conventions of the public sector make its financial record look even more unfavourable in comparison with private industry than if like was to be compared with like. Thus, for example, in 1938 the un-nationalized railway companies had gross receipts which exceeded working expenditure by £26 million and this 'profit' was available for either ploughing back or for distribution as interest and dividends to stockholders and shareholders. The nationalized railways also, in every year up to 1955, succeeded in making a working profit – one which fluctuated and was only above the 1938 level in four years, but a working profit nevertheless. However, in addition to working expenses, railway receipts were expected to be sufficient to cover certain 'central charges' and when these are also taken into account, the position looks much less satisfactory.

British Railways 1948–55 (£m.)

	1948	1949	1950	1951	1952	1953	1954	1955
Working profit	23.8	10.6	25.2	33.3	38.7	34.6	16.4	1.8
Central charges	32	34	36	34	35	37	38	40
Overall surplus of deficit	−8.2	−23.4	−10.8	−9.7	3.7	−2.4	−21.6	−38.2

The central charges comprised a number of elements – fixed interest payments to previous railway owners on the government stock which they had received in compensation, a contribution to the sinking fund by which such stock was to be redeemed over a period of ninety years, and fixed interest payable on new borrowing by the railways since nationalization. Whether or not the railways should have been expected to meet these charges (and a good case can be made out that compensation represented a gross overvaluation of railway assets at the time when the railways were taken over) the fact that the whole of railway capital is now in the form of fixed interest stock means that a failure to cover working costs appears as a definite loss rather than merely low or zero dividends to shareholders.

We are not prejudging the question of what rate of return nationalized industries should earn on their capital and how such capital should be basically valued. But blunt statements of overall surpluses and deficits without full explanation of the burden of central charges must have a damaging effect on the internal morale and external image of public industries.

However, the fact remains that the railways have failed of recent years to make even a *working* profit. Revenue has been insufficient to cover costs of operation quite apart from central charges. If they were still in private ownership, they would be able to meet none of their fixed interest obligations to debenture holders, let alone pay dividends to shareholders. The overall deficit has risen from £57·5 million in 1956 to £120–£130 million p.a. in the mid sixties.

Why Have the Railways Lost Money?

The answer lies in a great complex of factors which it is not easy to unravel. For our present purposes, a brief reference to just five of the reasons for the railways' financial plight will have to suffice.

(i) Failure of the railway managers to find out just *which* of their services were losing money. In 1951 a Traffic Costing Service was set up which gave, for the first time, *some* idea of the effect on costs of the density, volume, frequency, and type of traffic carried on various routes. But although the Transport Commission deserved credit for initiating these analyses which showed how inappropriate was the structure of charges which the railways had inherited on nationalization, it is clear that they did not do *enough* to overcome their traditional ignorance of the costs of carrying different traffics.

Certainly, as late as 1959, it was still a mystery just where the massive losses were being incurred. In that year the railways were subjected to the scrutiny of the Select Committee on Nationalized Industries, the Report of which echoed the plaintive admission of the Permanent Secretary to the Ministry of Transport that 'We find one of the most difficult things in the Ministry is to discover where money is actually lost – it is very difficult to get an answer to that.' Freight traffic was, in the opinion of a Ministry witness, 'probably making a substantial surplus'. Long-distance passenger services were 'generally profitable'. Those commuter services which had been electrified 'just about washed their faces'. Losses must therefore have been limited to stopping trains and unmodernized commuter services. But, as the Committee observed, 'this, however, seems a very small area of operation to which to attribute an operating loss of as much as £42 million in 1959', and it is difficult to avoid their conclusion that considerable progress remained to be made, and should have been made, in costing techniques.

A useful product of the Beeching era was the much more careful diagnosis which showed that in fact, of all rail traffic, only coal, and parcels and mails carried by coaching train, *fully* covered the cost of carriage. However, even when they knew which services were losing money, the railways were frequently prevented from cutting their losses by restraints on their commercial freedom.

(ii) The railways continued to be treated as an irresponsible monopoly long after they became subject to severe competition from road transport. Until 1953, for example, they were compelled to publish their charges – a sensible restriction on a monopolistic enterprise, but an absurdly convenient guide for the road competitor who could finely pare his rates to undercut the rail charge. Moreover, these charges had to be justified, up to 1962, before an anachronistic triumvirate known as the Transport Tribunal. The lengthiness of the legal proceedings before this body – both the Transport Commission and objectors employed counsel to argue their respective cases – generally meant that proposed charges increases were lagging behind increasing costs by the time they were implemented. And nearly always, the Tribunal had reduced the proposed increases according to some private criteria which were never explicitly defined. On three occasions, the Minister of Transport himself added to the Commission's burden by intervening either to delay or to reduce approved increases in charges, or to persuade the Commission to postpone its application to the Tribunal.

(iii) Although the railways had been instructed in the nationalization Act to pay their way taking one year with the next, they continued to provide what they knew were unremunerative services when they thought that to do so was in the public interest. Partly, this policy stemmed from ambiguities in the enabling legislation itself, partly from a traditional public service attitude which the railways had developed during their monopoly era. The railways accepted such responsibilities on a very substantial scale, and the extent to which 'these two approaches, the commercial and the often unprofitable public service, frequently conflict' was only gradually realized. The crucial questions of *who* decided what constituted the public interest, and of who paid for any consequent losses, remained ill-defined. The division of responsibility between Commission and Ministry was described by the latter as 'all very vague', and by Sir Brian Robertson, then Chairman of the Commission, as containing 'an element of enigma'.

(iv) In the period up to 1955 the railways operated with capital equipment which was rapidly depreciating. Expenditure on the railways was given a low priority in the national scale so that, in fact, considerable *disinvestment* took place during these years. Investment since, under the Modernization Plan, although ultimately cost-reducing, has frequently in the short run led to *increases* in costs as, for example, when dual systems of steam and electric traction were transitionally run in parallel.

(v) Throughout the post-war period, the railways have suffered as a result of the vast expansion of road transport. Since 1952 the railway share of passenger traffic has fallen from 21% to 11% (in 1965), and of goods haulage from 53% to less than 27%. In both cases, reduced shares have been accompanied by a decline in the absolute level of business done by the railways. Most of the new traffic has been carried by 'C' licence holders (those using vehicles only for the carriage of their own goods) and by the ever-growing number of private cars.

There is, of course, no necessary cause for lament at the passing of the railway hegemony – provided that the growth of road transport is a reflection of its superior economic efficiency. Unfortunately, it seems likely that to some extent the changes which have been taking place are the result of a public policy which has *distorted* rather than emphasized the relative economic advantages of the different transport sectors. In particular, there has been a failure to ensure that road users pay the true costs which are involved.

At first sight, it looks as though road users pay far *more* than the costs of roads. In 1965 road taxation (from licences and fuel duty) amounted to £742 million, and on top of that motorists had to pay purchase tax on new vehicles; expenditure on the construction and improvement of roads in the same year was below the £200 million mark. However, this expenditure cannot be equated with the true costs of roads. We also have to add the cost of the ancillary services without which use of roads would be impossible – policing, traffic control and signalling, and street lighting – and, much more important (if difficult to quantify), the *social* costs involved in road use arising from congestion, accidents, and damage to buildings and public health. Rough estimates suggest that the magnitude of these costs is greatly in excess of the amounts collected from road users in taxation.

Moreover, the aim should be not just to recoup road costs from users in aggregate, but also to relate the payments which they make to the highly varied costs which are incurred by different types of vehicles using different roads at different times. At present, road charges consist of petrol taxation and two overhead elements – vehicle licences (based primarily on engine capacity) and purchase tax on new vehicles (from which lorries and vans are exempt); this taxation structure completely fails to reflect cost variations. Road costs are averaged (to the extent that they are recouped at all), and the system involves cross-subsidization of urban by rural users, of peak traffic by non-peak, and of private by public transport. At a time when the railways are trying to relate their prices to increasingly sophisticated costing, the failure to bring home the real cost of road use implies a lack of comparability between road and rail operations which makes nonsense of investment and other policies based on their relative results

There is a similar lack of coordination and comparability between road and rail investment. Investment in roads is the responsibility of the Ministry of Transport and a vast number of local authorities. The Ministry itself has given high priority to arterial motorways between major industrial centres, and the distribution of remaining funds seems to have largely depended on the negotiating strength of the local authorities concerned and their good fortune in having plans formulated and approved at times when increased expenditure was announced. In the little consideration of alternative projects which has taken place, differences in cost seem to have been given more weight than probable rates of return. There is regrettably no evidence at all of any effort at carefully ranking alternative road projects as a basis for selecting the most economic use of scarce funds, or of comparison of road projects with investment in the railways. A *post hoc* analysis (not, of course, by the Ministry) was made to calculate the social costs and benefits involved in the construction of the M.1, which fortunately showed that high rates of social return could be expected. However, further studies have suggested that other, perhaps less grandiose, schemes for road improvement and widening, and a 2×2 lane M.1, might have achieved a higher ranking order than the M.1 project itself. Secondly, the same criterion should have been applied to investment in alternative forms of transport. The M.1 results have been particularly misused to make misleadingly favourable comparisons with rail investment, e.g. the Euston–Crewe electrification which is expected to yield a commercial return of only 5–7%. Such comparisons are obviously quite meaningless because the returns are calculated on non-comparable bases.

Thus no attempt has been made to establish the fundamental pre-requisite of road-rail and public-private coordination – that there should be comparability between the pricing and investment mechanisms of the different operators.

Other Public Enterprises

We have dealt with transport policy at some length because, in many ways, it has epitomized the government's general approach to the nationalized industries; although we shall not deal with them in the same detail, it is fair to say that the other public enterprises have been similarly constrained in their pricing and investment policies by both interference and the expectation that they would combine a public service outlook with commercial success. The fuel and power industries, for example, although in intense competition, price their products on very different bases and work within different constraints. Although a little more flexibility is now being introduced, coal has generally been priced on an average cost basis, a policy which involves subsidization of the loss-making half of the industry by the more efficient pits and areas. This meant that, when coal was in short supply in the immediately post-war years, it was uneconomically low-priced; in glut conditions, the burden of the marginal producers unduly raises the average price. The electricity industry, on the other hand, has made some efforts to adopt discriminatory pricing in order to even out the peaks of demand which cause a serious risk of over-investment. Meanwhile, the price of fuel oil, in the private sector, is determined by the few large producers according to profit-maximizing principles, with a heavy surcharge of taxation. Thus, although these sources of fuel and power are intensely competitive, each being a fairly close substitute for the others, policy has failed to achieve either coordination within the public sector, or a rational basis for competition between public and private suppliers.

B.O.A.C. were persuaded to buy British VC 10s when they thought that American aircraft would be more commercially suitable for their purposes. (The railways were similarly at one time forced to Buy British when better and cheaper diesel locomotives could be bought from abroad.) Urban users of electricity and buses have subsidized their rural counterparts. In the fight against inflation, the existence of a substantial sector of the economy under direct government control for a long time meant that when dampening down demand was the order of the day it was public investment which bore the brunt of the cuts; it is still public enterprise prices and incomes which, in such circumstances, are initially restrained. Until recently, the authorities have shown a marked reluctance to allow nationalized industries to diversify into potentially profitable secondary activities.

None of these restraints is necessarily to be condemned. All can be defensible if only they can be shown to stem from a consistent policy for public enterprises worked out by the government. What causes concern is the real doubt that any such framework for decision has in fact existed.

THE PURPOSE OF NATIONALIZATION

Too little thought has been given to the question of what exactly the nationalized industries should be expected to achieve. For the Labour government in the immediate post-war years, public ownership was perhaps an end in itself, to be justified primarily in the negative terms of avoiding concentration of economic power in private hands and ensuring that, instead of being exploited, consumers and workers would be the main beneficiaries of public enterprise activity.

If more positive economic advantages were considered at all, they were limited to securing economies of large-scale production and to the use of public investment as a compensatory device for offsetting the vagaries of the private sector and maintaining employment at a higher level than during the thirties. In the fifties the nationalized industries were administered by a government lacking interest in the basic idea of public enterprise, and presumably not entirely distressed at the difficulties in which the public industries increasingly found themselves. It is difficult to evaluate government policy during this period as there is little evidence that action was based on any hard thinking about the precise role of the nationalized sector.

Before going on to discuss more recent developments, it will be useful to set out what the policy *possibilities* are between which we have to choose. In deciding how public enterprises ought to behave, there are three very broad alternatives to consider. We can regard them as simply *commercial* enterprises, we can expect them to operate on rather more sophisticated *economic* principles, or they can be used as instruments of a wider *social* approach. In discussing each of these in turn we shall once again draw mostly on the transport industries for illustrations.

1. The Commercial Approach. Essentially, this consists of telling nationalized industries to ignore the fact that they are part of the public sector and to behave as though they were private concerns. In this case, the nationalized industry would be distinguished from its private counterpart only in terms of ownership: its surplus (or deficit) would accrue to (or be borne by) taxpayers as a whole rather than a group of shareholders.

At least, it is claimed, this solution has the advantage of straightforward simplicity. But even this is doubtful – except in the sense that it relieves the government of the burden of making difficult decisions. Problems for the managers of the public industries in formulating their policies, and for the community as a result of their policies, would still remain. For the fact is that private commercial behaviour is not simple at all, and is tending to become less so. It is increasingly recognized that private firms are not exclusively motivated by profit maximization; their objectives are frequently much wider and more complex. Consequently, the injunction to a nationalized industry to run itself like a private business does not prescribe any unique course of action as an outcome; the same profit level, for example, might be attainable with very different output and pricing policies.

However, the main drawback to the commercial approach is its narrowness. It leaves out of account so many considerations to which most people would attach importance. These can be brought into the picture by going on to examine the other two alternative policy bases.

2. The Economic Approach. Commercial and economic criteria are very often confused together and it may help to sort out the difference between the two by returning to the problems of transport policy, this time in the early sixties.

The 1962 Transport Act had been passed replacing the Transport Commission by Boards responsible for the different elements of nationalized transport. The railways' capital structure was drastically reconstructed, including a writing off of past losses. At long last they were freed from the inhibiting restrictions of the Transport Tribunal. The way was cleared for implementation of the policy laid down in a 1960 White Paper that 'the practical test for the railways, as for other transport, is how far users are prepared to pay economic prices for the services provided. Broadly, this will in the end settle the size and pattern of the railway system.'

Dr Beeching was recruited from I.C.I. as Chairman to work out the implications of this test and in March 1963 produced his famous report on *The Reshaping of British Railways*. If the Report had been fully implemented, it would have meant a halving of the route mileage from 17,000 to 8,000, a closing of nearly a third of Britain's 7,000 stations and halts, drastic pruning of passenger services and the elimination of 70,000 railway jobs. More positively, there would be concentration on providing transport in which the railways' comparative advantage over road is greatest – lengthy, through-journeys for homogeneous traffic capable of being organized into train-loads.

Now determining the size of the railway system in this way

involved the application of a purely *commercial* criterion, asking of each service – does it earn sufficient to cover financial costs? But failure to cover costs only shows that the service does not *pay*. We cannot conclude that the service is therefore *uneconomic*. The total economic benefits of running the service may still be greater than the costs which are incurred.

Firstly, provision of a railway service may indirectly yield important returns or costs to *non-users*. Their failure to show up in a commercial balance sheet does not mean that these 'social' costs and benefits are non-economic, and their inclusion may radically alter the apparent 'profitability' of a service. The decision to construct the Victoria line, the first underground railway to be built in London since the First World War, illustrates how the discrepancy between commercial and economic criteria can arise. It was reckoned that at present fare levels the line would lose £2·14 million per annum, and that nearly £1 million would be lost additionally each year on other London Transport routes as traffic was diverted from them. However, studies suggest that when social benefits are taken into account a very different picture emerges. The gains to users of other highly congested underground and surface routes would be so large that on this wider but still economic basis the return on the Victoria Line investment might be about 11%. Thus a project which is clearly economic would not have been undertaken if only commercial considerations had been taken into account.

Similarly, the potential savings of the Beeching closures would be to some extent offset by the social costs resulting from increased traffic on the congested road system. It is difficult to quantify accurately by how much cutting the size of the railway system would add to the problem but even a relatively small increase would have to be viewed in a context of congestion which was anyway increasing, and would therefore tend to become more significant year by year. Country towns, holiday resorts, and the new concentrated marshalling centres would all suffer particularly badly.

The Beeching analysis can also be attacked on the grounds that not enough attention was given to the question – 'in what circumstances can this service be *made* to pay?' And even conclusions about what did pay were fundamentally suspect inasmuch as they were based on current road–rail price relatives; as we have already argued, prices charged to road users totally fail to reflect the true costs involved.

An economic, as distinct from a commercial, approach, may therefore yield very different output and price policies. For example, on commercial grounds there is a strong case for reducing the size of the coal industry. But when we take into account the long-term fuel requirements of the economy the position is not so clear. If increasing foreign exchange expenditure on fuel oil is a consequence of a smaller domestic coal industry, is a policy of wholesale closures still justifiable? Perhaps – if resources released from the coal industry are redeployed in export industries which more than earn the necessary foreign exchange. But the argument weakens if either the resources used in the coal industry are so specific that they are incapable of efficient redeployment, or if it is not anyway a shortage of manpower which is the major constraint on increasing exports.

3. The Social Approach. Applying economic criteria to nationalized industries thus embraces wider considerations than judging them on commercial grounds. It is also possible to adopt still broader principles of evaluation. What is economically appropriate might at the same time be thought unfair, undesirable, or politically inexpedient. Are such considerations to be set aside as irrelevant? Are we interested only in establishing the principle that 'he who benefits should pay' – regardless of capacity to pay? Or should not the public enterprises, which are, after all, 'socialized' industries, be used to further social ends such as regional development, reduction of urban concentration, a more equitable distribution of income and so on – which might require moderation of a purely economic policy?

Recent Emphasis

We have now set out three broad lines of policy, distinguished by their width of objectives, according to which nationalized industries could be required to function. Which should be chosen? It is important to be quite clear that there is no simple right or wrong about any of the alternatives. None can be regarded as the *scientifically* correct solution. For behind them lie different political attitudes and concepts of social priority; the choice between them (or combinations of them) is essentially a matter of values. What is very doubtful is that the present operation of the nationalized sector reflects the consistent application of *any* well-considered set of principles.

In 1961, when the deficits of the nationalized industries were mounting to proportions which caused unwanted pressure on the Exchequer, the government finally attempted re-evaluation of the role of public enterprises in a White Paper on *The Financial and Economic Obligations of the Nationalized Industries*. One critic said that this document merely codified the muddle of Whitehall thinking, but at least it was an effort to formulate some sort of policy for public concerns. By and large, it remains the framework within which they operate today.

The approach of the White Paper was basically commercial, and tried to set the operations of public industries more firmly within the competitive market. In place of the vague obligation of the Nationalization Acts that revenues should be sufficient, taking one year with the next, to allow Boards to pay their way, the government now established definite financial targets for the major nationalized industries. Accordingly, 'Surpluses on Revenue Account should be at least sufficient to cover deficits on Revenue Account *over a five-year period*.' Moreover, provision from Revenue Account should include depreciation calculated at replacement cost and

adequate allocations to general reserves which will be available *inter alia* as a contribution towards their capital development. . . . There are powerful grounds in the national interest for requiring these undertakings to make a substantial contribution towards the cost of their capital development out of their own earnings and to reduce their claims on the nation's savings and the burden on the Exchequer.

Secondly, there was recognition that it is not good enough, given the scope and size of public investment, for nationalized industries to be what the Radcliffe Committee called the 'residuary legatees' for investment resources. The government now discuss investment plans for 'the next five years ahead and [are] ready to agree to long-term commitments as appropriate'.

Thirdly, 'the government recognize . . . that the industries must have freedom to make upward price adjustments especially where their prices are artificially low.' At the same time, however, the possibility remains of Ministerial intervention to restrain or postpone projected price increases. But the government might then adjust a Board's financial objectives in such circumstances, and be prepared to give 'a written statement of its views' which presumably the Board could defensively flourish at critics of its subsequent financial difficulties!

The White Paper, unfortunately, fell short of being an adequate policy formulation in a number of respects. The chief concern throughout was with *financial* considerations, and particularly with the effect of public enterprise operations on the Exchequer. Great emphasis was laid on the 'extent to which public corporations depend on the savings of others to finance their investment', and the Treasury analysis suggested that self-finance by public enterprises would 'reduce their claims on the nation's savings'. This was an astonishingly naïve view. The fact that public enterprises finance more of their investment from ploughed-back profits does not, of course, mean reduced dependence on national savings; all that is implied is that instead of savings coming from taxpayers or those who buy government bonds, consumers of the products of nationalized industries should be forced to save through higher prices.

What is most regrettable is that the White Paper concentrated on the issue of how public investment was to be financed to the exclusion of the much more vital consideration of the criteria according to which it should be undertaken. The real problem of how to decide what proportion of limited resources should be invested in nationalized industries, and the establishment of a coordinating procedure to ensure that it was then allocated between alternative enterprises and projects on a consistent basis, was ignored.

The White Paper proposals also failed to satisfactorily resolve the conflict which can arise in public enterprise operation because of their mixed objectives. We have seen that there are many grounds on which non-commercial policies can be justified, but acceptance of such obligations by nationalized industries in the past has been unsatisfactory in three respects. Firstly, the existence of a public service tradition has fostered an ignorance of just how extensive a proportion of their total operations non-commercial activities have been. Secondly, the responsibility for determining which non-paying services were in the public interest has fallen, by and large, on the Boards themselves. And finally, the financial shortfall caused by such activities has either been met by internal cross-subsidization of one group of consumers by another, or has led to overall deficits damaging both to the external image and domestic morale of the industries concerned.

It is not true to say that the 1961 proposals were designed only to make nationalized industries mirror images of private enterprises. It was recognized that

public corporations cannot be regarded only as very large commercial concerns which may be judged mainly on their commercial results; all have, although in varying degrees, wider obligations than commercial concerns in the private sector.

But that these 'commercially unprofitable activities . . . have been taken into account in fixing the financial standard for each undertaking', and that 'to the extent that commercially unprofitable activities are subsequently imposed from outside, a Board would be entitled to ask for an adjustment of its financial objectives', evades the really basic issues.

Perhaps the emphasis on a more commercial outlook from the nationalized industries may, as in the case of the railways, reveal for the first time the full extent of the public service element; to discover just what does, or might, pay, is clearly a useful preliminary to consideration of non-commercial obligations. But an important shortcoming of the White Paper approach is that it continues to blur the question of who is responsible for deciding which unremunerative activities should be undertaken, and why. The implication that this will still rest partly with the Boards themselves is quite unreasonable. For one thing, public service operations are part of a wider complex of public policy on which it is beyond a Board's competence to pontificate; and secondly, these are clearly *political* decisions which must, therefore, be taken by a publicly accountable political authority – the government itself (and not just central government. Local and regional bodies will often have an important part to play in such decisions). Moreover, the subsidies arising from non-commercial activities should generally be borne by the taxpayers whose representatives have decided that they should be undertaken rather than by other consumers of the product or service in question; and recoupment of such costs from the State must take a form which does not suggest a 'propping-up' of the nationalized concern.

The aim of public enterprise used to be couched in the straightforward terms of subordinating the profit motive to the interests of workers and consumers. There was also a time when economists thought in terms of simple pricing rules by which the profit motive could be replaced. At least it is now clear that the problems of operating public industries involve decisions of many more dimensions. Nationalized concerns have to be run in the interest of the *nation*, not just of that part of the nation which happens to consume their output. Choice has to be made between the different *principles* underlying alternative pricing methods; the notion that 'he who benefits should pay' may require substantial modification in the light of wider policy aims. Pricing policies must be such as to ensure comparability between industries competing in the same markets so that investment decisions can be a rational reflection of consumer choice. As well as narrow commercial considerations, wider economic costs and benefits and social priorities may also have to be taken into account. The authorities have yet to come to terms with these considerable problems involved in operating public industries.

CHAPTER 6

AGRICULTURE

DURING the 1962-3 negotiations on joining the Common Market, Britain's representatives in the discussions insisted that the terms for entry would have to include a safeguard for British farmers; ostensibly, at least, the negotiations ultimately foundered on this very issue – although discussion of agricultural technicalities was clearly only a façade for the testing of more basic political attitudes. But it is interesting that the government singled out agriculture as the major domestic interest to require negotiation. What makes agriculture such a special case? The Brussels negotiations are just one example of the extraordinarily paternalistic attitude which the State has adopted towards farming throughout the post-war period, and it is this high degree of protective attention which justifies our separate consideration of agriculture in this chapter.

Structurally, farming is organized very differently from the manufacturing sector of the economy. The movement towards integrated, large-scale production has, by and large, passed agriculture by. The typical British farm remains small in terms both of acreage (as compared with the New World or Commonwealth producers, though large in comparison with most European units) and of employment – nearly half of British farms have no paid workers at all and only 3% have ten or more. It is, on the other hand, an industry requiring very substantial capital investment. The capital tied up in the land itself and in farm buildings and in the shorter-term finance of machinery and stock, is very high in relation to gross output. However, despite its heavy capital requirements, farming is still organized mostly on an individual or family basis. Few British farms are formed into companies, and generally farms are independent units, only 8% being organized into groups of two or more. The typical British farm is thus a single-plant, single-enterprise firm of heavy capital outlay relying chiefly on family labour supplemented by casual workers at harvest time.

The State and Agriculture

State support of agriculture is highly comprehensive and takes a number of forms. Sometimes it is indirect, like the legislation permitting producers to set up Marketing Boards for production, sales and prices, as in the market for liquid milk. The Ministry of Agriculture sets a relatively high price for liquid milk, the market for which is partially insulated from foreign competition by the nature of the product, while milk used to make butter, cheese and other dairy products is sold more cheaply, at prices based on world prices for imported dairy produce. Domestic producers of such products are thus enabled to compete against foreign competitors by a process of joint product subsidization.

For some sectors of farming, support is by direct protection from foreign competition – import duties which raise the price of foreign products to levels which leave the market largely to home producers. This is on the whole exceptional in the British system of farm support and is of particular significance only for horticultural products. The duty on imported tomatoes, for example, fluctuates with domestic output, being very high at the height of the British season and then declining as home output falls off.

However, the most general form of State assistance is by means of subsidies. These are of two types. Increasingly, support is by direct production grants – financial assistance for drainage schemes, buildings, ploughing old grassland, use of fertilizers, etc., and provision of specialist services for farmers in the form of research, training, and advice. The cost of direct financial assistance has risen considerably over recent years:

1954–5	£50m.
1960–1	£104·5
1965–6	£108·1

But the major part and peculiar bulwark of British agricultural policy is the system of *price* subsidization. The Agricultural Act 1947, which still forms the basis of such support, laid down as one of the aims of agricultural policy the promotion of an agriculture which would be 'capable of producing such a part of the nation's food and other agricultural production, as, in the national interest, it was desirable to produce in the u.k.' This statement, though nebulous, has formidable implications. The amount 'which it is in the national interest' to produce is not, of course, an objective quantity; but the fact that it is mentioned in an Act of Parliament suggests that it is to be interpreted as a different amount from that which farmers would produce if left to their own devices. If the government intends that farmers should produce more than they otherwise would, then the only way in which this can be achieved, apart from coercion, is for the government to provide the necessary financial incentives. In other words, a target output which differs from that which would result from free market conditions implies acceptance by the State of responsibility for farming incomes and a need to manipulate the market so as to induce the required output.

The main way in which the government does this is by guaranteeing prices for the different agricultural products, which are fixed after February and March consultations between the Ministry of Agriculture and the producers' representatives, the National Farmers' Union. The farmers then get on with the job of producing the maximum output compatible with these price levels. When they come to sell their products, they do not at once get the prices which the government has guaranteed, because sales take place in competition with largely unrestricted imports from abroad. The market price is set by ordinary supply and demand forces, and because of low-cost foreign competition are well below those which would induce farmers to produce so large an output. The low 'world' prices which farmers at first receive are then supplemented up to the guaranteed level by 'deficiency payments' from the State. Support through guaranteed prices was further extended in 1956 in the form of 'Government Long-Term Assurances for Agriculture', which reduced uncertainty about the future course of guaranteed prices by pledging that changes in the existing level of support would not take place with any suddenness.

The cost of subsidies through guaranteed prices mounted during the early sixties to proportions which caused considerable alarm in government circles:

1954–5	£140m.
1959–60	£154·7
1961–2	£225·5m.

This rise occurred because the method of subsidizing agriculture by deficiency payments was 'open-ended'. That is to say, the amount paid depended on: firstly, the *volume* of home output for which prices had to be made up to the guaranteed level, and secondly, on the level of *import prices* which largely determined the return which farmers initially received. During these years, subsidy expenditure has increased both because of a decline in 'world' prices as surpluses have developed and also because home production has expanded. The embarrassing thing from the authorities' point of view was that such expenditure was unpredictable for any given year. Since 1964 the government has therefore re-established control over the amount to be spent by laying down minimum import prices for certain products and by limiting deficiency payments to specific levels of output. As a result, the bill for implementation of price guarantees was cut from £225 million in 1961–2 to £124 million in 1965–6.

When price subsidy payments are added to production grants, the total cost of direct governmental assistance to agriculture (i.e. excluding the operation of Marketing Boards and import duties) amounts to very large sums indeed:

1954–5	£190m.
1961–2	£342·6m.
1965–6	£243·7m.

Government assistance represents a very substantial proportion of farmers' net incomes; indeed, there are particular areas or types of farming for which subsidies comprise the *whole* net income.

Rationale of Agriculture Support

What possible defence can there be for a system which apparently encourages inefficiency with such inflexible generosity? One set of reasons justifying assistance to farmers on this scale arises from the peculiarities of agriculture in comparison with manufacturing industry. It can be argued on these lines that the difficulties of adjusting agricultural supply to changes in demand lead to much greater fluctuations of prices and incomes in the agricultural sector, and that this is coupled with an extreme immobility of resources, particularly labour, which makes farmers stay in the business even when profits and wages are well below what they could earn elsewhere. The consequences of this greater rigidity were evident in the run-down condition of British agriculture in the pre-Second World War period.

When war broke out there was a shortage of shipping space and a disruption of traditional sources of supply which necessitated a rapid expansion of home agricultural output to fill the gap. In these circumstances, food was required for survival; the cost in terms of resources was almost irrelevant, and a policy aimed at maximum production was clearly called for. But even with the return to peacetime conditions, the government continued to emphasize the need for expansion, and, although the reasons were never clearly articulated, the official case for a policy of massive support seems to have been based on two considerations. The first was strategic. It was felt that the war had shown the folly of relying on imports to too great an extent, and that it was therefore safer to produce a larger proportion of food requirements at home, even at higher cost, to reduce dependence on sources which might be cut off in the event of hostilities or political disruption. Secondly, Britain and Europe in the immediately post-war period were in the throes of the dollar shortage. Given a chronic incapacity to earn sufficient hard currency to pay for imports, domestic production which replaced imports from the dollar area could be justified even though it implied less efficient use of resources.

However, even for the period just after the war, these arguments were not particularly convincing. Strategic considerations demanded not so much a higher degree of self-sufficiency as preparedness for expansion, and this might well have been achieved at much lower levels of current output. The balance of payments argument, on the other hand, rested on the assumption of a continued dollar shortage; it was also often forgotten that expansion of home agriculture itself required dollar imports, particularly of feeding-stuffs, which eliminated some part of the gain in import-saving.

In the period since the 1947 Agriculture Act, the force of both arguments has been substantially diminished. Strategically, the case for higher agricultural self-sufficiency is weakened by the dismal consideration that any major disruption of world foodstuffs trade is no longer likely to be of the conventional kind.

And from the balance of payments viewpoint, the dollar shortage has not been with us for a long time; the strength of the traditional argument for countries specializing according to their particular endowments has been correspondingly restored.

Yet the government thinks in terms of still more expansion. In the ill-fated 1965 National Plan a further 18% increase in net output was envisaged by 1970–71 (produced, however, with substantially less manpower). Can continuing support for agriculture on a large scale any longer be justified? Perhaps the most important economic argument for its retention is that a high level of domestic agricultural output may still be a major factor in achieving balance of payments stability – although in a more roundabout way than the crude import-saving argument suggested. Today's more sophisticated version of the case stresses the difficulties of reversing the changes which have already taken place; to do so may have adverse effects on the 'terms of trade'.

It is granted that some of the resources at present used in agriculture could be more economically employed in manufacturing industry, and that in static terms the orthodox arguments for specialization hold good. That is, if instead of trying to produce our own foodstuffs we were to concentrate resources in producing things in which we have a competitive advantage, we could get our food supplies more cheaply by exporting manufactured goods to pay for them. But, it is objected, this argument assumes that everything else remains unchanged while these formidable adjustments are taking place. The necessary increase in the volume of exports even at present prices would be very large indeed. And how could this increased volume be sold? It would only be possible if there was a sharp *fall* in export prices. Similarly, the increase in the British demand for imported foodstuffs would lead to an increase in their prices. The terms of trade (the relationship between export and import prices) might therefore turn sharply against us and outweigh much of the gain from increased specialization.

There is almost certainly something in this case. The problem is to establish just how much, because the relevant variables are difficult to even roughly quantify. The argument does, however, seem weak in stressing only the price-effect of switching our resources from agriculture to other uses. It ignores the fact that there are also likely to be repercussions on incomes. If we buy more foodstuffs from foreign producers we at the same time increase their capacity to pay for our exports. And anyway, in current conditions of world food surpluses, it does not seem probable that increased reliance on supplies from abroad would lead to much increase in their price.

It is equally relevant to consider the other side of the picture – that achieving greater self-sufficiency does not only involve a waste of resources resulting from uneconomic agricultural production; we also have to take into account the increased difficulty in selling our exports if we restrict the market for foreign foodstuff producers and the income which they can thereby earn. It is frequently pointed out that the Commonwealth has been the most slowly growing sector of British foreign trade during the post-war period; what we sometimes forget is that the U.K. has also been the Commonwealth's most slowly growing market – and that at least one important reason for this has been a British agricultural policy limiting the expansion of Commonwealth food exports.

Thus, although there may be some economic justification for the protection of agriculture in the U.K., the case is not an impressive one. However, wider issues may be involved. There is a danger in thinking that merely to state the economic implications of a particular policy is to say all there is to be said. The labels 'economic' and 'uneconomic' have come to have highly persuasive connotations, 'economic' as a term of approval and 'uneconomic' as implying a *malaise* requiring prompt remedy. This is unfortunate. All that 'uneconomic' means is that, in a certain industry or as a result of a particular policy, the cost of obtaining a given output is greater than it could be. But to jump to the conclusion that all uneconomic industries and policies ought therefore to be eliminated is to argue that there are no noneconomic ends, the fulfilment of which might be *worth* the additional costs involved. We have seen that just after the war, the benefit of strategic security perhaps outweighed the economic cost involved in protecting farmers. Although this particular argument has become dated with the development of weapons of mass destruction, it may be that there are other consequences of supporting agriculture which might be thought similarly to justify the costs incurred. Is, for example, the retention of a rural pattern of life worth anything? Or the preservation of the English countryside? Can farms be regarded as at least gaps between towns which are fortunately difficult for builders to encroach upon?

It is not the job of the economist to answer questions like these; the role of economics is limited to showing the costs which would be involved in alternative policies. Only when we have sorted out the economic aspects of an issue from the non-economic can we come to a rational decision about what represents an appropriate balance between the two. However, even if we decide that there are sufficient reasons to justify a policy of supporting agriculture, the question still remains as to the best way of doing so.

We have to distinguish here between the financial and economic issues involved. At the financial level, the choice is about *who pays* for keeping more farmers in the business, at higher levels of income than they would earn in a free market. In this respect there is a major difference between our own practice and that of the Common Market countries. We have seen that British farmers are largely exposed to competition from low-cost overseas producers and are then compensated by *post hoc* payments from the taxpayer. European agricultural policy, on the other hand, shields domestic producers mainly by import levies which raise the price of low-cost imports to the higher home level. Continental farmers are thus supported directly by consumers who foot the cost of the subsidy bill by paying higher prices in the shops. This, then, is one set of alternatives. If we are going to assist agriculture, should the money come, on the whole, from consumers or tax-payers? They are not always the same people, and the British method, which roughly relates the financing of agricultural support to ability to pay, might therefore be thought more equitable than a system which distributes the burden according to the amount of food which families happen to consume.

Apart from the question of finance, and still given that the present level of agricultural support is thought justified, there is further scope for disagreement about the use to which farming subsidies should be put. In the British system, support for farmers continues, on the whole, to encourage increases in output; it is essentially based on the need to provide a living income for the marginal (least efficient) farmers. But surely any justification there may have been in the past for maximizing output has long since disappeared, and the emphasis now should be on improving the structure and efficiency of agriculture so that its dependence on the State can be reduced. The fact that an increasing proportion of assistance is taking the form of production grants rather than price guarantees might be regarded as evidence that this is just what is happening. However, most of these grants do relatively little to stimulate specific improvements. Fertilizer and lime, and calf subsidies, for example, which account for well over half the total, are essentially inducements to increase current output; efficiency is increased only in the sense that higher yields per acre are obtained so long as State support is maintained. What is far more important at this stage is to bring about improvements in productivity of a kind which reduces the *need* for such assistance.

A more positive approach to the question of agricultural support has implications which governments are only just beginning to face up to. A large proportion of British farms are too small or otherwise inadequate *ever* to be made economically viable. The corollary of trying to increase efficiency rather than output is that many of these farms would have to go – facilitating amalgamation into more economically sized units, and enabling support to be concentrated on those parts of the industry most likely some day to stand on their own feet. A policy of generously compensating small farmers out of the business rather than compensating them for their inefficiency might, in the long run, prove money well spent; the nation's food bill might thereby be kept at the low level which British consumers have traditionally come to expect.

CHAPTER 7

RETAILING

'THE trouble is that there are far too many people who don't actually *produce* anything' — is a common enough criticism of the distribution of Britain's working population, of which a large and increasing proportion (about a third) is employed in providing 'services', including over two and a half million in retail trading.

But this sector can only reasonably be dismissed as 'nonproductive' if we are very narrowly defining 'production' as output which has added *quantitatively* to inputs, i.e. as getting something physically greater than we started with. If so, then we would have to conclude that little else except agriculture is really productive, and even manufacturing industry would mostly be excluded on the grounds that it only involves qualitative changes in the materials processed.

This is not a very useful definition. But if, in order to cover manufacturing industry, we widen our notion of 'production' to mean 'the process of satisfying consumer wants', a good deal of *non*-manufacturing activity will also have to be included. Consumers can only be satisfied if output is made available where and when they want to buy it. Transport, wholesaling, and retailing are therefore as much a part of 'production' as manufacturing, as also are direct services – the provision of haircuts, holidays, domestic help, and so on. Indeed, the proportion of resources devoted to 'services' is often a rough measure of the opulence of an economy, the fact that people can afford to spend increasing sums on various types of services showing that their demand for more basic requirements of food, shelter, and consumer durables has been relatively satiated.

However, to stress that services are as much part of the process of satisfying consumer wants as agriculture or mining or manufacturing is not to say that, in present-day Britain, resources used in the services sector are *as* productive as in others. It is notoriously difficult to measure productivity of service industries because to a large extent their output must be assessed qualitatively, but the rough estimates that are possible rather suggest that productivity in this sector has been increasing more slowly than in manufacturing industry. And, although it is absurd to label retailing as a waste of resources in unproductive uses, it would be equally foolish not to consider the questions – are too many resources going into retailing, and are they being used in the most efficient way?

The existence of well over half a million retailing establishments in Britain implies that there is a shop for every ninety people. But, superimposed on the traditional network of small shops, with their advantages of tick, gossip, personal service, and just nearness, have been a series of formidable retailing revolutions.

The first was the emergence of department stores and multiple stores in the late nineteenth century. These represented the application to shopping of the lessons of large-scale production. The particular attraction of the department store was the variety of goods and services which it provided within a single establishment – a greater array than any Eastern bazaar could offer, and a good deal more comfortable. The aim of the department store was to make it worth while for the customer to forfeit the advantages of local shopping by making his single journey serve as a passport to many purchases. Multiple or chain stores, on the other hand, to begin with continued to specialize in particular lines of business. They had the advantage over the smaller independents (as also had the department stores) in economies of scale such as being able to employ specialist personnel, secure discounts from manufacturers for bulk purchases, order special exclusive lines, and use superior advertising techniques.

Threatened with such powerful competition, the small independents defensively retaliated by urging on manufacturers the need for their goods to be sold at uniform prices. With fixed resale prices, competition was diverted on to the independents' own ground – the provision of specialist services. The independents could hope in this way to retain a larger proportion of the trade; but the department and multiple stores still made a lot of ground by offering quite different services – palatial stores with deep carpets, escalators and lifts, liveried attendants, pretty and polite assistants, free delivery, extensive and anonymous credit, and after-sales services.

With the depressed conditions of the thirties, the temptation to break manufacturers' rules and enter the forbidden territory of price competition proved irresistible. More remarkable, however, was the reversion to service competition after the war when the widening gross margins of the big stores – due to a further gust of technical innovations such as cost control and electronic accounting – were largely absorbed in the provision of even more extensive facilities for the consumer.

It was this which opened the way for a further revolution in retailing, the creation of supermarkets. The essence of the supermarket is that it achieves the economies of scale like the department and multiple stores, but exploits its advantages in a different way. It not only buys cheaply, it sells cheaply too. The supermarket movement was a deliberate attempt to eliminate the service element in costs. Simply designed, space-saving stores; cash on the nail; carry it home yourself; and – above all – self-service: all effected substantial cost economies which could be passed on to the consumer through price cuts. The manufacturers came to appreciate that they could no longer afford to inhibit the supermarkets, which, with their mass orders resulting from a policy of rapid turnover and low margins, were fast becoming their major customers. As a result, retail price-fixing was broken in the market for groceries within a few years.

Success of the supermarkets prepared the way for Super-Save, U-Save, Grandway, Grandfare, Buyright, and others – the 'discount' stores. The distinction between the discount stores and the supermarkets is essentially one of scope. Like the supermarkets, discount stores aim at cutting costs through large-scale buying and the provision of only minimal services; but the range of goods on which they cut prices is extended to all sorts of consumer durables. Beyond the discount stores there lies the logical conclusion of the reaction from service competition in direct selling to the public by manufacturers, either through mail ordering or automatic vending. In fact, mail-order business is the fastest growing branch of retailing and it has been estimated that there are about five million active accounts handled by the companies.

Faced with changes which have directly attacked their previous line of defence, uniform fixed prices, the independents have this time struck back more constructively. The last decade has seen the development of voluntary chains – independents forming themselves into groups particularly for the purpose of buying, but also in order to provide services beyond their individual means. In this way, they are able to combine the advantages of small-scale independence with some of the benefits which their larger rivals can enjoy. By the middle of 1961, some 35% of grocers belonged to a voluntary chain. Further economies have resulted from extending supermarketing techniques to the wholesale link. Self-service warehouses are now developing in which the small buyer can wander round with a trolley collecting his requirements and pay cash as he leaves. He has to provide his own transport and time, and loses the benefits of credit and perhaps display and shop-fitting assistance, but gains in flexibility, time-saving in dealing with travellers, less susceptibility to pressure sales, smaller stocks, and lower margins for the wholesaler.

Despite these innovations, the small shopkeeper remains hard-pressed. Always something of an in-and-out business, the hazards and the rate of turnover are increasing. But the multiplicity of shops remains. Given the advantages of the larger units, is there not a serious waste of resources? *Why* are there still so many shops?

The answer lies partly in the fact that many shopkeepers are either satisfied with lower rates of return on their capital and effort than they could earn elsewhere, or grumble without being prepared to change. There is inflated optimism about likely profits and plenty of prospective entrants to fill the places left by those whom reality forces out. But many stay put, either not calculating their hours of work and worry in such a way as to give a truthful picture of their real rewards, or tolerating low profits because of the non-pecuniary advantages implied in those magic words 'being your own boss'.

From the demand side, too, the fact that consumers patronize small shops by giving them sufficient custom to make the owners think it worth while to stay in business should be an indication that the advantages of a multiplicity of shops are worth paying for. The customer in this case must be right. But is consumer choice made on a fair basis? Choice can only be free (and therefore direct retailing resources into those channels which reflect consumer requirements) if both large and small shop-keepers, independents, multiples, supermarkets, and discount stores, are able to display their relative advantages to the full. We must doubt that this, until recently, has been possible because of the continued prevalence, in the non-foodstuffs markets, of the practice of resale price maintenance.

Resale Price Maintenance

When Tesco Stores Ltd opened 'the largest supermarket in Europe' at Leicester in 1962, their chairman threatened that 'if the manufacturers don't like it they can lump it; they are not dealing with someone who can't fight'. This referred to the Tesco policy of selling a wide range of goods at prices lower than those fixed by the manufacturers. Within a year, they *were* fighting, but unsuccessfully. The firm of Kayser Bondor had taken them to court and secured an injunction preventing Tesco from selling women's stockings and underwear at prices below those which they had stipulated. Earlier in the year, the manufacturers of Gor-ray skirts had also clashed with Tesco, cutting off their supplies and compensating other local agents by allowing them to sell off their existing stocks at unrestricted prices. (On the morning following this announcement, the local Tesco manager had many offers of supplies from the local retailers whom the manufacturers claimed to be protecting.) The Tesco case was not something new. In May 1960 the Prestige group had also successfully fought a court case to prevent the Leeds Grandway discount store from selling their sponge mops at 18s. 11d. rather than at the fixed price of 30s., and one discount store was forced out of business through stoppage of supplies. At first sight, this all seems very peculiar. In an age when everyone complains of rising prices it is odd that attempts actually to reduce prices should lead to local uproar and recourse to the law to prevent price-cutting.

As we have seen, the practice of resale price maintenance seems to have originated around the turn of the century in the desire of smaller independent retailers to be protected by manu-facturers from the encroachments on their business by the newly developed multiples and department stores. Two varieties of restriction developed. There was individual R.P.M. – the imposition of fixed selling prices by a single manufacturer on an individual (and, if inefficient, grateful) retailer. And there was the more highly organized collective R.P.M. – manufacturers getting together and agreeing on the range of prices at which their goods should be sold in the shops and then collectively imposing their wishes on retailers. This was enforced through a complex machinery of inspection, warnings, and fines on price-slashers by private association courts, with the ultimate sanction of a collective boycott on retailers who persistently failed to toe the line.

Under the Restrictive Practices Act of 1955, collective resale price maintenance was made illegal. Individual price-fixing, on the other hand, was still allowed and specific legal recognition made the practice automatically enforceable in the courts. Why was this permitted by a government which, ostensibly at least, was trying to give the economy a more competitive outlook? Why was there no outcry from a public which had been complaining of rising prices since the war? Is there, in fact, a case to be made out in favour of R.P.M.?

Resale price maintenance imposes uniform selling prices on retailers. Whether they are large or small, efficient or inefficient, energetic or lazy, shopkeepers are allowed to charge only a single price for the product. There are a number of ways in which it might be claimed that the consumer benefits from such uniformity, the first of which is that it makes it possible to shop with more confidence. Finding the same branded goods selling at the same price in all retail outlets, the consumer feels some guarantee that he is getting what he thinks he is paying for. With the abandonment of fixed prices there would be an incentive for manufacturers to reduce the quality of their goods in order to remain price-competitive. Moreover, price-cutting would be heaviest on the popular branded goods, and, as these became less profitable, retailers would switch to alternative lines with the result that consumers would no longer be able to rely on the quality guaranteed by 'names'. Secondly, it is argued, price-fixing forces retailers to compete for custom by the provision of services which are beneficial to the consumer – credit, comfort, after-sales maintenance, and free delivery – which would not be possible with the narrower margins implied by unrestricted prices. The consumer further benefits with the multiplicity of shops which R.P.M. tends to encourage. Without price-fixing, many smaller and more out-of-the-way retailers would be driven out of business so that any consumer gain from lower prices would be outweighed by loss of convenience resulting from the concentration of retailing into fewer hands (with the danger of large monopolies being able to charge higher prices with impunity).

This case for R.P.M. is not at all convincing. Of course fewer services are likely to be provided without R.P.M.; replacement of benefits which *add* to prices by those which *reduce* them is, after all, the major object of the exercise. One authority has estimated that the saving to consumers might amount to £180 million per annum – about £3 10s. 0d. per person – and certainly foreign experience would seem to confirm this order of magnitude. Publicity in the court cases against discount stores has at least opened many eyes to the profit margins which sometimes prevail. Tesco, for example, after losing a court case, prominently displayed signs in their stores saying 'this manufacturer is forcing us to take an 87% mark-up on this product'.

It is just possible that consumers *prefer* the combination of higher prices and extensive services (although the success of the new price-cutting stores hardly confirms either this view or that put to the Lloyd Jacob Committee in 1949, by certain rather untypical women's associations, that housewives do not enjoy the trouble of 'shopping around'). The important thing is, however, that consumers should be allowed to choose. With R.P.M., consumer choice is limited to high prices with service and high prices without service.

The Resale Prices Bill

After several years of prevarication, the case for freeing prices was finally accepted by the government in its publication of the Resale Prices Bill in February 1964. The Bill was modified but not destroyed by the large number of amendments which threatened its passage through Parliament, and became law in April 1965.

The procedure for dealing with resale price maintenance is modelled on the Restrictive Practices Act which we described in Chapter 4. Indeed, its application is the responsibility of the Registrar and a strengthened Restrictive Practices Court. R.P.M. is not completely outlawed, but all agreements must be registered, and are liable to the scrutiny of the Court. It will no longer be possible for manufacturers to enforce minimum selling prices for their products under the threat of withholding supplies, unless they can show that retailers are using their product as a 'loss-leader', or that abandonment of fixed prices would result in a reduction in the quality or variety of goods offered, a reduction of retail selling outlets, withdrawal of after-sale services, or a 'general' and 'long-run' increase in consumer prices; moreover, parties to an agreement will have to convince the Court that its advantages to the public outweigh the ill-effects of continued price-fixing. The 'public' is defined as 'consumers or users'.

This is not going to be an easy set of rules to apply. The Bill protects manufacturers against retailers using their products as loss-leaders, i.e. being sold at or below cost in order to attract customers for other products. The problem of defining 'cost' – whether, for example, it should include a percentage for overheads and return on capital – make the loss-leader clause a potentially wide loophole. Again, there are going to be difficulties in proving that a manufacturer is withholding supplies from a retailer because of his price policy, rather than for legitimate reasons such as unsuitability of premises, uncreditworthiness, or inability to offer servicing facilities.

Recognizing how the climate of opinion was changing, certain manufacturers – notably I.C.I., Gillette and Distillers – discontinued R.P.M. even before its legal abolition. On the passing of the Act, many more producers followed suit and immediately freed their goods from price-fixing. However, some 700 firms decided to fight a rearguard action by applying for exemption from the new rules, and since the Court was not able to hear its first case till 1967, the impact of the new legislation has been significantly delayed. This, indeed, was probably the idea behind quite a large number of the exemption applications and the indications are that many will abandon R.P.M. when their cases are called. Just how thoroughly R.P.M. is destroyed will then depend on the severity of the Court's attitude to the remaining practitioners.

However, the pattern of retailing which finally emerges will not be merely a reflection of legal decisions. It will also be determined by what *consumers* want. If they do prefer service competition, as supporters of R.P.M. claim, then price-cutters with low margins will lose ground to the department stores and independents; if, on the other hand, they would rather have lower prices, it is the shops providing extensive services which will find themselves in difficulty.

The growing practice of issuing 'free' trading stamps, coupons and gifts to customers suggests that the abolition of R.P.M. will certainly not automatically eliminate all forms of indirect competition.

Considerable consumer gains have already resulted from the partial abandonment of price-fixing, with price cuts ranging up to 20% on a wide variety of goods. But are there any ways in which the consumer can *lose* by unregulated prices? Admittedly, shopping is perhaps less certain and budgeting a little trickier as prices fluctuate more. But it is a strange argument that prices should be kept high because there is a danger when buying a low-priced good that it might have been bought even more cheaply elsewhere! The fact that price-cutting on popular brands might lead to the introduction of new ones hardly seems serious either. Apart from anything else, this is just what happened *because* of R.P.M. – as retailers tried to avoid manufacturers' control by introducing their own unrestricted lines in competition. Moreover, the researches of consumer associations hardly support the illusion that branded goods are particularly reliable! Nor does there seem much basis for the view that manufacturers of such goods will suffer the complication of production planning which is sometimes predicted – providing that R.P.M. is abandoned on *all* branded goods at the same time. They should, after all, benefit from the larger sales which lower prices will imply.

The ending of R.P.M. may well lead to elimination of many existing retail outlets. Total employment in retailing is likely to fall (particularly when the effects of the 1966 Selective Employment Tax are also taken into account), and there will be a switch of employment to those enterprises most suited to benefit from the increased competition. It should be emphasized again, however, that the small shopkeeper will suffer only to the extent that consumers do not *prefer* the services which he provides. The shop at the corner offers advantages over large competitors in the town centre in a number of ways and is entitled to *charge* for them. A pattern may therefore develop in which shoppers make most of their purchases at low prices on an expedition to the main centres, and pay perhaps considerably higher prices for the odd items which they find it more convenient to buy locally. Indeed, the scope of service which could be offered by the small independent could easily be extended by an amendment to the Shop Act enabling him to stay open at unusual hours.

The most important way in which consumers will gain from the abandonment of resale price maintenance may not be so much from increased retail competition as from the stimulation which this gives to competition between *manufacturers*. Agreements between manufacturers, either open or tacit, not to resort to price-cutting can only be effective if prices are also fixed at the retail end. Once this guarantee is lost, the way is open for aggressive selling by efficient manufacturers and the restoration of price-competition to its traditional role of eliminating the less efficient.

To sum up, the economy without resale price maintenance will be tougher for both shopkeepers and manufacturers. The important thing is that consumers will be allowed to express their choices more freely. It is quite unreasonable to expect consumers to subsidize the quiet life which some retailers and producers have so far enjoyed, or that some consumers should cross-subsidize those who happen to prefer service competition.

Consumer Ignorance

We have been stressing in this chapter that the whole point of production is to satisfy consumer wants, and that every effort should therefore be made to remove obstacles which impede free choice by consumers. It might therefore be appropriate to end by mentioning another limitation on consumer sovereignty – the fact that consumers often lack the knowledge which is needed if their buying is to be done rationally. Pure economic theory assumes that consumers know all there is to know about the prices and quality of goods available in the market. We have noted, on the other hand, that one of the arguments for R.P.M. was that consumers need the guarantee of trustworthiness given by branded goods with fixed prices. Although it is very doubtful whether in fact the existence of R.P.M. gave this protection, the assumption which lay behind the argument – that consumers are *not* on the whole well informed – seems closer to the truth than that of economic theory.

If this ignorance arises because consumers just do not care or that it is too much trouble to find out and compare the prices and qualities of different goods, there is no problem. A problem does exist, however, when consumers are unable to obtain information which they would like to have, or when the information which is available is distorted. Two such obstacles to rational consumption seem to be important in present conditions.

The first is a side-effect of increasing affluence. With growing prosperity we spend increasing amounts on sophisticated durable goods – television sets, washing machines, motor-cars – all of which are highly complicated pieces of machinery. In these circumstances, most of us are just not technically qualified to assess the relative advantages of different models before buying, and, since they are durable goods of frequently changing specifications, even subsequent experience is largely irrelevant to later buying decisions. Secondly, there is the impact of the £500 million or so which is currently spent each year in Britain on advertising. In the absence of other sources of information, it might be argued that advertising performs the useful social function of increasing consumer knowledge. However, apart from being informative, advertising also seeks to persuade. If it generally only persuades people to do what they anyway would like to do, it also stimulates impulse or pressured sales which may be regretted later, and it is not the job of the advertiser to point out the faults of a product as well as the merits.

In this respect, a very useful job is done by the Consumers' Association, an entirely independent organization financed wholly from members' subscriptions. In their monthly bulletin *Which?* C.A. publish the results of rigorous tests of various brands of goods (bought in the shops, not special models supplied by the manufacturers) together with some evaluation of their suitability for different types of consumer. High standards of objectivity (producers are not allowed to use flattering quotations from *Which?* in their advertisements) and thoroughness in testing products means that the Consumers' Association provides a very valuable service, the need for which is shown by its membership of 445,000. Since many of these 'members' are libraries and other institutions, and the results of surveys are summarized in the Press and sometimes on television, the information is made available to a sizeable part of the interested public. Apart from enabling consumers to get better value for their money, C.A. also acts as a spur to manufacturing efficiency. It is not unusual, after a particular brand has been criticized in *Which?*, to find in the subsequent edition a note to the effect that 'This model has now been withdrawn . . .' or 'The manufacturers tell us that substantial modifications have now been made. . . .' Manufacturers are most of all kept on their toes by interested and well-informed consumers. On the whole, we get the prices and products which we deserve; if we don't bother, then we shouldn't grumble.

CHAPTER 8

THE LABOUR MARKET

THE spectre of mass unionism grown beyond control, monstrous but irresponsible, outdated and restrictive, is one which haunts not only right-wing extremists. Certainly, at first sight, the unions present an impressive picture of strength. Legally, they are secure and privileged. They have the right to do anything collectively which would not be illegal if performed individually; they can sue in respect of civil wrongs performed against them, but cannot themselves be sued as a collective body; they can impose political levies (from which members have to 'contract out') which they can use to buy parliamentary support. Total membership of unions has risen from about two million at the turn of the century to over ten million today. The annual revenue from this membership amounts to about £40 million, and reserves, following a period of relative industrial peace, stand at about £120 million.

In some ways, facts like this tend to exaggerate the power of the unions. Generally, for example, it is misleading to talk of 'unionism' or the 'trade union movement' as though it were a homogeneous body acting according to an agreed policy. Although the number of unions has declined by over a half from its 1920 total of 1,400, and over two-thirds of union membership is now concentrated in the twenty or so largest, trade unions continue to speak with many and often quite dissonant voices. There is frequently little in common between the aims and policies of such different organizations as the exclusive and traditional craft unions, the mass industrial unions embracing all workers in a particular occupation, the newer multi-industry groupings like the Transport and General Workers, and the most rapidly growing of unions – those for 'white-collared' and salaried workers.

Admittedly, at the head of some but by no means all of this multiplicity of unions stands the Trade Union Congress. It looks as if, in the fairly near future, its position will be strengthened, but so far it has been a hortatory, advisory, conciliatory body with very little real control over the affairs of individual unions. T.U.C. resolutions may sometimes be reflected in unions' policies, but if member unions decide to pursue alternative lines of action there is little that the T.U.C. can do to restrain them.

On the other hand, membership figures do not show the full extent of union influence. Sixty per cent of the working population are not trade union members, but a large number of these work in industries where wage-rates are pushed up by the unions to which they do not belong. The fact that many workers enjoy the fruits of union action without contributing towards their funds is, not unreasonably, resented by trade union members and underlies the case for the 'closed shop'. That so many are getting 'something for free' is particularly aggravating to the unions at a time when their finances, despite a marked improvement in the sixties, are not really as strong as they look. Their seemingly colossal reserves, in fact, average out at only about £12 per head of membership, and the greater part of their annual income is swallowed up in working expenses. The reason for this relative financial weakness is not hard to find. Between 1938 and 1956, for example, average earnings rose by 245%; during the same period, average union membership dues were increased by a mere 31%. Inflation, too, has whittled away the real value of union reserves which are held mainly in gilt-edged stock.

Collective Bargaining

One of the more extreme products of the policy of *laissez-faire* was the passing of the Combination Acts which banned worker associations during the first part of the nineteenth century and gave to the individual worker the unwanted right to negotiate his own contract with the individual employer. Wage bargaining was thus made 'free' – but hardly fair. The single employer, with his greater resources, and particularly when there is less than full employment, will always enjoy greater bargaining strength than the individual worker.

Today relatively few wage contracts are negotiated on an individual basis. In addition to union members and those non-members whose rates are nevertheless the result of union activity, a further slice of the working population (about three and a half million) makes its wage bargains through State-organized media like Wages Councils. All these are examples of collective bargaining – associations of workers to establish bargaining equality with their employers.

The aim of collective bargaining is improvement of working conditions – which could take many forms. In Britain, however, the unions have concentrated most of their efforts in securing increases in money wages. Since wages are costs as well as incomes, it is often argued that most trade union activity is self-defeating; wage increases cause rising prices which swallow up the money gains and leave workers no better off in real terms than they were before. To see whether there is any truth in this contention requires a look at the mechanism of wage increases.

A union puts in a wage claim. The employer grants it. Where does the money come from? Clearly, there are only three possible sources. The first is a reduction of profits. Secondly, profits may be maintained or even simultaneously increased if the wage increase is offset by an increase in productivity (output per man-hour) – due either to greater effort on the part of the individual worker, better organization on the part of the management, or greater capital outlay per worker. Thirdly, the wage increase may be financed by a higher selling price for the product.

Thus wage increases do not necessarily lead to corresponding price rises. If they come from reduced profits or increased productivity, union action will genuinely have improved the real incomes of its members. The only qualification is – *how many* of its members? The danger exists that wage increases may result in reduced employment so that the benefit from union action will be confined to those members lucky enough to avoid redundancy. Reduced profits may force marginal firms out of business; improved productivity may replace men by machines; increased prices may cut the demand for the product. This is particularly likely when a firm in a competitive market is faced with a wage increase which its rivals do not have to bear.

However, it may be a very different story if *all* firms are meeting similar wage pressures and are all passing on some part of their increased costs through higher prices. In the conditions which have typified the post-war economy, of *generally* rising prices, the responsiveness of demand to particular price increases is correspondingly reduced. We also have to remember that the worker has a dual role as producer and consumer. On the one hand, wages are *costs*, helping to push up prices; at the same time, wages are *income*, providing the means to buy the more highly priced output.

The fact remains that wage increases passed on as higher prices mean that the cost of living is rising. If some workers get more money, the result will be that other unions will put in defensive wage claims on behalf of their members – who are the consumers paying for the initial increase. Prices will consequently rise still further, and this leads to another round of wage bargaining. Is anyone better off?

Trade union activity certainly looks abortive when the wage/price spiral is presented in these terms. However, the analysis skips from the initial wage increase to the end-result of the wage round; we are missing the point that real benefits may accrue to some union members in the intervening process. Clearly, the union which is first in the annual wage round does secure an increase in the real income of its members, at least temporarily. Wages will have been increased and, unless the workers spend their whole increase on the product which they themselves produce, they will find that they are able to buy more for their money. And even the last in the wage queue will be achieving something in at least preventing the reduction in real wages which would otherwise occur. There may, secondly, be genuine gains for all of them if there are sections of the working community who, for one reason or another, do not take part in the wage round. Some money wages will have risen but not all prices. The effect will be a shift in real purchasing power from the relatively fixed-income groups to those who are more strongly organized.

The point that we are making is simply that trade unionists are not as stupid or ignorant of the economic facts of life as a superficial analysis too often suggests. The trouble lies rather in the narrowness of their allegiance. Trade union officials are hired by their own members. They are paid to do the best they can for those members. They are not paid to improve the lot of workers as a whole, and it is even less their job to think in terms of the national economy. The result is that much wage bargaining is a competitive struggle between *unions* rather than between unions and employers.

The Labour Market

The Economic Function of Wages

In the theory of an economy based on the price mechanism, wages play an important role in bringing about an allocation of resources which reflects consumer demands. The consumer, in distributing his expenditure among the variety of goods and services coming on to the market, in effect 'votes' for particular uses of resources. The entrepreneur collects the votes and recasts them in the markets for factors of production – land, capital, and labour. If more people are buying more of his goods he will be able to bid a larger volume of these scarce resources away from less popular competitors.

In pure economic theory, the market for labour is based on similar principles to any other. In the same way that the price of oranges is determined by the quantities offered for sale and consumer willingness to buy them, so wages represent the price which balances the supply and demand for labour. The theory only makes sense if the amount of labour offered in the market and the demand for labour from employers *are* sensitive to changes in the wage level. On the whole, this does not seem an unreasonable assumption. Higher wages can expand the labour supply in a number of ways – by bringing about an increase in the number prepared to work (possibly more female or retired workers being attracted into employment) or by inducing the existing labour force to work longer hours at the now higher rates or make greater efforts; admittedly, higher wages may cause some workers to *reduce* their hours and effort, but in present conditions the net effect of higher wages on the labour supply seems likely to be positive.

On the demand side, the amount of labour which a producer employs will depend on the net addition which he thinks further workers will make to his revenue. How much he can produce depends also on the amount and quality of equipment per worker; if this is assumed constant, then employment of additional workers will ultimately yield only diminishing returns, and it is also probable that, as output increases, the producer will have to cut his selling price to induce consumers to take up the larger quantities of his product coming into the market. A careful employer will, so far as he can, weigh the wage costs of additional workers against the net change in his revenue position which occurs as a result of employing them. He will offer employment to the point where this is just equal to the extra wages he has to pay. Other things being equal, we can conclude that the higher the wage-rate, the smaller will be the volume of labour which he finds it profitable to employ.

Wages in these circumstances act as signposts indicating the shift of resources between different uses which is dictated by changing consumer demands. For example, increased demand for motor-cars, either by causing price increases or enabling improvements in productivity to be made, will mean that the return from additional workers may now exceed the current wage. Car firms will be able to offer higher wage inducements to workers to move from those contracting sectors of the economy where the reverse situation exists.

Wages can thus be thought of as the result of two different mechanisms. When we were discussing collective bargaining, we showed that powerful worker associations can *push* up wages by applying pressures on profit margins or prices; on the other hand, our theoretical model suggests that wages can also be *pulled* up to reflect changing consumer demand. However, in practice, the economic function of wages in adjusting final output to the pattern of consumer preferences is decidedly blurred by imperfections in the labour market and by the intrusion of non-economic considerations.

WAGES IN PRACTICE

Immobility of Labour

To some extent the supply of labour can be varied by changing the numbers, hours, and efforts of the labour force within a given geographical and occupational setting. However, major structural adjustments in the economy may require movement of workers from one job to another and to different areas. In practice, shifts of labour take place only partially and slowly. Changing jobs may imply the acquisition of new skills which is not possible for some workers because of their inertia, age, or lack of ability. There may be institutional obstacles to mobility such as trade union apprenticeship rules, or social barriers to movement which break the labour force up into a number of non-competing groups.

Changing areas often involves expense, disruption of a family, loss of old contacts. For very understandable reasons, therefore, labour tends to be fairly immobile; labour shortages in some areas and occupations, indicated by high wage-rates, may do little to induce workers to move from less attractive alternatives. Higher earnings may similarly fail to perform their economic 'signpost' function in occupations which require long periods of highly specialist training. A shortage of doctors or dentists or university professors may cause an increase in their remuneration as their scarcity value becomes recognized, but this increase in earnings will not much increase their number now. The main effect will be to induce more people to begin the lengthy training (which may involve the building and staffing of more training institutions), and the labour force expands only very much later.

Fair Wages

In practice, it is obvious that the terms of wage bargains are not always couched in the language of the market-place and that even when they are, this is often only camouflage for quite non-economic considerations. It is all very well for economists to talk of labour as just another factor of production whose rate of hire is determined by the forces of supply and demand, but as human beings we also have ideas of fairness and equity, and these ethical notions obtrude a good deal in the process of wage determination.

One of the most popular set of arguments for wage increases stems from the existence of traditional differentials between and within industries. An appeal for social justice on this basis is a particularly useful weapon for wage negotiators since different variants of the argument from differentials can be used to support practically *any* claim for increased pay. The starting-point is the existence of a certain *traditional* stratification of the labour force. Those well placed in this conventional system can argue for wage increases because time-honoured differentials are being whittled away; those who are badly placed can bargain for larger increases on the ground that the traditional differential should be modified or eliminated. The inflationary potentialities of such arguments are most obvious where two opposing groups have different conceptions of what constitutes a fair differential, and secure compensatory increases every time the other temporarily succeeds in establishing the difference it considers just. This type of argument is frequently supported by pseudo-scientific evaluations of different kinds of work combined with the principle of 'comparability' – that it is only right that people doing similar work should receive similar pay.

Other arguments for wage increases have a rather more economic flavour which conceals the fact that they are frequently just as much ethically based. Thus, to argue that wages should rise because of increases in the cost of living rests on a belief in the sanctity of current living standards. To claim that wages should follow increases in profits clearly involves a value judgement about a fair allocation of revenues. (The argument tends to lose its attraction when the cost of living or profits are *falling*.) Even the generally accepted view that wages ought to rise in the case of improved productivity has a non-economic basis inasmuch as productivity increases are generally due more to improved equipment than increased worker effort. There is a lot of truth in Barbara Wootton's dictum that 'we are more interested in keeping our distances above other people than in the actual level at which our earnings make it possible for us to live'.

To what extent have 'fairness' considerations modified the wage structure which would have resulted from purely economic pressures? There may, after all, be a difference between what we want and what we get, and wage claims based on notions of fairness but camouflaged by economic arguments may be successful only when the economic basis *is* valid. Can it be doubted that the narrowing of differentials over the past few decades between manual and clerical/professional workers is largely due to increased supply of the latter as educational opportunities have been extended? And how can an employer grant wage increases, however well grounded in social justice, if to do so causes his sales to decline as a result of consequent price increases?

Full Employment and Collective Bargaining

The possibility that non-economic wage claims will cause unemployment because of reduced profits or sales is, however, largely eliminated when the State is pledged to maintain full employment and knows how to do so. In these circumstances it is up to the authorities to *offset* any employment repercussions of wage bargaining. Basically, maintaining employment means that spending must be kept at a level sufficient to absorb current output; any demand deficiency must be made good by the authorities – by techniques which we will be considering in the following chapter. By and large, the obligation to ensure full employment implies that demand is adjusted to wage levels rather than the other way round.

Given the guarantee that there will be no adverse consequences, producers are naturally only too happy to maintain good industrial relations by offering little resistance to wage demands. The way is opened for equity considerations to play an increasingly significant part in wage negotiations.

A further limitation on the economic role of wages arises from the fact that in this country collective bargaining mostly takes place on a national basis. Unions insist that the same rate is paid for similar work wherever it is done; employers in areas of labour surplus or firms of low productivity thus have to pay the same minimum wage-rate as those where labour is in short supply or particularly productive. Again, wage differentials between skilled and non-skilled labour have been narrowed by the industrial unions' practice of negotiating flat-rate increases for all their members.

Most of this discussion has been concerned with wage-*rates*. Wage-*earnings* – minimum rates supplemented by overtime, bonuses, and so on – may reflect purely economic pressures more faithfully. However, we can safely conclude that non-economic factors play a very important part in the process of wage determination. This is not necessarily a bad thing. To say that wages *ought* to be paid on a purely economic basis is, of course, just as much a value judgement as the considerations of fairness which in fact dominate wage discussions. All that we have pointed out is that the economic function of wages *has* become less significant; some of the problems which this causes are considered in Chapter 11.

PART III

ECONOMIC POLICIES

CHAPTER 9

EMPLOYMENT

BETWEEN 1921 and 1939 the average level of unemployment in Britain was 14%, and it was against this dreadful background that *The Times* declared in 1943 that

next to war, unemployment has been the most widespread, most insidious, and most corroding malady of our generation: it is the specific social disease of western civilization in our time.

In only a single post-war year, 1963, has unemployment briefly crept above the 3% which Lord Beveridge, in his influential *Full Employment in a Free Society* (1944), thought was the minimum which *could* be achieved; throughout most of the period it has been well below 2%. However, the virtual disappearance of general unemployment on any significant scale and the present policy emphasis on achieving rapid growth rather than just stability of the economy do not obviate the need to consider what are the determinants of the unemployment level. An extremely serious problem still exists for particular regions in Britain where unemployment has persisted at levels up to five times the national average. And secondly, although post-war conditions have certainly been exceptionally favourable in allowing the government to fulfil its responsibility, first accepted at the end of the war, of achieving 'a high and stable level of employment', success in eliminating general unemployment has also depended on the adoption of deliberate stabilization policies. These policies are based on the greater understanding which we now have about what causes unemployment, and the existence of high employment levels makes it no less important for us to consider how such a situation can be maintained.

Meaning of Full Employment

The concept of 'full employment' obviously has to be related only to those people who *want* jobs and who are capable of working. The fact that over half of Britain's population do not have jobs (or at least not jobs for which they are paid) is because they are housewives or too old, too young, or too lazy to want jobs or be able to do them. Voluntary unemployment of this kind is no problem; the purpose of a full employment policy is to provide work for those who require it – in Britain, about twenty-five millions.

Literally, full employment is something which can never be achieved. Labour exchanges will always have workers on their books who are in the process of moving from one job to another. or who are in occupations where there are seasonal variations in employment. 'Frictional' unemployment, as this is called, is inevitable, but can be reduced to very low proportions by facilitating contacts between those who want work and those who have work to offer. The most that 'full' employment can mean, therefore, is that about 98·5% of the working force is occupied at any one time.

A full employment policy cannot be a guarantee that the present occupational and geographical distribution of the working force will be maintained, that every worker can be sure of always doing his present work in his present area. Clearly, such a policy, even if practicable, would eliminate all flexibility in the economy and ultimately lead to a fall in the standard of living. Minimally, full employment means that there are enough jobs, of some sort, somewhere, to go round. On this basis, full employment could be statistically defined as the number of employment vacancies in the economy being equal to the number of people who are involuntarily unemployed. This definition allows us to refer to a state of 'over-full' employment – when, as it has for much of the post-war period, the number of vacancies *exceeds* the number of workers available to fill them.

However, do we really want to say that there is full employment even when the unemployed are in quite different areas and occupations from the vacancies? Supposing, for example, that the situation is like this:

Area	Vacancies	Unemployed
X	75,000	5,000
Y	5,000	75,000
Total		
	80,000	80,000

Total vacancies are equal to those wanting work, but, whereas the vacancies are concentrated in area X, the unemployed are mostly in area Y.

This may be no more than frictional unemployment if contracting industries in area Y are disgorging labour which is *then moving* to the expanding employment opportunities of area X. But what if workers are *not* moving, if the pool of unemployment in area Y consists of the same people out of work for lengthy periods rather than a constantly changing group of workers in the course of shifting jobs? It is this type of unemployment which has been the most untractable in post-war Britain.

REGIONAL UNEMPLOYMENT

While unemployment in the country as a whole has been kept at remarkably low rates, certain regions – in particular, N. Ireland, Scotland, Wales, and the northern part of England – have suffered from *persistently* higher levels of unemployment than the national average.

Percentage of Unemployed

	N. Ireland	Scotland	Wales	N. England	U.K
1954	7	2·8	2·4	2·3	1·5
1964	6·6	3·7	2·6	3·4	1·8
1954-64 Average	7·4	3·4	2·8	2·8	1·8

Regional disparities are not just a post-war phenomenon. There were similar differences in unemployment levels during the depressed inter-war years although the divergence was then between a national average of 14% and a rate in excess of 50% in areas like Northern Ireland, Central Scotland, South Wales, and the North-East of England. Before the war, the uneven spread of employment could be largely attributed to the decline of the old staple industries – mining, textiles, shipbuilding, and agriculture – and the concentration of the newer industries closer to the major consumer markets of the Midlands and South of England. Today, however, it seems that the problem arises more from the fact that the *same* industries are growing less rapidly in the older regions rather than that such areas have a less favourable pattern of output.

Extreme advocates of a free economy argue that this sort of situation is self-correcting and that market pulls and pushes will be sufficient to eliminate regional disparities. A very low national rate of unemployment implies severe labour shortages for the more rapidly growing areas, and this induces movement of unemployed labour from other parts of the country. At the same time, the increasing congestion of the more popular regions causes flows of capital in the opposite direction to take advantage of the surplus labour, capacity, and less-used social amenities of the relatively declining areas. Such shifts of resources are further encouraged by price considerations, with wages and rents rising more rapidly in the expanding sectors of the economy.

Unfortunately, market forces are more likely to accentuate regional disparities than to remove them. In fact, labour *has* moved on a very considerable scale: population in the southern counties, London and the Midlands has greatly increased at the expense of the traditional industrial regions. But since it is mostly the younger workers who are prepared to move, the poorer regions thereby become characterized by a working force which is on average older and less adaptable. Movement of labour may thus lead to an even *greater* reluctance of firms to move to the depressed areas and a *further* surplus of labour develops. Frequently, too, such areas have a heritage of labour troubles and restrictive practices built up during the decline of staple industries; wage-rates tend to be no lower than in areas of labour shortages because they are negotiated on a national basis; social capital – housing, transport and communications, and general amenities – have often been run down in the cumulative process of decline; the general aura of decay compares unfavourably with the buoyant optimism of the faster-growing regions.

Since market forces may perpetuate regional disparities, with the gap between poor and rich areas widening over the years, there is a clear case for government intervention to deal with the problem. The most important argument for government action is that it is intolerable that anyone should be involuntarily jobless for anything above a minimal period; in view of the financial and human costs involved, and the limited scope for labour movement, it is *not* enough that a similar number of employment vacancies should exist elsewhere. Secondly, in a period of expansion when labour is generally in short supply, any unemployment represents an obvious waste of resources. Thirdly, attempts to deal with local unemployment by raising the *general* level of demand will cause inflationary pressures in those areas which have consequently over-full employment. And finally, the present trend of concentration of population is leading to rapidly inflating social costs in a handful of over-congested areas.

In fact, regional policy dates back to the 1934 designation of four 'special areas' on which government assistance was to be concentrated. These were extended and renamed 'development areas' in the 1945 Distribution of Industry Act, which remained the basis of official intervention until the flurry of activity since 1958. The 1960 Local Employment Act tried to introduce more flexibility by replacing these large and statutorily defined regions by very much smaller 'development districts' where 'a high rate of unemployment exists or is to be expected, and is thought likely to persist'. 4·5% was the unemployment criterion used, but areas with lower rates could be included if the position was expected to deteriorate, and those with higher unemployment excluded if it was likely to be only temporary. Under the 1966 Industrial Development Bill, however, there was a reversion to a wider geographical basis for assistance, the new development areas covering most of Scotland, the north of England, Wales and western England.

Although the scope and scale of intervention has changed, the *type* of assistance has remained on the same lines throughout. The emphasis has been on diverting new enterprises into the areas of high unemployment by a combination of positive inducements and negative controls on their establishment elsewhere. The Board of Trade is empowered to build factories itself for lease or sale, or to provide substantial financial assistance to private firms who build their own. At the same time, control over alternative location has been exercised through the 1947 Town and Country Planning Act, under which firms have to secure an Industrial Development Certificate before building any factory or extension over 5,000 square feet. Various other incentives have been tried, such as provision in the 1963 budget for plant and machinery expenditure in certain areas to be wholly written off for tax purposes in its first year, and in 1966, 40% cash grants for investment in the development areas.

This sort of policy approach has been criticized on a number of grounds. Despite the fact that local unemployment has been with us for many generations, measures to deal with it have too often seemed designed to meet crisis conditions, with an emphasis on relieving immediate distress. Moreover, their effect has been dissipated in attempts to attract business to areas where unemployment was high without any consideration of their development potential. In fact, large parts of the less prosperous areas are probably dead ducks as far as economic development is concerned, and no amount of financial cajolery will induce enterprises to move in on a sufficient scale; although location of industry in already congested areas may not always be rational, we have to accept that businessmen do sometimes know what they are doing when they studiously avoid certain areas. The relative importance of the different factors which deter firms from moving into regions of high unemployment is a matter which deserves a lot more research than has so far been done. However, it is likely, in view of the reduced pulls now exerted by sources of power and raw materials, that the existence of substantial 'external economies' has become a prime determinant of industrial location. Many of the development districts, for example, were too small to provide such facilities as labour-training, communications, and social overheads on a sufficiently attractive scale; in others, the quality of amenities is so poor that it is probably better to start all over again.

In the past few years there has been an encouraging shift in the emphasis of government policy to a broader approach to ensure planned development for all regions. Areas with high unemployment are, on this wider view, not the only regional problem: in other parts of the country planned development means coping with over-full employment and mounting congestion. Once it is realized that further industrial concentration in the more prosperous regions may at times involve more social cost than social benefit, encouragement of industry to move to less buoyant regions becomes a positive contribution to national economic development rather than the philanthropic gesture it has resembled in the past. To assist in this process, the whole country is now divided into ten regions and in 1964–6 a machinery of regional planning was established in each of them. This comprises a Regional Council to represent local interests and a Regional Board made up of representatives of the Ministries concerned in each region. It is the function of these bodies to draw up development plans and to act as pressure groups for securing their implementation. Quite what impact these money-less, powerless agencies will achieve, and how incompatibilities between regional plans will be resolved within the framework of the national plan, remains uncertain. However, the new approach is certainly a good deal more positive than previous attempts to eliminate regional disparities.

REDEPLOYMENT

In the thirties it was decided that the greater mobility of capital made it easier to 'take work to the workers' than for labour to move from areas of high unemployment to those with greater employment opportunities. Despite the fact, as we have just seen, that labour flows can, in certain circumstances, *aggravate* rather than reduce regional disparities, the recent renewal of interest in how to increase labour mobility is still justified. Economic growth implies flexibility in the economic structure with decline in some sectors being matched by expansion of others. Some degree of labour mobility is therefore essential, both *geographical* – if only *within* a particular region – and *occupational*, to ensure that growing industries with high productivity are not starved of labour through hoarding in other sectors of the economy.

A recent governmental view seems to have been that redeployment can be achieved through unemployment. One of the justifications claimed for the policy of deflation in 1966 was that the sharp increase in unemployment would lead to a 'shake-out which will release the nation's manpower, skilled and unskilled, and lead to a more purposeful use of labour for the sake of increasing exports'. Similarly, the idea behind the Selective Employment Tax was to redeploy labour from service occupations (relatively low productivity) into manufacturing industry (higher productivity and a source of increased exports).

The trouble with both these measures is that they do only half the job. They *may* be effective in ensuring that labour is *released*; they do nothing to ensure that it is subsequently absorbed in the right occupations and areas. There is now some evidence to suggest that the problem is not chiefly that workers are *unwilling* to move, which is what has often been assumed. Financial allowances to cover the cost of movement and resettlement and the provision of extensive retraining facilities (since the workers released are on the whole not likely to have the skills demanded by their new employers) could probably do a great deal in overcoming labour immobility. There are already in existence a wide variety of ways in which a worker moving to a different job or area can secure government assistance. But it must be seriously doubted whether they are sufficiently well-publicized and easily available, and whether they are on anything like the right scale. Economic growth involves change and those who are prepared to adapt themselves should be generously rewarded for doing so rather than penalized by lengthy periods of transitional unemployment.

CYCLICAL UNEMPLOYMENT

Although structural unemployment was a serious problem even before the war, it was then dwarfed, although at the same time aggravated, by the existence of *general* unemployment throughout the economy as a whole. Such unemployment was termed 'cyclical' because it was associated with fluctuations in the level of national income, which from the nineteenth century onwards recurred in fairly regular nine-year movements. Four phases could generally be distinguished in a trade cycle: (1) the depression, a protracted period of high unemployment, excess plant capacity, and general pessimism about the future course of the economy; (2) a gradual recovery phase ultimately leading to (3) a boom of rising demand, high employment and investment, generally increasing prices and costs, and buoyant business expectations; and (4) the boom breaking into a recession phase leading sharply back to depression conditions.

It was only in 1936, with the publication of *The General Theory of Unemployment, Interest and Money* by John Maynard Keynes, that a break-through was achieved by economists in distinguishing the factors which determine the general level of employment in an economy. Post-Keynesian theorists, apart from elaborating and refining the basic concepts which Keynes introduced, have pursued the study of why income and employment tend to fluctuate *cyclically*. In the following sections, we shall adopt a similar programme – seeing first what causes general unemployment, and then briefly considering the nature of the trade cycle.

The Level of Employment

Personal savings are soon eaten up by a protracted period of unemployment, and it is the workers, with relatively little to fall back on, who are the hardest hit by a general slump in the economy. But, of course, employers suffer too. Some may be forced out of business, and others will find that their profit margins are cut; expensive plant and equipment will lie idle. The indignity, misery, and sheer economic waste of a trade depression are against the interests of *all* concerned.

Unemployed workers cannot buy many goods, and producers have difficulty in selling their output. Since this is clearly one problem rather than two, it may seem strange that producers do not break the *impasse* themselves – by restarting production. Surely, if they did so, the wages which they would pay to newly employed workers would provide the incomes with which their increased output could be bought? However, a spontaneous and *simultaneous* decision by all producers to expand output is not very probable; and, unfortunately, if only a few firms act along these lines, the results are not likely to be encouraging to them or to others. If, for example, a producer of television sets takes the plunge and re-employs laid-off workers, he will have difficulty in increasing his sales unless at the same time business expands in the rest of the economy. Although it may be true that a slump could be cured if most producers adopted expansionist policies, what is true for the whole economy may not hold good for its parts.

Another way of saying that there is general unemployment is that the level of spending in the economy is inadequate to absorb the output of goods and services which could be produced with full employment. How can such a situation come about? The basic reason is that decisions to spend and decisions to produce are often taken by separate groups in the economy, acting from different motives; at any given income level the possibility of spending and production plans precisely matching is therefore extremely remote.

On the one hand, expenditure is planned by three broad groups – private individuals and firms, central and local authorities, and foreigners (through their demand for our exports); the spending which they hope to do may be either on goods and services to be currently consumed or on 'investment' (the term being used here to refer to the process of adding to, or replacing, the *physical* stock of capital in the economy). Output, on the other hand, will be made up of domestic production, by private firms and public enterprises, *plus* imports; once again, we can make a broad distinction between the production of goods for immediate consumption, and output of capital (or investment) goods – plant and machinery. We therefore have:

planned spending   = planned consumption + planned capital formation

and

planned production   = planned output of consumer goods + planned output of capital goods

However, since we are talking about plans, what the various elements *intend* to do, there is no obvious reason why any of these quantities should exactly match. Demand and supply plans are, by and large, formulated independently, and it is therefore very unlikely that they will correspond. It would be a matter of fluke if 'planned spending' just equalled 'planned production', 'planned consumption' just equalled 'planned output of consumer goods', or 'planned capital formation' precisely coincided with 'planned output of capital goods'. But what happens if they don't?

Let us suppose that to begin with the economy is in a state of full employment equilibrium at a level of income and output of £30,000 million, but that, whereas supply plans for the coming year involve a similar value of goods and services being produced for the market, the amount of intended spending only adds up to £29,500 million. There is no reason why suppliers should realize that there is this discrepancy of demand until they come to sell their output. Demand deficiency will then show itself initially in an unwanted and unintended accumulation of stocks; in other words, the immediate result is that producers, in effect, supplement the overall demand themselves by 'buying' some of their own output. They will obviously continue to do so only if they think the decline in demand is temporary. Once they view it more seriously, producers will start to cut down output – not only to what they think will be the new level of demand, but also to allow for the surplus stocks which have been built up and which will have to be worked off. The final outcome of supply plans exceeding demand plans is therefore a *fall in income and employment*. In the opposite situation, when demand plans happen to be greater than intended output, the effect will be to *increase* incomes and employment.

Maintaining any given level of activity in an unrestricted economy thus precariously depends on what would be quite fortuitous correspondence between spending and supply plans. The major contribution which Keynes made to economic thinking was to stress that there are no forces within a free enterprise economy which automatically ensure that full employment is achieved. On the contrary, equilibrium of the economy, since it depends on intended demand equalling intended supply, is just as likely to be established at low as at high levels of activity. And above all, discrepancies between spending and supply plans, which are all too likely, are corrected by changes in the level of aggregate income (and generally, therefore, of employment too).

The Trade Cycle

General unemployment results from inadequate demand, and we have seen that inequality of spending and production plans tends to cause shifts in the level of income and employment. The next question which we have to consider is why income and employment fluctuate, not at random, but according to a fairly regular *cyclical* pattern.

Let us suppose, by way of illustration, that when aggregate spending falls short of supply plans by £10 million the cut in demand is concentrated, in the first place, entirely on the motor-car industry. Incomes of motor-car producers are thus reduced by £10 million as sales fail to reach the anticipated level. However, this is not the end of the story. Owners and workers of the car industry, with lower incomes, will in turn have less to spend on other goods and services. If they economize in their spending by, say, £8 million, then other producers, whose output they would have bought, will find that *their* incomes are cut by that amount. Consequently, they will be unable to maintain their previous level of consumption and their reduced spending will cause yet another round of income cuts. And so the process will go on.

Thus the effect of an autonomous fall in total demand is not confined to its initial impact on incomes; it sparks off a chain of repercussions and causes a *series* of adjustments in the level of income. To the extent that reduced incomes in one sector of the economy represent cuts in demand for the output of other sectors, the downward pressure on the income level will continue indefinitely. However, it is probable that, at each round, the reduction in spending will be *less* than the fall in income – because people do their best to maintain their earlier standards of consumption by drawing on past savings and cutting down their present level of saving. If this is so, the chain effects of an initial cut in demand will be finite. If, for example, people reduce their spending by only 80% of any given cut in income, the series of downward adjustments to the level of total income will look like this:

£10 million + £8 million (i.e. $\frac{8}{10}$ of £10 million) + £6·4 million (i.e. $\frac{8}{10}$ of £8 million) + £5·12 million (i.e. $\frac{8}{10}$ of £6·4 million) + £4·09 million (i.e. $\frac{8}{10}$ of £5·12 million) + ...

At each round, the secondary fall in income becomes less. Given that the 'marginal propensity to spend' remains constant throughout, we can in fact calculate that the overall fall in income resulting from an initial £10 million cut in demand will be £50 million. The value of the *multiplier* (the ratio of total income reduction to the fall in demand which started the process off) is therefore in this case five. If we look again at the example, it can be seen that if, for a given fall in income, people had reduced their spending by 90% instead of the 80% which we assumed, then the multiplier would have been greater: .

£10 million + £9 million + £7·29 million + £6·571 million + ...

The value of the multiplier thus depends on the 'marginal propensity to spend'. The higher this is, the greater will be the multiplier effects of any change in the total of demand in the economy.

In these examples, we have been able to predict the final outcome of demand disturbances because we have assumed that the relationship between income and spending is simple, known, and constant throughout the process, and that no complications arise from the existence of foreign trade. However, in practice, the multiplier is a very tricky concept to apply. Although it may be reasonable to assume that spending behaviour in face of income changes has some sort of pattern, it is not likely that *all* consumers will react in just the same way.

The extent to which spending plans are affected by income changes, and hence the value of the multiplier, will depend on how the initial demand cut is distributed throughout the economy. Reactions will vary according to whether the brunt is borne by individuals (and whether they are rich or poor), public authorities, firms, or foreigners. A very wealthy individual may wholly maintain his spending despite a fall in his income; workers, with less resources to fall back on, may have to cut their expenditure by the full amount of their income reduction. Again, if the decline in demand, instead of being concentrated on the home car industry, falls instead on the market for imports, much of the subsequent income impact will be 'exported'. In this case, the secondary rounds of income adjustment will chiefly work themselves out in other economies – though there will be some 'feedback' effect to the home country as, with their reduced incomes, foreigners will be unable to buy so much of its exports.

There are, then, extreme complications in using the concept of the multiplier operationally. We can, however, at least get from it an intuitive understanding that, given an autonomous change in the level of demand in the economy, the subsequent adjustment will tend to be an exaggeration of the original disturbance; the theory of the multiplier also shows that upward or downward pressures on income finally peter out. It does not, in itself, explain why there should be cyclical fluctuations in income and employment – although it helps to do so if we use it in conjunction with another hatchet from the economist's toolbox, the *accelerator* principle.

A look at trade cycle history shows that fluctuations take place to a much greater extent in the industries producing capital goods than in the consumer goods sector of the economy. It is the heavy industries – coal, steel, shipbuilding, and so on – which have always been the most severely hit by trade depression. The theory of the accelerator tries to show why this should be the case, and it does so by emphasizing the way in which the demand for capital goods is related to changes in the level of income.

We can explain the basic idea behind the accelerator by seeing what happens in an economy in which the capital stock is made up of 100,000 machines designed to last for ten years, and installed evenly over the past decade. We will suppose that each one is capable of producing £1,000 of output per annum. Then, if total demand in the economy is running at a level of £100 million a year, the capital stock is just appropriate.

Aggregate demand	Capital stock	Replacement investment
£100m.	100,000 machines	10,000 machines

The output of the capital goods sector which produces the machines will be used just to replace the capital stock as it depreciates – at the rate of 10,000 machines per year. But what happens if the level of demand somehow increases by £10 million? Since the capital stock was fully utilized in producing output worth £100 million, new machines will now be required.

Aggregate demand	Capital stock required	Investment	
		Replacement	Net
£110m.	110,000 machines	10,000	10,000

The capital goods industry will now be called upon to produce not only its previous output of 10,000 machines to replace the existing capital stock, but also a further 10,000 to meet the new demand. The table below illustrates the effect on the capital goods sector of this and some further changes in aggregate demand:

Time period	Aggregate demand (£m.)	Capital stock	Investment Replacement	Net	Total
1	100	100,000	10,000	0	10,000
2	110	110,000	10,000	10,000	20,000
3	115	115,000	10,000	5,000	15,000
4	120	120,000	10,000	5,000	15,000
5	110	110,000	0	0	0
6	100	100,000	0	0	0

Two interesting implications emerge from these figures. The first is that fluctuations in aggregate demand are greatly *magnified* by the time they reach the heavy industry sector. When total demand rises by 10% between periods one and two, the demand for capital goods actually doubles. Similarly, an 8·5% (£120 m. to £110 m.) fall in aggregate demand (between periods four and five) wipes out the demand for capital goods altogether. Secondly, the output of capital goods begins to decline while total demand is *still increasing*. Whereas the increase in demand from £100 million to £110 million led to an expansion in total investment, the further increase from £110 million to £115 million causes a 25% (20,000 to 15,000) *fall* in the demand for capital goods.

Thus the relationship between aggregate demand and investment is rather a complex one. Even when total demand in the economy is increasing, the industries producing machines do not necessarily enjoy stability. A careful examination of the figures in our example shows that the level of investment in capital goods depends, not so much on the absolute level of demand, as on the *rate at which it is changing*. Therefore, although aggregate demand continues to rise, once the *rate* at which it is increasing begins to fall off there is an actual *decline* in the demand for machines.

The accelerator principle certainly gives a plausible explanation of the relatively greater volatility of the capital goods sector of the economy. In the simple form in which it has been presented so far, it over-explains the problem which we set out to understand. The fluctuations which actually occur in the capital goods industries are nothing like as great as those which the naïve version of the theory would suggest. This is because our model is a gross over-simplification of what actually happens. We have been assuming, for example, that capital goods producers have a decidedly simple outlook; at each increase of demand they immediately respond by expanding output without waiting to see whether the increase is permanent and without, apparently, having learnt anything from past experience. In practice, of course, firms will be a good deal more cautious in interpreting increases in demand and to some extent will merely allow their order books to lengthen.

The theory also needs modifying to take into account other complications – that replacement demand may not be distributed evenly and that depreciation may be a function of other factors in addition to the age of the machine, that the capital stock may not have been appropriate to the level of demand in the first place so that increased output could be squeezed from existing capacity, and that the capital: output ratio may not be constant and uniform; by the time we have allowed for all this, the accelerator principle, like the multiplier, loses much of its pristine attraction.

Used together, the multiplier and accelerator theories provide some idea of the way in which the trade cycle works. Just where we start explaining the cycle is arbitrary, so we will suppose that to begin with the economy is in the throes of a depression, with widespread unemployment, and that an increase in total demand is suddenly achieved by an injection of new investment. From what has been said about the multiplier, we know that this initial increase in investment is likely to cause an even greater rise in a national income – because the original beneficiaries will partly pass on their higher incomes to other parts of the economy by their increased spending. With total income and demand rising, the accelerator mechanism will then come into play. Since the demand for capital goods is derived from the demand for consumer goods, a further spurt of investment will be induced as it becomes clear that a larger stock of capital is now required to cope with the increasing demand. This investment in turn will raise incomes still further and ultimately induce yet another bout of investment.

In conjunction, then, the multiplier and accelerator explain the momentum of the upward and downward phases of the trade cycle. Once begun, movements in the level of income and activity tend to feed on themselves. But we still lack an explanation of regularly periodic *fluctuations* in the economy; the simple theory of multiplier–accelerator interaction contains the seeds of *explosive* rather than cyclical tendencies in the economy, with any disturbance from equilibrium tending to be cumulative. A little more is therefore required to explain the turning-points of the trade cycle, that is, why booms and slumps should ever come to an end.

There are two general possibilities here which can just be mentioned. The first is to recognize that there will be *time-lags* in the working of the multiplier–accelerator process, and that spending and investment will not react immediately to changes in income in the way which we have so far assumed. If, for example, investment is partly dependent on changes in income which took place some time ago, the rate at which present income is increasing may be correspondingly slowed down; this, via the accelerator, will cause a definite contraction in the heavy industries with multiple repercussions on the general level of income. An alternative, or supplementary explanation of the turning-points of the trade cycle is that the economy may contain ceilings and floors against which potentially explosive movements can come to rest or bounce off. The ceiling may take the form of resources in the economy being fully employed (although expansion may still take place in monetary terms); a floor may exist in that total investment in the economy cannot fall below zero, so that when surplus capacity inherited from the boom has been worked off during a slump (which may take some considerable time) investment demand will begin to rise again as more plant becomes necessary even to reproduce the existing low level of output.

Even from this brief and highly simplified account of the causes of cyclical unemployment one vital policy conclusion should be clear. Left entirely to its own devices, the economy will almost inevitably be subject to periodic bouts of less than full employment as a result of the failure of independent decisions about use of resources to add up to the appropriate total. If full employment is our aim, then we must accept the need for a 'managed' economy. Fluctuations in income and employment can only be moderated by a deliberately counter-cyclical policy on the part of the authorities, and the forms which this can take will be the subject of the rest of this chapter.

STABILIZATION POLICY

Since a private enterprise economy does not behave as we want it to, what can the State do to make up for its deficiencies? Elimination of general unemployment involves solving the problem of inadequate demand, and, if private spending is insufficient to absorb planned output, there are clearly two general ways in which the authorities can help to stabilize employment and income at a high level. Either policy must be directed at stimulating additional spending by the private sector, or the State must itself undertake compensatory expenditure to make good any shortfall.

During much of the post-war period the economic situation has been the opposite to that of the thirties; aggregate demand has often *exceeded* the supply of goods and services which the economy would produce at constant prices, and the problem for the authorities has been how to cope with an inflationary rather than a deflationary gap. Stabilization sometimes involves stimulating demand, and sometimes spending requires dampening down. In the following discussion of stabilization policies, we will therefore consider methods by which demand can be changed in either, rather than just one, direction.

Monetary Policy

In Chapter 2 we described the armoury of monetary weapons by which the authorities could try to influence the economy, and, in particular, criticized the idea that demand could be limited by concentrating a 'credit squeeze' on bank lending; all that tends to happen is that potential borrowers are diverted from the banks to the many other sources of finance which exist in a developed economy. However, it was also shown that the Bank of England and the Treasury are able, to some extent, to manipulate the level of interest rates in the economy, and it is now time to consider just what can be expected from this power to vary the price, as well as the availability, of credit.

Monetary policy used to be thought of as a particularly powerful form of control inasmuch as interest-rate changes affected *both* the elements of aggregate demand – consumption and investment. It was also claimed to have the virtue, which more direct measures lacked, of anonymous and general applicability. However, on all these counts, the traditional case for relying on monetary regulation of the economy has received something of a battering in recent years.

In the first place, it seems highly unlikely that consumption is really sensitive to interest rates. The amount which people consume depends essentially on the amount they earn, and also on the institutional channels (banks, building societies, government debt, etc.) through which saving is facilitated, rather than on the interest which their savings could earn them. Certainly, even the most spendthrift might try to save a bit if the rate of interest were to shoot up to 25%, and those who now save might not think their thrift was adequately rewarded if it fell to 1%. But how many of us adjust our savings because of interest changes of the conventional magnitude, say from 4 to 5%? Some observers have suggested that the considerable rise in personal saving in Britain since 'dear money' was re-introduced in 1951 is evidence that interest rates *do* have an appreciable effect on consumption; an equally plausible explanation of this phenomenon is, however, that the post-war 'spending spree' ended at about this time, and that people then returned to a more normal savings pattern. On the whole, interest changes probably have much less influence on the total amount saved than on the *way* in which the total is distributed. Although people may not cut down their spending because of a rise in the general level of interest from 4 to 5%, they may well switch their savings to a building society if building society rates rise more than those of the banks.

If interest rates do not affect consumption very much, the effectiveness of monetary policy depends on its impact on the *investment* component of aggregate demand. Once again, however, there is now considerable scepticism about the view that the cost of borrowing funds is a sufficiently significant factor for high interest rates to deter investment and low rates to encourage it, to any useful extent.

Decisions about building new factories or installing new equipment are, above all, characterized by uncertainty. Firms have remarkably little data on which to base their investment decisions. They know, perhaps, something of the past and present profitability of similar investments (although they will not even have this guide if they are launching a new product or process), and they may, through market research, get a reasonably accurate picture of the present extent of the market and its distribution among their rivals. But information of this kind is of limited usefulness. What is really required is some knowledge of the future. What will be the capacity of the industry and the demand for the product during the life of the asset in which they are considering investing? Which government is going to be in power, and what will be its policies on taxation, growth, nationalization, and restrictive practices? How are consumer tastes likely to change? What will be the rate and direction of technological development? These are the sort of things which firms would like to know. In fact, even such a basic consideration as how long the plant which they are thinking of installing will last, is essentially a matter for conjecture. The manufacturers will give some idea of its *physical* life, but what is important is when it will become outdated, and it is very difficult to predict the probable rate of obsolescence.

The entrepreneur can hedge against these risks and uncertainties in a number of ways. The first is to get as much of his money back as he can within the more predictable near future. However, the shorter the period over which the investment is made to pay for itself, the less sensitive it is likely to be to changes in interest rates. Suppose, for example, that an investment of £50,000 is being considered. The cost of borrowing this sum is not limited to interest payments; depreciation allowances will also have to be set aside so that the principal can be repaid. The relative importance of these two elements in capital charges will vary according to the 'pay-off' period:

	Pay-off period	
	(A) 5 years	(B) 20 years
Interest @ 5%	£2,500 p.a.	£2,500 p.a.
Depreciation	£10,000 p.a.	£2,500 p.a.
Total capital charges	£12,500 p.a.	£5,000 p.a.
Change in capital charges resulting from an increase in interest to 6%	£500 p.a.	£500 p.a.
(Proportionate change)	4%	10%

Annual interest (since we are treating it simply) is the same for both the five-year and twenty-year investment – £2,500. The amount which has to be set aside for depreciation allowances, on the other hand, depends on the pay-off period; if depreciation is spread evenly over the years, it will amount to £10,000 per annum in case (A) and only £2,500 per annum in case (B). The important thing from our present point of view is that interest payments therefore form a much smaller *proportion* of capital charges in the shorter-term investment. The significance of this can be seen if we consider the impact on capital charges of an increase in interest to 6%. In both cases, this adds £500 to annual capital costs; but whereas, if the pay-off period is five years, this represents a 4% increase in total capital charges, the proportionate change in the case of the longer-term investment amounts to no less than 10%.

We can conclude that the shorter the period over which an investment is expected to pay for itself, the more interest payments are swamped by other capital charges and the less sensitive investment is likely to be to interest-rate changes. Investigations suggest that, for the reasons we mentioned earlier, much of manufacturing investment has a very short pay-off period and is therefore not likely to be much affected by changes in the cost of borrowing.

Another consequence of uncertainty is that investment decisions tend to be non-marginal. Given the risks involved, investment projects are not even considered unless their expected return is substantially *above* the cost of borrowing. In other words, a firm considering investment is more likely to rank its projects as in II than I:

	Anticipated Yield	
Project	I	II
A	5%	15%
B	6%	20%
C	7%	25%

If projects are ranked marginally, with *A* expected to earn 5%, *B* 6%, and *C* 7%, an increase in interest rates from 5 to 6 will exclude project *B* which will no longer show any return over the cost of borrowing. If, however, because yields are only 'anticipated', firms insure themselves by only contemplating high-yielding investment as in II, the amount of investment is unlikely to be much affected by interest changes of the conventional magnitude.

In general, the fact that they have inadequate information at their disposal means that firms have to rely to a large extent on guesswork and hunches about what *may* happen. In such circumstances, the general *mood* of entrepreneurs is a matter of considerable importance. The same data may be very differently interpreted by a business community which is optimistic about the future prospects of the economy than by one which is infected with a 'wait-and-see' caution. Thus, in the gloomy climate of the thirties, cheap money policies were not sufficient to stimulate the economy on to an upward path – what, after all, is the point of borrowing funds, even at low interest, if it is doubted whether they can be profitably used? Similarly, rising interest rates in post-war years have generally failed to damp down investment because of the continued buoyancy of business expectations securely based on the government's commitment to underwrite full employment.

Doubtless, the rate of interest has *some* effect on investment outlay; and perhaps larger changes (amounting to 'changes in gear') would have more. But, to the extent that monetary policy *does* work, its impact is likely to be unfortunately selective. It is the public sector (in which a large proportion of the really long-term investment in the economy is concentrated) and the fastest-growing firms in the private sector (which are most dependent on external finance) which will probably be most affected, and it is by no means obvious that these are the areas in which any necessary cuts in demand are least damagingly made.

Moreover, it is too slow. Investment plans are neither formulated nor executed hurriedly; changing interest rates will alter not so much the present level of investment as plans for the next period – which may prove too late to be useful but difficult to reverse.

Fiscal Policy

Monetary policy aims at stimulating or discouraging demand by changes in the price and availability of credit. Similar pressures can be brought to bear on the private sector by manipulation of the taxation structure. Consumer spending can be regulated by changes in income- and purchase-taxes; capital formation can be influenced by variation in the level of profits tax, investment allowances, and so on. However, fiscal policy can also be used more directly as a stabilizing device. The government is the major spender in the economy. If, therefore, the level of aggregate demand is expected to be inadequate to maintain full employment or so high as to create inflationary pressures, the State can adjust its own spending to compensate for the deficiencies or excesses of the private sector.

We generally think of taxation as the means of financing the host of services now provided by the State. In fact, budgetary policy has a much wider significance. It is a powerful weapon for influencing the general level of activity in the economy as a whole. Taxation represents a withdrawal of purchasing power from private hands, and government expenditure the injection of demand. If it is assumed that both of these effects are *net*, then a budget deficit – expenditure exceeding revenue – will have an expansionary impact on the economy; a budget surplus will deflate the level of aggregate demand below that which would otherwise have resulted. In both cases, the overall changes in economic conditions will be magnified by the effects of the multiplier.

Deliberately to unbalance the budget is against the canons of orthodox finance and 'common-sense'. A budget deficit is still popularly regarded as showing that the Treasury has not done its homework properly, or even that the country is in some sense 'going into the red'. A budget surplus, on the other hand, is welcomed as implying that the government has enough left over to permit cuts in taxation. However, the view that the State ought not to spend more than it can raise from tax revenues rests on a false analogy with private individuals.

We can spend more than we earn only by drawing on past savings and credit; ultimately we finish up in the bankruptcy court. The State, on the other hand, being a collection of all the individuals within its frontiers, is not similarly limited. A budget deficit certainly means that the government sector of the economy is living beyond its income, but the same is not true of the economy as a whole. All that happens is that national resources are shifted from the private to the public sector. This is a process which has to be initially thought of in *real* terms. The government obtains a larger portion of the nation's output than it is able to pay for from tax revenues. To bid those scarce resources away from the private sector, the necessary finance has to be raised through borrowing. Deficit financing means that the National Debt is increased, and the analogy with individuals suggests that this is just storing up trouble for the future. The State may manage, by deficit budgeting, to obtain a larger share of the national cake now, but it does so only by shifting the burden of indebtedness on to future generations. Borrowing now implies paying interest later and ultimately repaying the principal.

The comparison continues, however, to be misleading. Interest *will* have to be paid, but the important question is – who to, and who by? It will be paid to those individuals who have bought government bonds, and it will be paid out of taxation on other (and sometimes, the same) individuals. The *real* effect will already have taken place with the initial re-allocation of resources from the private to the public sector. All that remains for later generations is a mere transfer payment from one section of the community to another. This can be called a 'burden' only to the extent that higher taxation may be required to service the debt; this might, by its disincentive effects, depress the level of output. More probably, however, the original deficit financing will have helped to expand output; out of the higher incomes which result the same tax rates will yield larger revenues. As for the necessity for repayment, involving as it would a much larger transfer, why should it ever happen? Given the unimpeachable credit of the British government, maturing debt can be replaced by new borrowing. Only to the extent that the debt is held by foreigners, the result of external borrowing, does it represent a real burden to the economy.

We have so far been working on the assumption that any taxation represents a *net* reduction and any government expenditure a *net* addition to the level of demand in the economy. In practice, this is not so. A tax yielding £10 million will only cut demand by that amount if all of it would otherwise have been *spent*; if, for example, firms and individuals would actually have saved £3 million of it, the net effect of taxation is to reduce spending by only £7 million. Similarly, the way in which the government *uses* its revenue determines what addition it makes to total demand. Expenditure on goods and services represents a 100% injection of new demand (unless there are adverse effects on private spending); expenditure on transfer payments for example – revenue used to pay interest on the National Debt or welfare benefits – will increase demand only according to the propensity to spend of the recipients.

It therefore by no means follows that a balanced budget is 'neutral' in its effects on the economy. The impact of a budget on the economy depends, not just on the relation between aggregate government revenue and expenditure, but on the *net* effect of the different types of taxes and uses of revenue which are possible. Generalization is therefore difficult. What we *can* say is that, if all revenue is directly spent by the State on goods and services, a balanced budget will always tend to *stimulate* the economy; neutrality in these circumstances would imply budgeting for a surplus. But a balanced budget *could* have the effect of dampening down the economy – if taxation and transfer payments resulted in a shift of purchasing power to those sections of the community with a lower propensity to spend.

To some extent, a modern welfare economy is self-regulating, containing elements which automatically counterbalance cyclical tendencies. Two examples of such 'built-in' stabilizers are progressive taxation and the payment of unemployment benefits. In the recovery or boom stages of the trade cycle, generally rising incomes mean that more and more people fall into the higher tax brackets; there is thus a greater than proportionate increase in tax revenues, and total spending by the private sector is consequently restrained. In the same way tax revenues will fall off more rapidly than incomes during a depression period, and, to that extent, private spending can be maintained; demand during a slump will be further supplemented by increased government expenditure on unemployment benefits and National Assistance.

However, the existence of these 'built-in' counter-cyclical elements in government expenditure and taxation is not in itself a guarantee that the economy will run smoothly along at the full employment level. To repeat the point which we made earlier, there is no doubt that a good part of the post-war success in maintaining full employment has been due to the fact that governments have made positive attempts to implement stabilizing policies based on the increased understanding which we now have of the working of the economy.

Unfortunately, knowing what causes cyclical unemployment does not altogether mean that therefore we can control it. Successful stabilization requires that a recessionary condition is correctly diagnosed early enough for countering action to be taken, and the measures used to redirect the economy must be rapid but controllable.

On each of these counts, our present stabilization techniques must still be judged decidedly blunt, hit-or-miss instruments of regulation. We still lack finesse in forecasting the future course of the economy and, even when the need for action is finally appreciated, both monetary and fiscal policies are slow – both to implement in the first place and in their impact on the economy. Moreover, since they are even slower to reverse, there is a real danger that attempts to iron out fluctuations may instead aggravate them or cause a new 'policy cycle'; measures taken in Period Two to deal with a situation which arose in Period One may only begin to take real effect in Period Three, by which time conditions may call for a complete reversal of the policy.

Problems such as these chiefly arise because full employment is not the only end of economic policy. With our present economic knowledge, there is no insuperable difficulty in a government maintaining full employment – provided that it is prepared to pump up demand to the necessary level. What is much more doubtful, however, is whether demand can be regulated to a level which *just* ensures full employment without any excess which might cause inflation and balance of payments difficulties; it can also be questioned whether full employment is compatible with achieving the maximum rate of growth of the economy. These are matters which we will touch upon in the following chapters.

CHAPTER 1

GROWTH

THE immediate economic problem in the 1930s was the elimination of unemployment. But among those seeking an explanation of the periodic fluctuations in economic activity were some who saw in such cyclical movements evidence of an even more serious trend problem. The thesis of the 'stagnationists', as they became known, was that increasing difficulty might be expected in maintaining high levels of employment in the mature economies of America and Europe. On the one hand, they argued, the process of saving had been greatly facilitated by sophisticated institutionalization, in the development of life and social insurance and the growth of self-financing by big businesses; at the same time the well of investment opportunities was drying up as the great growth impulses of earlier phases of development became exhausted. Population increase was slowing down (in Britain attention was already being paid to the economic implications of a declining population); the 'passing of the frontier' meant that there was no longer any thrust to economic progress resulting from territorial expansion; the impact of great new capital-consuming industries became less as economies developed. Investment thus became increasingly inadequate to absorb the savings which were being generated in mature economies, and secular stagnation with intensifying bouts of unemployment could therefore be anticipated.

These fears seem to have been triumphantly belied in succeeding decades. Not only has employment in the United Kingdom been relatively stabilized at a level exceeding the estimates of even the post-war optimists; at the same time, substantial economic progress has been made. National income in 1965 was something over three times as large as in 1948 – not, of course, that this meant that people were three times better off. We have to allow for the very large rise in prices which had taken place, and the population among which the national income was shared had increased by about 10%. But even when both of these adjustments have been made, the fact remains that *real* national

174

income *per head* was over 50% higher in 1965 than it had been just after the war. Given also that redistribution of income has also taken place (although there is now some scepticism as to its extent), there is no doubt that the standard of living of the majority has substantially increased.

The economy has grown to an extent which many people in the thirties would have regarded as inconceivable, and yet the growth record of the United Kingdom in the post-war period is widely regarded as unsatisfactory. Such dissatisfaction can hardly be based on a comparison with the past; the problem does not seem to be one of a declining rate of growth. Long-term comparisons of national income figures are difficult and dangerous, but the recent rate of increase of output per head, at about 2·5% per annum, is as high, or higher, than that achieved even at the climax of nineteenth-century development, and is certainly greater than that of any other similar period. Perhaps we are now in too much of a hurry, and forget that a growth rate of 'only' 2½% or less has been sufficient to increase national income per head over six times in the past century and a half. Anyway, since history endorses the recent record of the economy as distinctly encouraging, the basis for current anxieties about United Kingdom development must be looked for elsewhere.

It lies, of course, in comparison with the recent achievements of other economies. First, there is the quite remarkable development record of the U.S.S.R., which neither difficulties in making accurate statistical comparisons nor the difference in political systems can make entirely irrelevant. The U.S.A., on the other hand, has achieved a rate of growth which has been little better than that of Britain during recent years. The problem here is that the base from which the United States is progressing is substantially higher than our own and that therefore even if we manage to achieve the *same* rate of growth, the absolute difference in standards of living will diverge even more rapidly during the future.

Most distressing of all, however, is the comparison between British growth and that of economies which are more similar in their background and problems. In particular, it is felt that we should, during the post-war period, have been able to grow at least as rapidly as other Western European economies. Listing such economies on the basis of the main growth indicators generally shows Britain to be at or near the bottom of the league. Admittedly, the figures have to be handled very cautiously – international comparisons of standards of living involve all the difficulties of intertemporal comparisons within a single economy in a more acute form. But the indices of gross national product, of national income per head, of industrial production, all point to a remarkably faster increase in the continental European countries and Japan than in the United Kingdom.

It might be objected that such figures are misleading because most of these economies were starting from a lower base in having to make up for their greater losses during the war. But by and large, post-war levels of income had been re-achieved by the early fifties; whether our comparisons are for the period since 1938, or since 1950, or since 1957, Britain still lags heavily.

Investment and Growth

If they can do it, why can't we? A good deal of attention has recently been devoted to the differences between the British and European economies which might help to explain the discrepancies in growth rates. One hypothesis is that the fast growers have been willing to devote a larger proportion of their resources to investment purposes; by sacrificing the enjoyment of current consumption they have been able to build up a capital stock which ensures an accelerated growth of output during future years.

Investment may be either net or gross. Net investment is an *addition* to the national stock of capital, whereas gross investment includes replacement of that part of the stock which has become worn out or obsolescent. Net investment in the United Kingdom has been running at about 5–6% of the net national product; all the West European countries have exceeded this, achieving rates of between 10 and 20%. On the other hand, the higher capital stock which the United Kingdom started off with implies that a larger volume of *replacement* investment has been necessary. Comparison of the proportion of national products going to gross investment narrows the margin between the British performance and that of other European countries; but once again the British rate of about 15% lags behind the 17–18%

of France, 22–25% in West Germany, and nearly 30% in Norway.

Elementary economics textbooks used to describe how Robinson Crusoe, using his hands alone, could catch only two fish a day. By going without for a single day, he had the time to make a net with which he could then increase his catch to four a day. And, of course, it *is* true that the process of capital accumulation is a vital prerequisite of economic development. On the other hand, it is dangerous therefore to jump to the conclusion that it is a *sufficient* condition for economic growth, and that *any* increase in investment is bound to accelerate the rise in standards of living. Clearly, a number of qualifications are necessary.

First, investment must be related to population. Is the capital stock being shared among an increasing, decreasing, or constant number of heads? Again, if population is increasing, it is also important to know *why*. If it is due to a fall in death-rates, the number of 'aged dependents' will be increasing and the consequent expansion of investment in, for example, old peoples' bungalows can hardly be expected to induce faster growth. Similarly, population increase as a result of a recent rise in the birthrate implies higher investment in such things as larger houses and educational facilities to cater for the increased proportion of 'young dependents'; there may be a very long gestation period before such investment yields returns in the form of healthier and better-educated workers. However, the population increase may be concentrated in the working force itself – as a result of immigration of young workers or an earlier 'baby boom' reaching working age. When we concentrate on this most important element in population growth we find that Britain's investment *per worker* in *manufacturing industry* – which is the most likely to encourage growth – has, since 1938, been higher than that of many major rivals in the growth race, including West Germany and the U.S.A.

However, in general, it is not just the quantity of investment which counts in inducing economic growth but also its *quality* and the relationship between actual investment and investment *opportunities*. For example, countries like West Germany, starting more nearly from scratch after greater war-time devastation, may as a result have succeeded in installing up-to-date plant and equipment on a more comprehensive scale than would have been allowed by piecemeal replacement. Again, it must be doubted whether the large proportion of British investment by public enterprises has been undertaken in a way which is conducive to growth. It seems probable, from what we said in Chapter 5, that the lack of coordination in the public sector, and the failure to evaluate alternative investments according to consistent criteria, must have seriously reduced the average productivity of investment in Britain.

Another major slice of British investment has been on defence; expenditure has ranged from 10% of the gross national product in the period following the outbreak of the Korean War to 7% in more recent years. Obviously, investment on defence is basically non-productive in the sense that output in future years does not increase as a result, except to the extent that civil applications of defence research and innovation are possible. On the contrary, expenditure of this magnitude imposes a number of strains on the economy which may act as a brake on economic growth. In particular, defence expenditure is concentrated on the basic fast-growing and export-conscious engineering and metal-using industries, and something like 3–4% of the limited working population is absorbed in the armed forces. This is not to question the wisdom of devoting so great a proportion of resources to defence, and it does not follow that releasing these resources would necessarily lead to a corresponding increase in other investment. But although the scale of the defence effort must naturally be a matter for political decision, the question nevertheless has economic aspects. Firstly, defence expenditure may partly explain why Britain's rate of growth is less than those economies which are not similarly burdened, e.g. West Germany; however, that it can be no more than a contributory factor is shown by the fact that France, with a higher proportionate defence burden, has nevertheless grown more rapidly. Secondly, the political nature of defence decisions does not obviate the need for as careful an assessment as possible of the costs of alternative defence projects and, more widely, of the relative efficiency of defence outlay and economic strength as sources of political influence in the world.

'Investment' is thus very much a hold-all term; emphasis on

achieving a high rate of capital accumulation may therefore be misplaced unless the nature and quality of the investment and different investment needs and opportunities are also taken into account. Blunt comparisons of the amounts invested by different economies is not likely to yield any significant clue about the nature of economic growth and how to foster it. It is not therefore surprising to find that in fact there is no close correlation between investment and growth. Norway, for example, directing nearly double the proportion of its resources to investment that Britain does, has only managed to grow at about the same rate.

This is not, of course, to argue that investment is irrelevant to economic growth. It may quite possibly be the case that the rate of growth in the British economy *could* be increased by more rapid capital accumulation, but whether this is so would depend on what form the additional investment took. Certainly, present investment could be directed into more growth-conducive channels. But high investment cannot be regarded as *the* factor determining growth. It is at least equally important that the investment should take place in a favourable context with regard to other factors of production and general attitudes.

People and Growth

Britain not only comes near the bottom of the growth league, its population has also been growing less rapidly than that of the U.S.A. and Western European countries. To what extent can this have been a contributory element in Britain's relatively slow progress? We pointed out earlier that if population growth is concentrated in the very old or very young sections of the community, additional investment is needed which is either nonproductive or requires lengthy gestation. But although a growing population means more mouths to feed as well as more hands with which to work, it may in certain conditions have stimulating effects on the *per capita* rate of growth. An atmosphere conducive to growth may be created by the fact that total demand is expanding, and this may be backed by the real economic advantage of reduced costs as production takes place on a larger scale. Again, the need for a larger capital stock may mean that improved techniques are introduced more rapidly.

More important than growth in total population is expansion

of the working force, and its flexibility. In this respect, many Western European countries do seem to have had a definite advantage over Britain. West Germany has benefited from a steady influx of refugee immigrants of working age (it is interesting to see how wage-rates sharply increased following the building of the Berlin Wall); as industrial production increased the demand for labour, Italy has been able to draw on an army of unemployed and under-employed in the less-developed South; in France the proportion of the working population employed in agriculture has been about a quarter (as compared with the United Kingdom, 4%), which could be slowly siphoned off into more productive industrial employment as demand rose. To some extent, Britain may have suffered in having already reached a more mature structural distribution of its working force.

As with investment in physical capital (and indeed we could regard it as part of the same problem), the question also arises as to the *quality* of the population, and in particular, of the working force. Is Britain investing enough, and sufficiently wisely, in *human* capital – education and other social services? To some people, to think in terms of improving the stock of human capital is repugnant as it reduces people to the status of *things*. But since most social expenditure is productive inasmuch as it goes to improve the health, skill, and morale of the working force, it is surely reasonable, if difficult, to attempt calculations about the relative 'yields' of physical and human investment. The results of such investigations do not tell us what *ought* therefore to be done, but it is always useful to know what are the economic costs and benefits involved in alternative policies. But although expenditure on, for example, education, is certainly not 'above' economic analysis, little research has been done to confirm or deny the feeling that Britain's slower rate of growth can be partly attributed to inadequacies in our educational system.

Attitudes to Growth

Study of the much more acute problem of how to launch very poor countries into the take-off to higher living standards soon showed that some of the most formidable obstacles to economic development lie in the existence of socio-religious attitudes which clash with the requirements of a dynamic economic society. Growth in a mature economy like Britain may be similarly inhibited by taboos, shibboleths, and a general outlook inherited from a very different age. We could doubtless do a lot better if only the idea of growth were really to catch on, to the point where people were sufficiently enthusiastic about the idea of economic development to accept the costs which are involved.

But perhaps the growth race is not really worth the carrot? After all, by world standards, Britain is already extremely rich. On the other hand, the amount of overtime worked in this country hardly suggests that people are satisfied with their present living standards, and it cannot be denied that there are a substantial number of people in Britain who remain shamefully poor. It could be argued that what is now required is not more wealth so much as a more equitable sharing out of what we already have; but redistribution of present incomes seems a poor solution to the problem when all that could be achieved by it could be more easily secured by just a few more years of growth at, say, 3% per annum. And, if a more equal distribution of income is our aim, it is, anyway, probably a good deal easier to make sure that the *increase* in national income goes mostly to the poorer sections of the community than it is to redistribute existing incomes.

Then again, faster growth does not *have* to imply just increasingly conspicuous consumption. Increased opulence could also take the form of more leisure as improved productivity enables the same output to be produced with less effort; the growth increment could be used to redress the 'private affluence, public squalor' imbalance – by, for example, the implementation of the recommendations of the Newsom, Robbins, and Buchanan Reports; countries which find it relatively easy to grow could devote part of their gains to reducing the dreadful disparities which exist between rich and poor nations.

Altogether, it requires neither an exclusively materialist outlook nor very much imagination to think how the very considerable gains from growth (a doubling of the national income in less than a quarter of a century given a 3% annual rate) could be deployed. What is not so obvious is that the benefits outweigh the costs of trying to *maximize* growth. These costs primarily arise from the need to ensure that resources are constantly flowing to the growth sectors of the economy, with the corollary that stagnant and uncompetitive elements are ruthlessly pruned. Increased flexibility means that workers must be prepared to learn new skills and move to the areas where the skills are demanded, and that firms cannot expect to continue to make the same profits by selling the same lines in the same markets; there is no room for policies of 'making' work or for enjoying a quiet life behind protective restrictions. The implications of maximizing growth have been nicely expressed as the need, not just to accept change, but to welcome it. Are we prepared to accept so fundamental a change in outlook? Perhaps not, but an analysis of the costs of growth is still a very useful exercise. It helps us to decide, if we do not want to go the whole way, just how far we *are* prepared to go. And secondly, it may be possible to introduce measures which reduce the costs of growth. In this respect, some consideration must be given to the scope for planning.

PLANNING

'We are all planners now.' But the way in which a Conservative government, pressed by business interests, was suddenly converted to the idea of planning in the early sixties, is still a little surprising. However, 'planning' can mean very different things according to what it is expected to achieve and how it is intended to do so.

Whatever its scope and form, planning involves alteration, in accordance with a central policy, of the pattern of output which would result from free enterprise. Just how much that pattern is changed depends on the aims of planning policy. The ends of the private sector may be fully accepted by the planners who confine themselves to showing private concerns how they can best achieve them. On the other hand, the purpose of planning may be to modify commercial criteria – by a balancing of economic and non-economic considerations, and the calculation of *social* costs and benefits. Clearly, the degree to which planning can be equated with 'interference' depends on what the planners are trying to do. The 'weak' variety may just require the authorities to encourage those conditions in which basically unconstrained enterprises can do their job most efficiently; 'strong' planning, on the other hand, will involve more direct intervention from above.

French Planning

Undoubtedly, one of the reasons for planning becoming more generally fashionable in this country during recent years was its apparent success in France. A particular attraction of the French example was that it ostensibly demonstrated the possibility of 'planning by consent'. Planning, it seemed, could be relatively painless, imposed from below rather than above, and designed to assist rather than conflict with private commercial interests.

French planning at least creates the impression of containing a considerable do-it-yourself element. Thus, the nominal head of the planning hierarchy is the Economic and Social Council, which is an assembly comprising the heads of employer and worker organizations, and some government departmental officials. Similarly representative membership is found in the twenty-five or so sectionally directed Modernization Commissions, each of which is concerned with a particular industry or aspect of policy such as finance, man-power, or regional planning. In between is the *Commissariat du plan* whose 140 economists, engineers, educationists, and administrators provide the expertise of the system; this extra-departmental body influences policy by coordinating, proposing, and advising, but has no powers of decision or financial control or implementation.

In practice, however, it is the *Commissariat du plan* which plays the vital role. It is the Commissariat which actually initiates the Plan for a coming four-year period by drawing up a general picture of developments in the economy which would be implied by different assumptions about the overall rate of growth. The sort of question which it sets out to answer is – what will the economy look like in four years' time, and how will it have got there, if the rate of growth is 3%, or 4·5%, or 6%? Consultations then take place with the Economic and Social Council about the validity and implications of the alternative rates, and only at this stage does the government select, on the basis of the general sketches which have been made available, the maximum rate of growth which it thinks is compatible with the various ends of policy. It might, as for example in the Fourth Plan which covered the years 1962–5, reject 6% as being likely to overstrain the balance of payments, and decide that 5% would therefore be a more feasible target. This choice is made only on the basis of *general* studies, and the next step is to determine whether, or how, things will work out in practice. This work falls to the Modernization Commissions which check the assumptions of the blueprint plan and show what its implications will be for their particular sectors or industries. In the case of the Fourth Plan, the result of these investigations and discussions was that the overall growth target was increased to 5·5%. The Economic and Social Council then debates the plan in a plenary session and the government makes a final decision.

A good deal is made of the point that French planning is 'indicative' rather than 'imperative', and that implementation of the plan therefore requires no special administrative machinery. It is expected that the private sector will conform to the general lines of the plan since it is in its interests to do so; the government merely influences the economy by providing a general framework within which the plan may be effective and by offering financial and fiscal incentives where necessary. However, this is a rather misleading picture of the French planning mechanism. In fact, the authorities play a much more active role in seeing that the plan is fulfilled than apologists of the system generally admit. In particular, they keep a tight rein on the capital market to ensure that funds flow into the channels indicated by the plan, and this, coupled with the existence of a large public sector, means that a substantial proportion of total investment in the country comes under direct government control.

Judged in terms of achievement of its targets, French planning has been generally successful (although there is now rather less confidence in French economic circles about the adequacy of indicative planning). And throughout the post-war period the French economy has managed to sustain a considerably higher rate of economic growth than the u.k. It is easy to conclude that this has been *because* of planning. Even though this may be true, it is difficult to isolate the effect of planning from other possible causal factors. It is also dangerous to generalize the French experience into the conclusion that planning is a necessary element in attaining high growth-rates – the German and Italian 'economic miracles' clearly show that this is not so.

Our understanding of how to make economies grow is very far from complete, but at least it is clear that the process of economic development is a complex of many factors. It is no good searching for *the* determinant of economic growth. Nor does it necessarily follow that a slow-grower can expand more rapidly by simulating this or that condition found in fast-growers. International comparison of planning experience may therefore be largely irrelevant to our own problem: high growth-rates elsewhere may have been achieved *despite* planning or because of the existence of other favourable conditions. All that matters is whether, if *we* plan, *we* can expand more rapidly than we have in the past without it.

British Planning

Until very recently most people in Britain have thought of planning as implying State direction of the economy through a system of controls – along the lines practised by the two Labour governments during the years 1945 to 1951. During this highly abnormal period the authorities were faced with the immense problems of reconstructing the economy. Consumers were ready to make good their war-time sacrifices by indulging in a vast spending spree; industry, on the other hand, was run down, partly devastated, and mostly still geared to war purposes; the balance of payments had been acutely weakened by the loss of overseas investments, the acquisition of new liabilities, and the breakdown of traditional patterns of trade. Demand from consumers for all the things which for so long had been missing from the shops, demand for new houses to replace bomb damage, demand for new factories and machines to meet peacetime needs, demand from overseas countries which had built up substantial credit balances during the war – all this added up to a pressure on resources which had to be contained if it was not to lead to an explosion of prices or balance of payments disaster.

In these circumstances, the government had no real alternative to maintaining the system of controls on the economy which had been created during the war. The problem of ensuring that enough resources flowed into investment, and that the investment was according to the most pressing social priorities, could only be solved by direct and comprehensive regulation of the economy; instead of being able to enjoy the peace, consumers and producers continued to be harried and frustrated by a complex system of rationing, licensing, and restrictions.

Planning therefore came to connote austerity, the black market, and red tape. In fact, of course, the problems of the immediately post-war years were highly exceptional and necessitated equally extreme policies. The Labour government itself began dismantling the control system as the easing of economic pressures made such comprehensive regulation less necessary; most of what was left was thrown, rather prematurely and indiscriminately, on to the Conservative 'bonfire of controls' after 1951, and, during the following decade, regulation of the economy was largely confined to 'global' fiscal and monetary measures.

And now we are all planners again! However, recent experiments in planning are very different from the control machinery of 1945–50. Influenced by, and partly modelled on the French system, it is indicative rather than imperative, guiding but not directing. It is, in fact, more French than the French.

The first step was to establish a National Economic Development Council, immediately rechristened 'Neddy', which began operations in early 1962 with the job of establishing the conditions necessary for maximum economic development compatible with 'soundness' in the economy. This was a wide enough brief to lead it to consider most aspects of the British economy.

The Council originally comprised some twenty industrialists (representing public as well as private enterprises), trade unionists and independent members, with the Chancellor of the Exchequer as chairman. This upper tier was linked by the Director-General to the Office of over a hundred technical specialists.

The Council began work quickly and within thirteen months had produced two major reports, the first of which was a blueprint for the growth of the economy over the period 1961–5. Its aim was to find out what would be the implications for different sectors of the economy of an annual rate of growth in gross national product averaging 4% – substantially higher than any growth-rate previously sustained by the economy. On the basis of an industrial inquiry into the impact of faster growth on a cross-section of seventeen private and public industries, and some heroic assumptions about the relative rates at which imports and exports could be expected to increase, it was concluded that 4% growth was quite on the cards and could be achieved with available manpower providing that it was fully used. A second report, in April 1963, was a sensible, if not original, catalogue of institutional 'obstacles to quicker growth.'

During the first years it certainly looked as if N.E.D.C. was making a favourable impact. Despite the fact that its blueprint was produced a year *after* the start of the plan period, Neddy was able to report, in March 1964, that the economy had been shunted from virtual stagnation on to a growth path sufficient to make up for earlier arrears and was getting close to a 4% average for the whole period. Unfortunately, most of this progress was attributable to the fact that the economy started with substantial excess capacity left over from the last deflation, and the rapid rise in output was due mainly to increased use of previously idle plant and manpower. As soon as this slack was taken up, imports began to rise far more rapidly than the planned rate and the economy was once again plunged into a balance of payments crisis at the end of 1964. The measures taken to deal with it meant that output was virtually stagnant during 1965.

At this time, the planning machinery itself changed with the creation of a new Department of Economic Affairs which at once absorbed most of the N.E.D.C. experts. The new Minister became chairman of N.E.D.C. which had its membership increased to provide more government representation. With planning initiative passing to the Ministry its role was effectively reduced to that of a discussion group for top people with particular responsibility for supervising the work of the potentially useful score of 'little Neddies' – Economic Development Councils for particular industries or sectors of the economy which function as channels of information and a check on the effectiveness of policy measures.

Within eleven months, the D.E.A. had produced, in September 1965, the first National Plan for the U.K. covering the period 1964–70. The Plan was based on a growth rate of 3·8% – slightly less than the Neddy target but none the less sufficient to achieve a 25% increase in national output by 1970 if it were fulfilled. The Plan pointed to an incipient labour shortage of some 400,000 at this growth rate – to be met by an increase in the growth of labour productivity, by reducing regional unemployment and by increasing activity rates (i.e. attracting new workers into employment). With regard to the balance of payments, the Plan called for increased exports at the rate of 5% per annum (a marked improvement on past performance) with import growth held at only 4% a year.

Any plan must be judged on two grounds. First of all, it should provide an analysis of the direction and magnitude of the changes in different sectors of the economy *required* if a given growth rate is to be achieved. And then it must tell us *how* it is all going to be done. Criticism has been directed at the National Plan as lacking in both these respects. Doubts have been voiced both about the questionable basis of its general analysis, and how it would be implemented. It is one thing to indicate the *need* for increased labour productivity or exports and quite another to ensure that they are achieved.

Planning for a higher rate of growth than has been experienced in the past can obviously only be successful if some of the previous obstacles to growth are removed. To what extent can we expect indicative planning of the present type to help in doing this? We can distinguish a number of roles which the present planning machinery *may* play in accelerating economic development:

1. *Investigation* We have stressed several times in this chapter that knowledge of the growth process is very inadequate. It is not difficult to find plausible arguments for the theses that the British economy has not grown faster because of: too little investment, too much investment mis-directed, restrictive practices on the part of the workers, restrictive practices on the part of poor quality management, an over-valued pound, fixed exchange rates, insufficient flexibility in the economy, and so on. What we do not know is the relative importance of these various factors, whether some of them are important at all, and whether there are others which have been too much neglected.

The D.E.A. could obviously contribute a good deal by its inquiries into different aspects of the growth process. So far, all that has really been done is to point out the need for such studies; only when more work has been done in defining the obstacles to growth will we be in a position to set about overcoming them.

2. *Asserting Priorities* For the first time, we now have institutions exclusively concerned with the problems of faster growth. Their mere existence puts an emphasis on the goal of national economic development which makes its achievement more likely. They ensure that whenever discussion of priorities takes place, the case for growth is fully presented. They can suggest policy alternatives which may never emanate from more hidebound Treasury pundits. Their opinions may help to bolster the weak-hearted and imbue the more cautious elements in government circles with a sense of the importance of keeping the economy moving on its upward path.

3. *Target-setting* By setting targets for the economy and showing what could be done, planning increases the likelihood that it will be done. To suggest a growth-rate which the economy is capable of achieving and to show its implications for different sectors gives a standard by which progress can be judged; it also helps by creating growth-consciousness and buoyant expectations about the future course of the economy. But target-setting, as we shall be emphasizing later, is only useful if it is thought that there is a real possibility that the targets will be reached.

4. *Market Research* To have a picture of how the economy will look if it grows at a certain rate facilitates long-term planning by public and private enterprises and by policy-makers in the government itself. Once an industry realizes that its demand will be increased by simultaneous expansion in the rest of the economy, output can be more boldly pushed to the limits indicated by long-term estimates; on the other hand, certain investments which industries are considering may be shown to be unwarranted, and mistakes which would otherwise have been made can thereby be avoided; seeing in advance the obstacles and bottlenecks which are likely to arise enables measures to deal with them to be prepared well in advance.

To return to a very important point, however, it is vital that the business expectations which planning succeeds in creating are in fact fulfilled. Confidence in planning will not be enhanced if firms which expand find that the programme has failed to work out for the economy as a whole. Indeed, unless there is faith in the estimates of the future rise in demand, enterprises will be very reluctant to expand at all. Unfortunately, this is just what seems to be already happening. In their March 1964 report *The Growth of the Economy* the council admitted that

several of the industries consulted fear that steady and rapid growth will not be sustained. Unless they can be convinced to the contrary, there may not be sufficient investment to maintain rapid growth after 1966.

How right those industries were! By 1966–7 the government had embarked on a policy of (by post-war standards) severe deflation designed to maintain foreign confidence in the pound. The National Plan had got off to a very bad start indeed and it was freely admitted that there was no longer any prospect of its targets being fulfilled.

Showing the feasibility and implications of a given growth-rate can certainly have a stimulating effect in itself. But success of the policy must depend more on changes being made to a system which has failed in the past to produce the results. In this respect, purely 'indicative' planning obviously has severe limitations. The French system, for all its emphasis on 'planning by consent', also involves seeing that the course charted by the planning bodies is in fact followed. Firstly, there is the fact that the government is involved in the planning process and commits itself to its implementation; and secondly, the government has considerable sanctions at its disposal to see that this is done.

In Britain, the government has certainly *involved* itself in the planning process by the creation of a special Department of Economic Affairs. What remains in doubt is the extent to which it has committed itself to the planning targets or the means by which it would hope to achieve them.

At the moment we are in a situation in which an increase in the growth rate causes external pressures to which anti-growth measures are regarded as the only acceptable short-term solution; this is what is meant by a policy of 'stop–go'. Given the fact that whenever the rate of growth is accelerated exports tend to increase less rapidly than imports, it is useless to talk in terms of sustaining the growth-rate at a higher level until something is done to remove this balance of payments constraint. Growth can clearly have no priority in a programme of policies until a satisfactory external position is achieved either by domestic measures such as an incomes policy (see Chapter 11) or by some fundamental adjustment in our international position (see Chapter 12).

Even when this question of priorities is sorted out, it is very doubtful whether purely permissive planning, despite its attraction of establishing growth as a collective responsibility, can have sufficient impact to achieve its aims. Ineffectiveness will soon rob indicative planning of the general acceptability which is its chief virtue, and it seems probable that future discussion will sooner or later be shifted to the problem, not of whether the planning mechanism should be given teeth, so much as of the form that they should take.

CHAPTER 11

INFLATION

REMINISCENCES about the good old days when a pound was a pound and 'for a shilling you could get . . .' generally omit the fact that the incomes on which this paradise was based were also very much smaller. Certainly the *cost* of living was lower, but so also was the *standard* of living, and these two indexes are frequently confused. The cost of living shows how much money has to be spent in order to obtain the same quantity of goods and services at different times. The standard of living, on the other hand, is a measure of the degrees to which people are *really* better or worse off, because it takes into account *both* prices and income changes. If the basket of goods purchased by a typical family unit rises in price by 10%, then the cost of living has increased; if the income earned by that family has meanwhile risen in the same proportion, then its standard of living is unchanged.

In this chapter, we shall be concerned with the rising cost of living – increases in the general level of prices in the economy (which in the post-war period have been accompanied by an improvement in the standard of living inasmuch as average incomes have risen faster). But, before going on to analyse the nature and causes of inflation and possible ways of controlling it, we should not beg the question of whether it really *is* a problem. Why worry about rising prices? Obviously, hyper-inflation leading to complete destruction of confidence in the monetary system is to be avoided at all costs, but explosive inflations of this kind seldom occur. Is there much cause for concern if the rise in prices is gradual and the real value of incomes increases meanwhile? There are a number of reasons for regarding even this as a situation to be improved upon.

Why Bother about Inflation?

There is, first of all, the effect of rising prices on saving. If, before the war, an individual saved £100, he was sacrificing an immediate claim on the resources of the economy which could be measured by the volume of goods and services which £100 would then buy. That physical volume of resources was released for investment purposes – adding to the stock of capital to produce more consumer goods in the future. When the same individual comes to spend his savings today, he is still able to reclaim £100 money value of resources. But the quantity of goods and services which he will be able to buy will have declined in real terms by some two-thirds. There must be a lot of people who, thirty years ago, thought that they had assured themselves of a comfortable old age by buying a life insurance policy of, say, £1,000, and are now discovering just how inadequate it has become. Admittedly, with increasing incomes they should have been able to increase their premiums annually, but this partial hedging against inflation does not alter the fact that the amount of goods they finally take out of the pool will be less than the *real* sacrifice which they originally made.

Inflation might also be thought unfair because of its effects on the distribution of income. It reduces the real value of debts, so that those who spend more than their current incomes are persistently favoured at the expense of creditors. And again, success in matching rising prices by at least equal increases in money incomes depends primarily on bargaining strength; there will be some sections of the community whose incomes are relatively fixed and whose real purchasing power is therefore continuously eroded.

Inflation is therefore generally inequitable. There are also some purely economic reasons for thinking that rising prices should be controlled. Saving may be rendered so unattractive that insufficient resources are released for the investment on which the future growth of the economy at least partly depends; ultimately, the futility of saving might come to be reflected in reduced incentives to earn. A second reason for trying to control inflation is the effect of rising prices on the balance of payments. Increases in the domestic price level tend, at least under a system of fixed exchange rates, to cause balance of payments difficulties as exports become relatively expensive and imports relatively cheaper.

However, although there are good grounds for trying to regulate inflation, it is important to keep the problem in perspective.

Clearly, the economic drawbacks of inflation depend on how much and how quickly prices are rising. Balance of payments difficulties, which are probably the most important single factor behind British concern at inflation, do not result from the fact that prices are rising as such; what counts is the rate of inflation in comparison with that of our major rivals. As for savings, inflation of the quite severe form experienced in Britain since the war has not prevented a considerable *rise* in the level of personal thriftiness, although it may have altered the relative attractions of alternative methods of saving.

Obviously, inflation must be prevented from getting out of hand. But is a *gradually* increasing level of prices too serious a problem? There are some who argue that such a state is positively conducive to growth – through its effects of reducing the real burden of debt and creating a generally favourable, if illusory, climate of expectations about returns on investment. Without adopting this view (the supporting evidence is far from conclusive), we may still think that the cost of eliminating an annual price rise averaging, say, 1–2% is excessive – *if* to do so causes increased unemployment or rather slower growth.

Unfortunately, we do not really know enough about the relationship between employment, growth, and inflation to provide precise choices of this kind. In the circumstances, it at least seems sensible not to regard price stabilization as an end in itself. Instead of concentrating our efforts wholly on trying to stop prices rising, we might also consider ways in which to counteract their effects. If it is questions of income distribution about which we are particularly worried, then it should not be beyond human ingenuity to devise methods of offsetting the unequal impact of rising prices. Or if it is the balance of payments which causes most concern, we should consider, if our prices are getting out of line, allowing the exchange rate to alter rather than letting the brunt of adjustment fall on the domestic economy.

CAUSES OF INFLATION

In the same way that the prices of particular goods are determined by the forces of supply and demand in a market, so the general level of prices in the economy depends on the relationship between aggregate spending and the volume of goods and services which the productive process makes available. The fact that prices are rising *means* that expenditure is exceeding the value of output measured at constant prices. How can such a situation arise?

The pressure on prices can come from either the supply or the demand side of the equation. Supply conditions can change as raw materials become more expensive, profit margins widen, or wage costs increase. As a result, prices may be forced up as firms try to recoup their higher costs from consumers; what look like higher costs to firms are also higher incomes for wage-earners and sellers of raw materials, so that spending can rise correspondingly. On the other hand, the amount which people plan to consume and invest may add up to more than the output coming onto the market (measured at constant prices); the excess demand can then only be satisfied in monetary terms – which involves a rise in the general price level.

In principle at least, we can therefore distinguish two varieties of inflation. Cost inflation originates in the *push* of increased costs on prices; demand inflation is due to the *pull* on prices as output is insufficient to meet the total claims which are being made on it. A considerable controversy has been taking place over the last decade or so as to whether post-war British inflation has been caused by cost or demand pressures. The trouble is that once they have got going, both cost and demand inflation operate through the now familiar mechanism – of rising prices followed by rising incomes which in turn lead to further price rises. The argument is therefore chiefly about causation. Cost inflationists claim that it is increased incomes, particularly wages, which are *causing* the rise in prices, and point as the root of the problem to the power of trade unions to force wage increases even when total demand in the economy is not excessive. The demand inflation school, on the other hand, argues that inflationary pressure only reaches the labour market *after* it appears in the market for final output. It is the fact that sellers find excess demand for their products and are therefore able to raise prices which *then* leads to either the unions exploiting the situation by pressing their wage claims, or employers themselves bidding up earnings in order to attract scarce labour to enable them more fully to meet the demand for their products.

There is no doubt that there has been a state of excess demand in the economy during much of the post-war period. It has shown itself in the labour market in the excess of employment vacancies over registered unemployed which has frequently existed, in the drift of actual earnings above the union-negotiated wage-*rates*, and in the willingness of employers to hoard labour during temporary recessions. It is equally likely, on the other hand, that wage increases have reflected *more* than just excess demand, and that there has been an independent inflationary pressure from the cost side which has at times been the major cause of rising prices. Particularly in the early fifties, inflation was at least accentuated by the rise in import prices due to devaluation and adverse terms of trade; there are some who argue that the effects of this phase have not yet fully worked themselves out. Again, the fact that firms tend to fix their prices on the basis of their costs *plus* a margin for profits suggests a greater sensitivity of prices to supply influences than to demand changes.

CONTROL OF INFLATION

If inflation is caused by excess demand, the way to tackle it is to bring about cuts in spending. It is often popularly supposed that this could be done just by reducing the quantity of money in circulation; if the money is not there, then it cannot be spent. However, this sort of reasoning ignores the fact that expenditure is a *flow*, so that a given quantity of money can be used to service quite different levels of transactions by being used more or less intensively. In other words, a contraction in the volume of money can be offset by an increase in its average rate of turnover – by a change in its 'velocity of circulation'. In a highly developed monetary system, the existence of institutions which can activate idle balances of money by offering in exchange very near-money assets means that there are very wide limits to the possible velocity of circulation. Of course, a policy of contracting the money supply must ultimately succeed in reducing the level of demand, but perhaps only if it is pushed to a degree which would severely damage the monetary system.

The role of monetary policy is more properly thought of as one of indirectly influencing demand via changes in interest rates, and, when used in conjunction with fiscal measures, will always enable the authorities to damp down the level of spending. In a number of ways, however, this control is imperfect, and it would be optimistic to assume that the authorities have sufficiently fine diagnostic and control techniques to allow them, delicately, to manipulate demand to a level which is just right. To try to establish a level of demand which is precisely appropriate to full employment output is to continuously court the danger of inflation as demand overshoots. Complete elimination of demand inflation therefore requires that the authorities have room in which to work. Instead of trying to maintain a level of absolutely full-employment demand, they would have to operate from a situation in which there was a certain degree of excess capacity in the economy to give them some margin of error.

But what if rising prices are primarily due to the push of costs? Recent empirical investigations, both of the post-war period and over the past century, have showed that the wage-rate changes are closely related to the level of activity in the economy, rising unemployment being associated with moderation of the rate at which wages increase. It can therefore be argued that a policy of deliberately creating excess capacity in the economy is one which kills two birds with a single stone. As well as directly tackling the problem of demand inflation, at the same time it enables the authorities to subdue cost inflationary pressures by reducing the bargaining strength of the trade unions. But how can such measures be reconciled with the other ends of economic policy – the maintenance of full employment and achievement of a high rate of growth? Proponents of the excess capacity thesis claim that the clash of priorities is not a serious one. The pool of unemployment required would be relatively small, perhaps only 3–4%, and this would be a price worth paying for the consequent benefits. With regard to economic growth, although such a policy might *initially* have depressive effects, business expectations would soon become buoyant again as the level of excess capacity became stabilized and therefore accepted as a norm. It is argued that in fact this situation would be far more conducive to growth than the stop-start consequences of trying to maintain absolutely full employment: competition would be stimulated, and the balance of payments would benefit as rather slacker home demand forced firms to make more energetic efforts at selling abroad.

This approach to the problem of inflation is, however, open to a number of criticisms. Even if it is granted that a 3–4% unemployment level would be sufficient to restrain prices (which in itself seems optimistic), we have to remember that this is an average figure. Over-full employment exists in certain parts of the economy, and to create excess capacity in these sectors implies *very* much higher rates of unemployment in the already depressed regions. In terms both of value considerations and the economic waste involved, such a policy does not seem likely to command general acceptability.

Secondly, it is doubtful whether a policy of creating excess capacity would anyway have the success in curbing cost inflation which is predicted for it. The fact that in the past wage pressures were reduced when certain unemployment levels were reached does not necessarily mean that the deliberate creation now of a similar degree of excess capacity will have the same restraining effects. In the pre-war context of regular trade cycles, the emergence of a significant amount of unemployment would be taken as a sign of worse to come. In the post-war period, it would be regarded as a temporary divergence from full employment. In both cases there would be good reasons for the trade unions refraining from wage claims. It is, however, very unlikely that they would respond in the same way to a 4% rate of unemployment at which the authorities clearly intended to *stabilize* the economy. Much more probably, wage pressures would be renewed as soon as the unions became adjusted to the new situation.

Moreover, although wage rises may be the most important pressure on prices, they are not the only element in costs. To bring about conditions in which firms operate at less than full capacity will lead to some increase in their unit costs as expensive overheads are recouped from a less than optimum output. Far from eliminating cost inflation, such a policy may therefore, at least in the short run, positively stimulate it. For similar reasons, domestic deflation can hardly be expected to create a favourable basis for increasing our competitiveness in foreign markets.

There is no doubt that creation of sufficient excess capacity must in the end be successful in checking demand inflation.

What is far from obvious, however, is that the complete elimination of demand pressures on prices is worth the cost which would probably be involved. Particularly is this so when it seems unlikely that the policy would be effective in curbing cost inflation. Cost inflation, it is now fairly generally agreed, can only be tackled by a more direct limitation of the rate of incomes increase, and in the rest of this chapter we shall examine some of the thorny issues which arise from the concept of a national incomes policy.

NATIONAL INCOMES POLICY

The rationale of a national incomes policy is extremely simple. Wages and dividends, which are incomes to their recipients, are also costs of production which firms will try to recoup in their selling prices. Price stability therefore means that incomes should not be allowed to rise faster than the consequent increase of costs can be absorbed by improvements in productivity. This is all that an incomes policy sets out to achieve, but when an attempt is made to map out some of its implications, the immense complexities of the problem soon become apparent.

Every Chancellor since the war has emphasized the need for incomes to be kept within the limits set by productivity increase in the economy, but relatively little progress has been made in seeing that this could be done. Something was achieved during the years 1947–50 when a call for restraint came in a White Paper *Statement on Personal Incomes, Costs, and Prices*; the T.U.C., loyal to a Labour government pursuing a general economic policy with which they agreed, accepted that wage increases would have to be moderated, but at the same time insisted that there were far more bases for exceptional increases than the White Paper had suggested. Despite these loopholes, the rise in money wages was certainly damped down. However, with prices shooting up after devaluation in 1949, loyalties became overstrained, and although the T.U.C. continued to agree with the government's policy it was forced to accede to its members' demands for 'greater flexibility'.

Next to nothing was achieved in the way of controlling incomes for the next decade. Successive governments tried, with no real success, to check rising incomes by persuasion and exhortation, by arbitration, and by the creation of general economic conditions in which trade union bargaining power would be reduced. The indecisiveness of policy during these years made Mr Selwyn Lloyd's demand for a 'pay pause' in July 1961 all the more shocking to trade unionists. Six months later the idea of an incomes policy was given more definition than it had so far had in the publication of another White Paper *Incomes Policy: the Next Step* which (a) showed that many of the criteria used to justify wage increases lacked any real economic basis, (b) introduced a 'guiding-light' of 2 to $2\frac{1}{2}\%$ as the safe limit for future annual increases, and (c) laid down certain principles which might justify above-average wage increases.

In November 1963, the policy was given institutional expression in the setting-up of the ill-fated National Incomes Commission. N.I.C. was to consider whether, in particular cases put before it by the government or either of the parties concerned, there were circumstances which justified income increases of more or less than the guiding-light (increased, after Neddy had done its homework, from 3 to $3\frac{1}{2}\%$). While keeping in mind the desirability of limiting the total increase in incomes to the long-term rate of increase of national production, it could take into account considerations of fairness, manpower needs, industrial policies and practices, and the likely repercussion which one settlement could have on another. High hopes were entertained of a body which could act as a forum for continuous restatement and review of government policy, and which, for the first time, was given the job of judging claims or settlements in national terms rather than just trying to find a *via media* between two sides of a dispute.

In practice, N.I.C.'s usefulness was totally undermined by the refusal of the trade unions to have anything to do with it. Ostensibly, the unions' boycott was on the grounds that the Commission represented an evasion of responsibility by the government and an attack on traditional principles of negotiation. However, the impression that the whole matter had been handled clumsily and high-handedly seems confirmed by the speed and relative ease with which the Labour government secured, by the end of 1964, a 'declaration of intent' from both trade union and employer organizations on the necessity of preventing price increases and the conditions in which this could be achieved. N.I.C. was given up as a bad job and a fresh start was tried with the formation of a National Board for Prices and Incomes. The Board works by looking at cases referred to it by the government of increases in prices or incomes and evaluates them according to criteria laid down by the government from time to time. Basically, its function is to decide whether there is any justification for deviations from an independently determined 'norm' – in cases, for example, of productivity improvements or where much below national average wages are being paid. The Board got off to a surprisingly vigorous start – fourteen cases in its first year – and has served both to delay the introduction of increases and to encourage the replacement of built-in inflationary bases for wage increases like cost-of-living scales by non-inflationary linking to productivity improvements.

The strategic role of the Board was enhanced by the passing of the Prices and Income Act in June 1966. This provided for a *zero* norm for wage and price increases for the next six months to be followed by a further six months of severe restraint. Moreover, the standstill was to be compulsory and the government equipped itself with legal sanctions for use against offenders.

However, it is one thing to achieve a temporary freeze of incomes (particularly when, as in this case, it is accompanied by general deflationary measures) and another to restrain the growth of incomes over a long period. The vital issue is what sort of policy is evolved after the freeze when the economy moves into an expansionary phase once again.

Prerequisites of an Incomes Policy

If we have learnt anything from the dismal history of post-war efforts at introducing incomes restraint it must be that there is no chance of success until two basic conditions are met:

1. Planning incomes involves other sorts of planning too. If incomes are to be restrained, we first of all have to know within what limits. This means estimating the rate of productivity increase, and itself implies some degree of forward planning of the economy. Even more far-reaching in its implications, however, is the fact that an incomes policy can only succeed, or for that matter even be introduced, if *real* standards of living are

rising rapidly. Unless this is so, different groups in the economy will concentrate on trying to increase their share of the limited national cake at the expense of the others. It is no good trying to restrain incomes within the meagre improvements of national production achieved during many post-war years. Policy must instead be directed at jacking up growth-rates towards the rate of increase of incomes which has become accepted as normal, and at sustaining growth. This, of course, is something of a hen-and-egg situation. Growth is impeded by excessive increases in money incomes; income restraint depends on rapid growth. But the trade unions are not likely to prove more cooperative until they at least see, firstly, that growth has a high priority in government policies, and, secondly, some evidence of its ability to implement them. In this respect, it must be seriously doubted whether the present toothless planning will be regarded by the trade unions as a guarantee that they would not be the losers if wage pressures were moderated.

2. Even more obviously, an incomes policy must be an *incomes* policy. A wages policy is not enough. Even a mellower climate of faster growth will not eliminate interest in questions of income distribution. A policy of restraining only wages will therefore be doomed even if the standard of living of wage-earners is rising steadily – because they will also be concerned about their position in relation to other groups in the economy. Equity therefore demands that a wages policy is coupled with an equally severe attitude towards profits and managerial incomes. In this respect, it is not sufficient to refer vaguely to the possibility of profits restraint if and when the need should arise. Very reasonably, wage-earners will want to know the details of such a policy now before they commit themselves to restraint of their own incomes.

Moreover, it is important to remember that 'incomes' connote *earnings* and not just wage-rates. Earnings may be well above nationally agreed rates because of overtime working, bonuses, and the willingness of employers to pay more than the basic rate in order to attract scarce labour. The various ways in which wage-rates can be supplemented add up to the phenomenon of 'wage drift'. Wage drift is a usually economic element in the wage mechanism, helping to shift labour to where it can be most efficiently employed, but the guiding-light by which increases in wage-rates are to be judged must take into account the probability that earnings will be swollen in excess of these rates. And once again, fairness requires that the same degree of control is exercised on those Inland-Revenue financed fringe benefits which are an important part of non-wage incomes.

Having emphasized the need for an overall incomes policy, we shall now look in turn at some of the difficulties which arise in deciding about the form which a wages policy and a profits policy should take, and how they should be implemented.

Wages Policy

In an earlier chapter, we have already mentioned one of the basic difficulties with regard to wage restraint. Wage-earners are not a homogeneous mass organized in a single bargaining body. Individual trade unions try to increase the standard of living of their members even if the economy is not growing – at the expense of less astute or weaker unions, or by cutting into the share of unorganized workers or into profits. Trade union officials are paid to look after their own; they are not watchdogs of the working class as a whole or immediately concerned with national welfare. Certainly it may be the case that, by pushing for excessive wage increases, the unions reduce the size of the cake from which they are trying to increase their slice. But it will only be in their interests to refrain from such demands if other unions are playing according to the rules which ensure that growth takes place. Two problems arise – what sort of rules should be set, and who should impose them?

One possibility is that control over wage-earnings should be imposed from above and indeed it seems likely, in early 1967, that the government will renew its powers to compel at least delays in price and income increases which it considers unjustified. However, any element of compulsion in wage regulation will certainly be bitterly opposed by trade unionists and construed as an attack on the right of free collective bargaining for which they struggled so long. An alternative would be a do-it-yourself regulation by the trade union movement itself. But what is the trade union movement? It is a collection of some 600 very different and quite independent units loosely affiliated to a central organization, the T.U.C., which lacks any power of effective control.

Many observers have therefore singled out trade union sectionalism as the crux of the wage problem. It is suggested that British trade unions are either too big or too small. They are too big in the sense that wage agreements are negotiated at a national level and set at rates which may have little significance in particular regional or factory conditions. Alternatively, they are too small in that there is no central trade union authority with the power to bargain for the movement as a whole and then to impose its decisions on members. Comparisons have been made suggesting that either bargaining at the factory level as in the U.S.A., or more centralized negotiations between a single trade union authority and a single employer organization as in Sweden, would have less inflationary potential than the British system. In fact, a development along these lines now seems very probable. Since the end of 1965, unions affiliated to the T.U.C. have been obliged, under the government's 'early warning' system, to submit wage claims to a vetting committee of the General Council; the T.U.C. has to keep the government informed about such claims and can also let a union know whether or not it thinks its claim is a wise one (although, even if it doesn't, a union can still go ahead after a short delay). A step further in self-imposed restraint came in March 1967 when the executives of 155 unions (accounting for over 99% of the affiliated membership) gave general approval to a scheme whereby all wage claims would be scrutinized by an incomes policy committee of the General Council according to criteria laid down after consultation with the government; there was also talk of regular negotiation at a national level with the employers' confederation. The government, however, while agreeing that some such arrangement may be the long-run solution to the problem, has so far refused to accept that the degree of restraint necessary in the immediate future can be achieved by such means.

The question of the nature of the rules to be applied is equally perplexing and goes some way to explain the reluctance of trade unions to forfeit their autonomy to a central body. Even if it is agreed that national wage increases must be kept within the limit of the rise in national productivity, the problem remains of distributing the permitted total among particular industries and wage-earners. The first general possibility is that wages could be related to productivity on an industry-by-industry basis. If productivity is rapidly improved in the motor-car industry, then its workers will receive correspondingly high wage increases; if productivity remains constant in transport, then transport workers will receive no increase. Such a system would amount to restoring to the wage-mechanism something of its theoretical function as a system of signposts to resources, with higher wages in the expanding industries tending to attract labour from less productive uses.

But, at a practical level, can we really imagine workers in slow-growing industries being prepared to see others receive the full benefits of growth in the economy? It can be argued that they could always move to other areas and jobs, and that if they stayed where they were then they must regard the non-pecuniary benefits as equal to the money-wage differential. But this is to exaggerate economic rationality and to underestimate non-economic considerations. The wage system is now firmly established as a traditional and 'fair' structure of differentials (which different groups still, of course, try to modify). A policy of wages related to industry productivity increases would be a reversal of the whole process to which people have been accustomed and, therefore, very difficult to implement. Anyway, would it be fair? And doesn't 'fairness' count as much as 'economic' considerations? A further practical difficulty arises with regard to the service industries which, in a mature economy like the U.K., employ a large proportion of the working force. Partly, the problem of this sector of the economy is that productivity is more difficult to increase than in manufacturing industry. But secondly, even when it is increasing, it may not be measurable. How would teachers or government employees, for example, fare under such a system? A final disadvantage of the 'industry-by-industry' approach is that the 'industry' unit would still in a sense be too large. The system of wage-fixing would remain at a national level. National productivity in the motor industry might be high and that on the railways low. But if wage-rates for the whole economy are set on that basis, how would the railways in the Midlands be able to attract the labour supply which they might well be able to use economically?

A second general possibility for 'wage rules' is that the 'growth increment' should be equally distributed regardless of variations in productivity increases. If the estimated limit to wage claims is 4%, then all wages should be raised by that amount. Given an effective profits policy, this would imply that product prices would fall in those industries where productivity was rising faster than the national average, and rise where the productivity increase was below the national average. As these price adjustments became reflected in demand changes, unemployment would ultimately arise in contracting industries and release labour for the expanding sector where labour shortages would be experienced. Quite apart from the obvious practical difficulty of insisting that declining concerns should continue to grant uniform wage increases, the success of such a policy would be limited by its dependence on labour actually responding to market pressures. In fact, labour mobility tends to be low, and it would be difficult to restrain incomes in the expanding industries from rising by more than the agreed national rate of wage increase as a result of wage drift.

The problem of wage drift, of earnings increasing more rapidly than wage-*rates*, is one which has to be faced in any variant of incomes policy. When output rises, earnings automatically begin to increase as a result of more overtime, higher piecework earnings, and production bonuses. If, therefore, national productivity is expected to rise by 4%, and these 'built-in' factors are likely to increase earnings by 2%, the safe limit for wage-*rate* increases is confined to the remaining 2%. Of course, taking probable wage drift into account in calculating the 'guiding light' makes the whole business of income restraint less attractive by reducing the permitted increases. It is also open to the objection that if wage drift did *not* take place to the anticipated extent, workers would have been robbed of their rightful share of the growth increases; moreover, the opportunities for wage drift greatly vary from industry to industry.

In general, to concentrate only on nationally set wage-rates (and in particular those which the government can itself directly influence as an employer, or through Wage Councils or arbitration) is to ignore the complexity of the mechanism by which wage-earnings are determined in Britain. With the immense flexibility which it affords for making quite different payments on the basis of the same national minima, it is difficult to avoid the conclusion of one authority that 'the present machinery of national wage negotiations is not very receptive to injections of productivity considerations as fuel'.

Profits Policy

The fact that profits form a much smaller proportion of production costs than wages is no reason for excluding them from an incomes policy. As we have already stressed, it is futile to expect wage-earners to accept limitations on the rate at which their earnings can rise without at the same time making it clear that similar rules will apply to other income recipients. An incomes policy must be fair and *be seen* to be fair. Although the difficulties of devising and implementing a policy of profit restraint have so far received relatively little attention, they are unfortunately just as considerable as those of a wages policy.

The least that a profits policy can aim at is to ensure that profits do not rise faster than wages. In other words, the proportion of national income going to profits must at least be kept constant. Social policy or the trade unions (as the price of cooperation in an incomes policy) may demand more: that the share of profits is actually reduced. The difficulties which will be discussed below would then, of course, apply *a fortiori*.

There is very little to be said for imposing maximum limits to the rate of profit which firms should be allowed to make. Admittedly, high profit margins may sometimes be possible only because a firm is in a position to exploit a monopolistic situation, but more generally they reflect particular enterprise or efficiency. It is obviously important that a profits policy should not discourage more go-ahead firms by narrowing the differential which they are able to earn over the return in less progressive concerns. However, attempts to limit profits other than by fixing maxima come up against a formidable problem of company taxation – that firms may take profits tax into account by setting prices which will yield them the after-tax profits which they consider appropriate. Company taxation may thus be regarded as a surcharge on costs which, in conditions of full employment, can be passed on to consumers through higher prices. Studies seem to show that just this sort of mechanism has been operating in post-war Britain. Unfortunately, too, the businesses which are likely to find it most difficult to recoup their tax burden from consumers – those selling primarily in foreign markets or those facing particularly severe competition at home – are the least suitable candidates for discriminatory pressure.

In view of these difficulties, and since an incomes policy essentially has to ensure that the burden of restraint is shared between different classes of income-earners in a way which is *personally* equitable, it is perhaps more sensible to concentrate on controlling profits at the stage when they become personal incomes. However, a call for voluntary dividend restraint, which is the most that has been attempted so far, is obviously not enough. A more acceptable approach might be to introduce a new tax on unearned income based on the difference between the rates at which dividends and wages are on average increasing. Thus, if the dividends paid out by firms were to grow faster than average wage-earnings, the tax-rate on dividends would be adjusted to equalize the two rates of increase. Presumably, dividend earners would then be entitled to rebates if wage-earnings instead increased more rapidly than dividends.

Even the introduction of a highly flexible tax on unearned income would not, however, fully satisfy the demands for equity because it concentrates only on distributed profits and ignores the benefits which also accrue to shareholders from that part of company profits which is ploughed back into the firm. Undistributed profits provide the basis for higher dividends later, and the argument that payment of the dividends tax would merely be postponed assumes a continuity of policy which might in practice not be the case. Anyway, shareholders also benefit from the increase in share prices which results from undistributed profits. Effective taxation of capital gains is therefore an essential element in workable policy for profit regulation.

Conclusion

Listing the difficulties of devising and implementing an acceptable plan for incomes shows just how far we still are from success.

Most of the problems which we have outlined still have to be faced. The T.U.C. leadership, let alone the rank and file on whom the success of a wages policy ultimately depends, is suspicious and uncooperative when wage restraint is mentioned. This attitude is hardly surprising when set against the background of a decade in which the economy has grown only hesitantly, and in which attempts at income restraint have been unfairly concentrated on wages alone. Nothing fails like failure, and the present prospect for an incomes policy is only likely to brighten when the trade unions are somehow convinced of the authorities' determination and ability to make the economy grow and to limit *all* incomes equally.

CHAPTER 12

BRITAIN IN THE WORLD ECONOMY

THERE is a general feeling that Britain has made a poor showing in the post-war world economy. Statistical support can be found for most arguments, and in this case we can point to the fact that the British share of world trade in manufactured goods was about 33% in 1913, dropped to 22% by 1937, and has since fallen below 14%. But, to a large extent, this deterioration merely reflects Britain's head-start in the process of industrialization; as other economies developed and world trade in manufactured goods expanded, it was natural that the proportion coming from Britain should decline. What really counts is not so much a country's share of world exports as whether its trade is increasing in absolute terms. A diminishing share of a rapidly increasing volume of world trade may represent a perfectly satisfactory state of affairs.

By and large, this is what has been happening. In view of the war-time disruption to traditional trading patterns, the continued progress of competitors less involved in the war, and the loss of a substantial portion of overseas investments, the British recovery and development since 1945 has been remarkable. Official estimates at that time suggested that if balance of payments equilibrium was to be re-established, the volume of exports would have to rise by no less than 75% above its pre-war level. In fact, what seemed an extraordinarily ambitious target has been greatly exceeded. The volume of exports has been raised by about 140%, while import volume has increased by only some 40% above that of 1938. At the same time, the structure of exports has been much improved by a healthy diversification replacing the traditional dependence on a narrow range of staple products.

This very substantial achievement has been partly masked by a deterioration from the particularly favourable terms of trade of the thirties. Nevertheless, whereas imports were then financed by merchandise exports only to the tune of some 60%, the visible export: import ratio has now become very much more favourable.

U.K. Balance of Trade 1958–65 (£m.)

	Imports	Exports and re-exports	Trade Gap
1958	3,375	3,407	+32
1959	3,638	3,522	−116
1960	4,137	3,733	−404
1961	4,041	3,892	−149
1962	4,092	3,994	−98
1963	4,366	4,287	−79
1964	5,005	4,471	−534
1965	5,044	4,779	−265

In the magic year of 1958 merchandise exports actually exceeded imports for the first time in British balance of payments history, and, with the exception of 1960 and 1964, the trade gap has never recently amounted to more than a few per cent of the import bill.

Yet we still suffer from balance of payments crises. There are two reasons for this. One is the fact that net invisible earnings are now of relatively little help in bolstering up the account. And secondly, the balance precariously depends on the level of activity in the domestic economy.

1. Invisible exports have consistently earned more than we have spent on invisible imports and contributed towards increasing the surplus on current account, or reducing the size of a deficit. However, the extent of this contribution has markedly declined. In the pre-war period, net invisible income was sufficient to pay for about one-third of British merchandise imports; in recent years this proportion has been less than 5%.

U.K. Balance of Payments on Current Account (£m.)

	Trade Gap	Net Invisibles	Current balance
1962	−98	+191	+93
1963	−79	+184	+105
1964	−534	+122	−412
1965	−265	+129	−136

A breakdown of these figures shows that the dwindling significance of net invisible income has been due to a combination of a fall in net investment income and a rise in net government expenditure. The increase debit on government account is chiefly

211

because of extended and more costly military commitments, and although our investment *income* has risen substantially it has been offset by an even more rapid increase in debits – the financing of both short-term debts (sterling balances) and the influx of long-term foreign capital.

2. Although it represented an enormous adjustment to the traditional structure of the British balance of payments to have achieved even a rough balance between visible imports and exports, the precariousness of this balance is exposed whenever the rate of growth in the economy begins to accelerate. In these circumstances, imports tend to rise a good deal more rapidly than exports. Partly, this is an inevitable short-term phenomenon; getting the economy moving again after a period of stagnation means that firms have to build up their stocks of raw materials and semi-manufactured goods without which exports cannot be expected to increase. Partly, on the other hand, the tendency for imports to rise disproportionately can be taken as a sign that the economy has not yet been fully adjusted; imports can still be made roughly to balance exports if demand in the economy is deliberately restrained below full capacity level. Once the economy is given its head at all, the effect is sharply to increase the demand for imported manufactured goods as well as the materials needed for domestic production.

A satisfactory balance of payments on current account *plus* a sufficient surplus to provide for a flow of foreign investment *plus* sustained growth of the economy add up to the need for an even greater volume of exports than we have so far achieved. How can this be done?

EXPORT PERFORMANCE

Although we have stressed the very considerable progress which has been made during the post-war years in chasing an export target which itself has continuously shifted, it is still true that British exports have generally failed to grow at the rate of our major competitors. Between 1954 and 1960, for example, world manufactured exports rose by 77%; during the same period, British manufactured exports increased by only 38%.

To some extent we can attribute this to the liberalization of trade which has taken place over the last decade. Consumers in markets which were relatively tied to Britain in the highly discriminatory trading system of the immediately post-war period have since become free to experiment with alternative sources of supply. Losses due to the removal of trading restrictions do not carry any necessary implication that British exports have been relatively uncompetitive, but it is possible to argue, as the National Economic Development Council did in its report *Export Trends*, that the greater availability of goods has made foreign buyers more price-conscious and that

so far as export prices of manufacturers are concerned, there seems to have been both a rise in prices compared to other countries, and a relation between the rise in prices in particular countries and the rate of increase in their exports of manufactures.

Some confirmation that prices are important is given by the remarkable upsurge of British exports in 1963 when the economy emerged from a dose of deflation at a time when Western European countries were experiencing relatively severe inflation. But this peculiar combination of circumstances throws no light on whether British exports have in the past generally tended to be uncompetitive, and any firm conclusion in this respect is made difficult by the extreme unreliability of international comparisons of costs and prices.

Another school of thought suggests that the relative lack of success of British exports has been due to an inappropriate commodity structure. Certainly, it is true that before the war, British exports tended to be concentrated on products in which world trade was expanding least rapidly. Whether this has been so in more recent years, however, is highly dubious. In 1963 the National Institute of Economic and Social Research undertook a detailed analysis of the issue. The director of the project, Professor Barna, came to the devastating conclusion that

there is thus, over the whole field of trade in manufactures, a systematic relationship. The faster world demand is expanding for a product group, the more inferior is Britain's share.

However, the other members of the research team, using the same material but comparing the British record with that of eight other major countries rather than just the United States and West Germany, concluded that Britain's export pattern was only 'fractionally less fast-growing . . . than the "world" average' and that 'commodity pattern analysis does not go far to explain either Britain's falling share in world trade or her balance of payments weakness'.

Similarly, British trade may have been inhibited by its ties to traditional markets. Nineteenth- and early twentieth-century international trade mostly took the pattern of advanced industrial countries exporting manufactured goods to less-developed primary producers in exchange for foodstuffs and raw materials. With the spread of industrialization and the divergence in consumption levels of rich and poor countries, this very basic form of specialization has tended to give way to an international division of labour on a more sophisticated basis. The type of trade which is now most rapidly expanding is that between relatively advanced countries. Second fastest is that between other countries at roughly similar stages of development, with the trade between rich and poorer economies relatively stagnating.

In view of these trends, concentration on Commonwealth markets may go some way to explaining the relatively slow growth of British exports. Although the proportion is declining, some two-fifths of British trade in 1961 was still with Commonwealth countries. But, whereas during the period 1954–61 U.K. exports to the Commonwealth expanded by only 16%, sales to Western Europe meanwhile grew by 58%. Moreover, major rivals like the United States, Japan, and West Germany were all succeeding in increasing their exports to the Commonwealth very much faster and consequently reducing the British *share* of the market. Although this was perhaps primarily a reflection of the dismantlement of import controls and erosion, through time and bartering, of the system of Commonwealth tariff preferences, it does not augur well for the future – particularly when Britain similarly represents the most slowly growing market for Commonwealth exports.

It is also often claimed that even when goods are being sold in the right markets at the right prices, export sales are limited by poor design, quality, delivery dates, and general salesmanship. Although it is unfair to generalize from particular instances, the accumulated evidence suggests that there must be something in this argument. *The Economist* published in 1963 a series called 'Spies for Prosperity', in which it invited its foreign correspondents to submit examples of such failings in different parts of the world. The results make gloomy reading and leave the nasty impression that the fault may lie, as *The Economist* man in Austria said,

in the old British habit of regarding all foreigners as inferior. This is not seen as a conscious thought, but as an ingrained British habit of mind.

Even attempts to adopt a more cosmopolitan outlook have their dangers. The correspondent from Sweden wrote:

I cringe at the thought of any British manufacturer attempting to address Swedish customers in their own language. Indeed, some have tried, with grotesque results. . . .

But how can such a parochial attitude be overcome? It seems improbable that manufacturers can ever be imbued with the spirit of that rather ill-judged slogan 'Exporting is fun!' If it cannot be made fun, then policy must be directed towards making it a paying proposition. This, indeed, was the purpose of the emphasis in the fifties on restraining home demand, the official attitude being that dampening the domestic market would force producers to look abroad for new customers. That this is unlikely to be the effect now seems to be generally accepted. Manufacturers have always argued that success in export markets essentially rests on a thriving, cost-reducing home basis. Admittedly, an easy, protected home market is unlikely to induce ventures into more competitive foreign territory. But there are other ways of stimulating competition than by the deliberate creation of cost-increasing excess capacity. One possibility is to resort to devaluation. We argued in Chapter 3 that this would probably be beneficial to the balance of payments although it is admittedly difficult to predict its consequences very precisely. Moreover, it is perfectly permissible under the rules of the International Monetary Fund which provide for an alteration in the exchange rate of a currency when an economy's balance of payments is in 'fundamental disequilibrium'; it is not difficult to argue that this is precisely Britain's position today. Both

Conservative and Labour governments have, however, eschewed the use of devaluation as a possible way of dealing with the problem. This abhorrence of devaluation seems to have stemmed less from doubt about its technical efficacy than the notion that it would be an inappropriate policy for a country occupying such an important role in the international monetary system.

Devaluation or not, it is clear that a sustained increase in exports will not be achieved unless domestic prices can be restrained at least from rising faster than those of our rivals. In this respect our main hopes will have to be pinned on progress towards a national incomes policy. Again, since price is not the only consideration in improving export performances, measures are required which will more generally stimulate competitiveness among British sellers – both abroad and also in competing with imports at home. However, policies aimed, for example, at reducing restrictive practices or encouraging mobility of resources in the economy will have only long-term effects on efficiency. What happens to the balance of payments in the meantime? Do we forfeit growth for external stability until the economy is sufficiently adjusted to expand without straining its international payments position? Or are there any stopgap policies which can help to keep the economy moving while more fundamental adjustments are being made?

In this respect there are three general possibilities. The disturbing impact of growth on the balance of payments could be contained by (i) re-introducing some degree of control over the amount which we import, or (ii) cutting down on our present level of foreign commitments and hence the necessary balance of payments surplus which is required, or (iii) meeting balance of payments deficits during the adjustments period from our reserves and unexhausted borrowing rights.

We shall be considering these alternatives in the following sections, but at the same time we shall widen the discussion to consider some general issues of trade policy and Britain's position in the international financial system.

TRADE POLICY

In the world-wide depression of the nineteen-thirties most countries tried to maintain domestic employment by protecting their producers against foreign competition by means of (*a*) tariffs which raised the prices of imports above those of home produced goods, (*b*) import quotas setting limits on the quantity or value of imports which would be allowed in, or (*c*) exchange control which meant that importers had difficulty in obtaining the necessary foreign exchange to finance their operations.

Since the Second World War strenuous efforts have been made to remove these impediments to the free flow of world trade. In 1947 an attempt was made to set up an International Trade Organization to organize the breakdown of the barriers to trade. In fact, the I.T.O. was never established because the United States Congress refused to give its blessing, but in its place the negotiators managed to achieve a looser expression of their ideals in the form of the General Agreement on Tariffs and Trade. G.A.T.T. is a treaty arrangement (there are now forty-four full signatories) under which the members agree to negotiate trade concessions within a regulated framework; the most important rule is that liberalization must take place on a most-favoured-nation basis – that concessions negotiated between any G.A.T.T. countries must be automatically extended to all members.

A great deal has been achieved in the several series of G.A.T.T. negotiations which have so far taken place, and in October 1962 a major obstacle to further progress was removed by the United States Trade Expansion Act which gave the President powers to negotiate tariff concessions on a scale which he had up to then been denied. In fact, he is now free to reduce tariffs on nearly 90% of imports into the U.S.A. The way was thus cleared for the major bout of G.A.T.T. negotiations known as the 'Kennedy Round'. This was an attempt to hurry along the process of trade liberalization. Rather than lengthily negotiate concessions product by product, it was proposed that members should agree to a general linear cut of 50% in *all* import duties. However, although the impact of such an 'across the board' reduction in trade barriers will have more far-reaching effects than previous rounds, the process certainly did not prove to be any more expeditious. As the Common Market countries (and particularly the French) pointed out, a linear cut was unfair inasmuch as many of the U.S. tariffs were to begin with very much higher than elsewhere. Even to cut them by half would not therefore reduce them to a level at which foreign producers could competitively enter the American market. The negotiations were consequently prolonged over the question of lopping off certain of the U.S. tariffs *before* the 'across the board' reductions could be agreed to.

Two Arguments against Free Trade

Although we are all happy enough when other countries reduce their trade barriers and make it easier for us to export to them, many people feel rather uneasy when *we* expose ourselves to more foreign competition. Is it not rather unnecessarily asking for trouble?

1. If tariffs are reduced on imports from other mature industrial economies like the United States or Germany, there is clearly the danger that some of our own producers will be forced to the wall. In these circumstances, are we not prepared to 'Buy British', even if it does mean paying a little more? At least we should thereby be ensuring employment for British workers, and keeping the profits for ourselves.

2. If, on the other hand, imports are allowed in from less developed economies like India or Hong Kong, do we not expose our own producers to 'unfair competition'? Goods from these countries are cheap because of the appallingly low wages which are paid there, and it seems inequitable that British firms, just because they pay a good living wage, should be made to suffer as a result. Then again, to buy goods from low-wage countries is almost to encourage employers there to employ sweated labour. Perhaps if we boycotted them things would improve?

Neither of these arguments makes very much sense, at least in present conditions. In Chapter 3, we showed that the whole point of international trade was to allow countries to specialize in production for which they were best suited. Tariffs, by distorting the real underlying pattern of costs, may therefore stifle trade which would otherwise have been beneficial to all countries concerned. The only case in which it is economically reasonable for us to buy from inefficient home producers rather than from their more efficient foreign competitors is if, as a result, some of our own resources become permanently unemployed. Provided, on the other hand, that foreign competition merely stimulates movement of workers and capital into more productive lines, all that we need worry about is ensuring that these shifts take place as rapidly and painlessly as possible.

The arguments against allowing imports from cheap labour economies is even less convincing. Once again, we showed in Chapter 3 that the basis of international trade is that different countries have different endowments of the factors of production – land, labour, and capital. We import bananas from areas which are endowed with more favourable climatic conditions, we export motor-cars because we possess highly developed capital equipment. Why, therefore, should we refuse imports from countries whose one great advantage is their plentiful supply of labour? (We should also be very careful in using this argument against India in case the United States, for example, should then use it against us, and refuse *our* exports on the ground that they come from a low-wage country!)

However, although very substantial benefits can and do accrue from trade between countries specializing according to their comparative costs of production, we should not jump to the conclusion that *any* move towards freer trade should therefore be unequivocally welcomed. Dogmatic enthusiasm for freer trade may be particularly misplaced when liberalization takes place within regional trade blocs rather than on a world-wide basis. This is because (*a*) some of the apparent gains from such blocs may in fact be nothing of the sort, and (*b*), to the extent that there are real gains, they may aggravate rather than moderate the growing gap between the rich and poor countries of the world.

Regional Trade Blocs

1. *The European Common Market* In January 1963 British hopes and fears, which had been so violently excited during the 1962 negotiations, were finally quenched by the French dismissal of the U.K. application to join the European Economic Community (the E.E.C.). Now, in 1967, fresh overtures are being made. From an economic point of view, just how much does it matter whether or not Britain gets into the Common Market?

The E.E.C. is an example of a customs union (although it is

also a great deal more if trade liberalization and 'harmonization' of social and economic policies are, as the founders of the Common Market intended, tentative steps towards full political integration). In accordance with the G.A.T.T. rules for setting up customs unions, all obstacles to trade between the Six – France, West Germany, Italy, Belgium, Holland, and Luxembourg – are to be completely eliminated; meanwhile, the varied tariffs against non-members which at present exist will be adjusted towards a common external tariff which will be, on average, no higher than the former level of protection. It is now expected that these changes will be completed well ahead of schedule; the final tariff cuts are due to be made in 1968.

One way in which economic benefits can be expected to arise from the E.E.C. is that the removal of internal barriers to trade facilitates a re-allocation of resources according to real relative costs. If, for example, German coal can be produced at lower cost in terms of resources than Belgian, but was over-priced in the Belgian market because of high tariffs, removal of those tariffs will lead to increased imports of German coal and a freeing of Belgian resources for use in more productive lines. Although this may initially look rather like a loss to the Belgian economy as their inefficient producers are displaced, there will be genuine gains to the Community as a whole – providing that redundant workers and capital in Belgium are fairly easily shifted to more productive occupations.

However, although there may thus be genuine gains from 'trade creation', there is also the danger that a customs union will cause losses because of 'trade *diversion*'. The freeing of internal trade coupled with adjustments towards a common external tariff may lead to shifts in demand in favour of Community producers and at the expense of outsiders. This is just the sort of change which commonsense would label a benefit but is it really so if the effect is to make it possible for high-cost domestic producers to oust *lower*-cost foreign competitors from the market? Such a switch to less efficient sources of supply must surely be regarded as a loss item in the balance sheet.

Much-quoted as evidence of the success of the Common Market are statistics showing the great increase of trade between members since its inception (by over 60% during the first four years, for example). Such figures have, however, to be interpreted cautiously, and, quite apart from the fact that they include trade diversion as well as trade creation, we cannot regard them as a straightforward index of the benefits resulting from freer trade. An initial problem is to decide how much of the increase can be attributed to the removal of trade barriers and how much would have taken place anyway. There was, after all, a similar burst of intra-trade earlier in the fifties, and it is at least plausible to argue, as some have done, that the reduction of tariffs was made possible by the fact that trade was autonomously growing so rapidly rather than that trade increased *because* they were reduced. Again, freer trade only leads to more economic utilization of resources if the underlying differences in comparative costs are faithfully reflected in producer prices. This may not be the case because, for example, of widespread monopolistic elements in industry which may distort prices from comparative costs just as much as import duties do.

Moreover, the gains from increased trade may, after a point, become quite small. We have already stressed that benefits arise only to the extent that it becomes possible to substitute low-cost imported goods for higher-cost domestic output, thus releasing resources for more economic use. If a tariff of 10%, for example, led to British consumers buying a home product costing £10 rather than an imported equivalent which without the tariff could have sold at £9 10s. 0d., the gain from removing import duties amounts to only 10s. per unit sold. Estimates made of the probable effect of British entry into the Common Market suggest that the impact on British national income of eliminating tariffs would amount only to a fraction of 1%. Quite possibly, a gain of so small an order would not in itself be considered worth the risk of increased balance of payments difficulties which might also result.

However, there may be other considerations, apart from the classical benefits reputed to follow from freer trade, which also have to be taken into account. It is argued that only the establishment of a large economic unit like the E.E.C. can extend members' markets to a size which makes it possible for the economies of large-scale production to be fully exploited. Certainly there are industries – like electronics, chemicals or aero-engineering –

where the technology of both research and production calls for massive scale which cannot be based on relatively small domestic markets like the British. However, the Anglo-French Concord project shows that technical collaboration may well be extended across market frontiers; for many goods, too, the mass production argument is based on the doubtful premiss that there is a similar degree of conformism in European consumer tastes as there is in the U.S.A. or U.S.S.R. What the heads think may be as important as how many heads there are.

Other proponents of closer economic ties with Europe rest their case on the shock effects which entry into the Common Market would imply for the British economy. Relatively sudden exposure to competition may lead to an accelerated breakdown of outdated restrictive practices and a widening of business horizons. The extent of this 'competitive jolt' would, however, depend on the ability of the E.E.C. authorities to prevent extensions of international cartelization which might have stifled competition at birth; although the executive body, the E.E.C. Commission, is armed with considerable powers in this respect, it has not so far secured the support of national governments which is a necessary basis for effectively using them.

The positive economic benefits which Britain might have derived from freer trade as such if we join the Common Market are probably not very substantial. On the other hand, entry would urgently require a new look at policies as diverse as those relating to taxation, labour law, the financing of social services, agricultural support, and the sterling area. One element in the cost of *staying out* lies in the lesser likelihood that any such fundamental re-examination will otherwise take place. Also to be taken into account is the fact that as E.E.C. trade becomes freer and the common external tariff is erected, British exporters will be facing an increasing degree of discrimination against them. For example, when the Common Market is fully established, German motor-car manufacturers will be able to sell their cars in France free of duty; British exports, on the other hand, will have to meet the external tariff of 30%. A competitive disadvantage of this order must ultimately have the effect of dampening down British exports to Europe. That this has not so far happened is due to the exceptionally rapid rise in total demand of the Six.

All that we have done here is to look very briefly at some of the economic implications of joining the Common Market or staying outside. It can hardly need emphasizing that whether or not we join Europe is a question involving issues far beyond these.

2. *The European Free Trade Association* E.F.T.A. is an agreement between Britain, Sweden, Denmark, Norway, Finland, Switzerland, Portugal, and Austria. Once again, there is provision for elimination of internal trade barriers, but E.F.T.A. is an altogether looser form of organization than the E.E.C. Members are free to set their own external tariffs, agricultural commodities are mostly excluded from tariff cuts, and there are no proposals for unifying the Association's economic policies. From the outset most of the members of E.F.T.A. have regarded it as a stepping-stone to union with the Six rather than as a genuine long-term alternative; the schedule for dismantling trade barriers is kept in line with that of the Common Market so as to minimize the necessary adjustments should a *rapprochement* ever become feasible.

There are a number of reasons why E.F.T.A. cannot be regarded as a formidable rival to the E.E.C. Several of its members do far more trade with the Six than between themselves and can therefore ill afford to be excluded from the Common Market. It is very doubtful if Austria, for example, could afford to stay outside this bloc indefinitely. Then again, the potential gains from freer trade are much less significant in E.F.T.A. than in the E.E.C. This is for two reasons. Firstly, the level of tariffs in the E.F.T.A. countries was much lower to start with so that the impact of their removal is likely to be correspondingly less. Secondly, the E.F.T.A. economies are much more complementary than competitive; no major redistribution of resources will therefore result from freer trade.

Rich and Poor Countries: North *v.* South

The most serious of the criticisms which have been directed at the European trade blocs is that they are essentially 'rich men's clubs' which facilitate trade between advanced economies but do nothing to assist the plight of the poorer half of the world. With regard to the E.E.C., this is not altogether fair. Associated to the Community are all the ex-dependencies of the full members, and there is provision both for generous investment by the Community in the poorer countries and for relatively free entry for most of their products. But most of these ex-dependencies are essentially primary producers and therefore complementary to the Six themselves. When it is a question of whether or not to allow cheap manufactured goods into the Common Market, policy is a great deal less liberal.

Britain, on the other hand, is one of the freest markets in the world for the produce of undeveloped countries and it would be tragic if part of the price for entry into the Common Market is imposition of stricter import controls on, say, the manufactures of India, Pakistan, and Hong Kong – particularly after the government has so far resisted the demand for such measures from home producers. Even if we manage to persuade the Community to accept the Commonwealth on similar terms to its own ex-colonial associates (not a likely possibility), the fact remains that a large part of the poorer half of the world lies outside the British and E.E.C. ex-dependencies.

G.A.T.T.-type negotiations have resulted in extremely rapid growth of trade between advanced economies. Meanwhile, undeveloped countries have found that the demand for basic commodities has grown far more slowly, and that, when they have attempted to diversify by moving into the processing and manufacturing stages of production, the problem has been how to sell their output in face of continued resistance from their richer customers. In this respect, the 1964 United Nations Conference on Trade and Development (U.N.C.T.A.D.) is of major significance. Although relatively little has actually been done as a result of U.N.C.T.A.D., this was nevertheless the first time that the poorer countries, the Seventy-Five as they became known, had united in a pressure group to demand that something *should* be done to reduce obstacles to trade with rich countries and pave the way for faster development.

Undoubtedly, measures along these lines are far and away the greatest contribution which the rich North can now make towards solving the appalling problems of the poor South. What we have to recognize is that it is no use making grandiose pronouncements about a Development Decade, or pledging 1% of our national incomes towards aid to less-developed economies if at the same time we make it difficult or impossible for them to compete in international markets. 'Trade not aid' may not be a wholly true slogan, but what is certain is that aid *without* trade will not take us very far.

Imports and Growth

Perhaps at this stage we can now return to one of the more parochial questions which we set out to answer in this section. If the result of faster growth in the British ecomony is to cause, at least in the short run, acute balance of payments difficulties, should we reduce the pressure by resorting to restriction of imports? In view of what we have just been saying about the benefits of freer trade and the substantial progress which has been made in this direction, such a policy might seem highly retrograde. By cutting imports, would we not be achieving higher growth at the expense of others – and, ultimately, also reducing their ability to buy from us?

Everything here depends on the sort of choice which has to be faced. Suppose, for example, that if we do not control imports, balance of payments difficulties will force the authorities to reduce the rate of growth by dampening down domestic demand. Then imports will fall anyway – and perhaps by considerably more than would have been necessary if they had been more directly controlled. At least import control would have the advantage that cuts could be made in less-essential imports rather than across the board. And since these would be mainly the products of more advanced economies, poorer countries would not be made to share the burden of slower British growth as they so far have.

In practice, however, it might be difficult to persuade other world traders, in the present G.A.T.T. context, that *some* import controls are better than a general reduction resulting from deflationary measures. The difficulty was illustrated by the outcry when Britain imposed a temporary 15% surcharge on a wide range of imports to meet the balance of payments crisis in October 1964. However, by the time that the first cut in the surcharge was announced in February 1965, there were signs

BALANCE SHEET FOR STERLING DECEMBER 1962

Assets (£m.)		Liabilities (£m.)	
		Short-term (Official)	
Gold and foreign reserves		'Sterling balances' (U.K. Treasury Bills, notes, government bonds, etc.)	2,391
		Temporary deposits with, and loans to, local authorities	71
			2,462
		Short-term (Private)	
U.K. banks' external claims in:		'Sterling balances' (accounts in commercial banks, etc.)	1,475
Non-sterling currencies	1,010	Loans to H.P. houses	105
Sterling and sterling area currencies	894	U.K. banks' external liabilities in:	
Other U.K. external claims in:		Non-sterling currencies	1,038
Non-sterling currencies	(200)	Sterling area currencies	120
Sterling area currencies	n.a.		2,738
	2,104		

Long-term (Official)

Official lending	543	Loans to the U.K.	1,930
Subscriptions to international financial organizations (except I.M.F.)	141	Overseas holdings of British government stocks (except those shown above)	(600)
Government holdings of non-sterling securities	(385)	Overseas holdings of U.K. local authority mortgages and stocks	(110)
	1,069		2,640

Long-term (Private)

Portfolio investments	(3,000)	Portfolio investments in U.K. companies	(735)
Direct investments (except oil, insurance, and banking)	(3,500)	Direct investments (except oil, insurance, and banking)	(1,400)
Net assets abroad of U.K. oil companies	(1,100)	Net assets in U.K. of overseas oil companies	(700)
		Other identified	(350)
	(7,950)		(2,835)

United Kingdom's I.M.F. Position

U.K. subscription to the I.M.F.	696	I.M.F. sterling holdings (cash and non-interest-bearing notes)	517
TOTAL OF IDENTIFIED ITEMS	12,821	TOTAL OF IDENTIFIED ITEMS	11,192

Figures in brackets are precarious estimates and/or known to be incomplete. Several items, e.g. direct investments of banks and companies, individual holdings of real estate, and trade credit, are omitted from both sides because they are not available.

that the argument was being understood and accepted – at least by our E.F.T.A. partners.

BRITAIN IN THE INTERNATIONAL FINANCIAL SYSTEM

So far we have been treating the balance of payments as an essentially insular problem. However, much of the official concern about the balance of payments stems from the fact that Britain acts in the capacity of an international banker with which many other countries make deposits (sometimes representing the whole of their international reserves). The pound sterling is used as an international currency for settling debts between economies with quite different internal monies. For its part, Britain tries to maintain a regular net outflow of long-term development capital for users of the system.

Some idea of the international ramifications of sterling can be obtained from the attempt by the Bank of England, in the March 1964 issue of its quarterly bulletin, to draw up a comprehensive balance sheet of Britain's external assets and liabilities. This is reproduced on pages 226–7. The figures suggest that the U.K. is substantially indebted both on short-term account (minus £2,094 million) and as a result of the long-term lending and borrowing operations of the official sector (minus £1,571 million). However, private long-term overseas investment has been well in excess of similar investment by foreigners in Britain and, when this is added to the balance sheet, Britain emerges as a net creditor in the world financial system to the extent of £1,629 million.

The Bank of England itself was anxious to point out that drawing up a balance sheet of this kind is not an exercise of great practical significance. On the one hand, such a gigantic task necessarily involves a certain amount of inspired guessing, and many of the estimates are therefore 'precarious' or 'known to be incomplete'. Secondly, as can be seen from the accounts, the assets and liabilities are hotch-potch totals of everything from perfectly liquid money balances to solid investment in factory buildings. From a policy point of view, what matters is not so much the totals themselves as how they are made up and the relationship between the different parts.

The Strength of Sterling

We have already shown that faster growth in the British economy will tend, at least for a while, to cause imports to rise more rapidly than exports. Unless net invisibles fortuitously increase to fill the widening trade gap, this will mean that the balance of payments on current account will move into deficit. Providing that such a deterioration is not expected to be permanent, it can be met by falling back on reserves. What we are concerned with now is the extent to which U.K. reserves provide a cushion for balance of payments weakness in view of the likely calls which can be made on them.

The usual basis for analysing the problem is to compare two totals – the amount of gold and foreign exchange held by the British authorities (the Exchange Equalization Account), and sterling which is held by non-residents in the form of short-term assets such as Treasury Bills or bank accounts. If these are taken to represent Britain's immediately mobilizable reserves and immediately realizable liabilities, the position certainly looks decidedly unhealthy:

	August 1937 (£m.)	*December 1945* (£m.)	*December 1962* (£m.)
U.K. gold and foreign exchange	605	610	1,002
'Sterling balances'	476	3,694	3,866

Whereas before the war Britain's reserves were well in excess of its sterling balances, the war brought about a colossal rise in short-term liabilities while reserves remained at about the same level (in money terms at least). Sterling balances rose because, with the British economy geared to war production, we could only pay for imports by giving claims against ourselves. These balances, therefore, to a large extent represented pent-up demand which would have to be met in the post-war period. By and large, this was done, and the sterling balances of today are of a rather different nature. But the short-term assets: liabilities ratio has not markedly improved.

For a number of reasons, however, comparison of reserves and sterling balances is an inaccurate and over-simplified index of the economy's ability to ride balance-of-payments weakness.

To see why this is so, we will look a little more carefully at each side of the account.

1. *Reserves* All that we have so far included under the heading 'short-term assets' are the quantities of gold and foreign exchange held by the British authorities. The basis for this, as a glance at the Bank of England's balance sheet for sterling shows, is that nearly all the other asset items are either fairly illiquid or not under the direct control of the authorities. In both cases it would be extremely difficult to mobilize them to counter excessive pressures on the pound.

However, in addition to these reserves, there are a number of secondary lines of defence against an attack on sterling: (*a*) In an emergency (mostly at the Fund's discretion) our right to buy foreign exchange from the I.M.F. can be exercised and nearly double the resources available in our own reserves; (*b*) Britain also has a claim on the supplementary pool of foreign exchange provided by the ten-nation Paris Club agreement; and, (*c*), further assistance might be forthcoming from central banks in other countries. The scope of cooperation between central banks was shown in the November 1964 sterling crisis when the British government raised credits of $3,000 million within twenty-four hours from sources other than the I.M.F.

Admittedly, it would not be reasonable to include these as British external 'assets' – since to use them would involve a corresponding deterioration in our liabilities position. But if we are interested, not in mere book-keeping, but in finding out what resources are available for countering pressures on the pound, exclusive attention on the item 'Gold and foreign exchange reserves' is very misleading.

2. *Pressures on the Reserves* We now turn to consideration of what it is that the pound has to be defended *against*. Sterling is under pressure when the number of pounds being sold (for foreign exchange) exceeds the number of pounds being bought (with foreign exchange). In Chapter 3 we saw that such pressures could result from both current trading and capital movements.

Most obviously, calls on reserves can arise from Britain itself having a current payments deficit. However, similar effects can result from the trading operations of the group of countries known as the 'Sterling Area'.

The Sterling Area (which still consists chiefly of Commonwealth countries) originated in the naturally close ties between Britain and its nineteenth-century Empire. A number of monetary links were gradually forged. Sterling came to be accepted as a means of settling debts arising from transactions even when the U.K. was not one of the parties involved; it was also generally adopted as a basic for domestic currencies – sometimes, indeed, overstamped pound-notes were themselves the medium of exchange in colonial territories; lacking developed financial structures of their own, these countries used the British money market as an outlet for their surplus liquid funds; London was looked upon as a major source of long-term capital and wide use was made of its unrivalled insurance, banking, and shipping services.

The Sterling Area did not become known as such until, with the breakdown of the Gold Standard in the 1930s, a group of economies preferred to align themselves with the pound. The association was a loose one with no formal rules of membership. It was merely that certain closely linked economies found greater interest in maintaining exchange stability with Britain than the rest of the world, and permitted relatively free flows of trade, capital, and labour to continue at a time when the world economic climate was highly restrictionist.

A further distinguishing feature of the Sterling Area is that members tend to pool their foreign reserves in London. Given that Britain was a major outlet for liquid funds and that most of their trade was transacted in sterling, it was convenient for the rest of the Sterling Area to sell in the British foreign exchange market any foreign currencies which they earned, and to hold their reserves in the form of sterling balances – on the understanding, of course, that these pounds could always be converted into foreign exchange should the need arise. This was not very likely with the pre-war triangular pattern of trade: its normal surplus with the non-sterling world was used by the rest of the Sterling Area to meet its traditional trading deficit with Britain. At times in the post-war period, however, the rest of the sterling bloc has *also* incurred net deficits with the outside world and therefore reinforced rather than dammed the drain on reserves.

Balance of payments swings can easily amount to £300 or £400 million in a year. These, as the Radcliffe Committee commented, can hardly be regarded as very large changes in comparison with total foreign transactions on current account which is currently in excess of £10,000 million but they are far from negligible when compared with reserves that have generally been less than £1,000 million.

An even more serious threat to reserves comes from capital movements. There are a number of reasons why foreign holdings of sterling may be run down. Firstly, sterling assets may be drawn on to finance accelerated development; this, for example, was the case of India which systematically reduced its sterling balances during the immediately post-war period. Secondly, funds held in London because of attractive interest inducements may be withdrawn when the differentials between the major financial centres is altered. Finally, and most alarming of all, there is the prospect of capital flowing out for speculative reasons – because of lack of confidence that the external value of the pound can be maintained.

However, it is not good enough to regard short-term sterling balances as a measure of the potential pressure on sterling from capital movements. The fact that large quantities of sterling are held in a liquid form means that they *could* be withdrawn easily. But they are not necessarily held in this way because they are *likely* to be withdrawn. A large part of sterling balances is made up of working balances and minimal reserves of foreign banks, firms, and governments, and is no more likely to be reduced than similar British holdings abroad (shown on the assets side of the balance sheet for sterling). Sterling balances no longer represent the pent-up demand which they did just after the war.

The potential pressure on the pound is none the less enormous – although less than a simple reserve/liability statement might suggest. Swings in the balance of payments plus capital movements (which may largely be the 'leads and lags' we discussed in Chapter 3) can add up to a movement out of sterling which could soon eat up our meagre reserves of gold and foreign exchange. However, these can be supplemented by drawings on the I.M.F. (though in 1967 these are largely exhausted) and finally by co-operation from the major central banks. With massive external support, it looks therefore as though the pound *can* always be saved. But is it worth saving? The cost of maintaining sterling as an international currency must be measured in terms both of the greater frequency with which balance of payments crises are likely to recur and of the loss of autonomy which we suffer in selecting policies to deal with them.

Whenever the growth rate of the economy is increased, imports tend to grow faster than exports. Expansionists argue that the consequent balance of payments difficulties will only be temporary and that if only the growth rate is maintained regardless of the external imbalance then exports will ultimately rise to the necessary level. Whether this theory is right or wrong we shall never know, given the present position of sterling in the world financial system: it is not possible to test it. For as soon as any weakness in Britain's current account is detected a 'confidence' crisis begins to take shape which will ultimately require resort to raising external support for the pound. And this support cannot be used as a buffer to enable domestic expansion to continue unimpeded: the price of such support is always that the British government subject the economy to measures which will immediately restore the external balance – i.e. reduce the level of demand and activity to the point at which imports are reduced by the required amount.

If, as many economists now believe, the balance of payments is in 'fundamental disequilibrium' control of domestic demand is anyway a necessary element in the solution of the problem. Only in this way can resources be released for increasing the proportion of output going to exports or import-saving. We have argued that a major factor in ensuring that such a switch *does* occur is by making British goods more price-competitive. Here again, the international ramifications of sterling mean that certain policy possibilities like devaluation or import controls have to be excluded because of their unacceptability to Britain's foreign creditors; the government is forced to rely on working out an effective incomes policy as the whole solution rather than just one part of it. Similarly, the scope for relieving pressure on the balance of payments by reducing the outflow of long-term capital is severely limited by the expectation that Britain will continue to play its traditional role of banker to the Sterling Area.

A good case can therefore be made out that the British economy is suffering from over-exposure. Our balance of payments is not a problem *because* the pound is used as an international currency. But the necessity to maintain a 'strong pound' both aggravates any underlying weakness and severely limits the number of ways in which it can be dealt with. However, to agree that this is so is easier than to see what steps can be taken to reduce Britain's commitment. Even negotiated 'funding' of sterling balances – voluntary agreement by holders effectively to lengthen the British debt by accepting repayment of them over an agreed number of years – would be a gamble replacing the possibility of a severe drain on reserves by a definite commitment to repay liabilities in regular instalments.

Solutions such as this, anyway, miss the point that many holders of sterling do not *want* their balances repaid. Sterling liabilities represent an important part of a stock of world liquidity which is already only precariously adequate to maintain the present growth of world trade. The British assets/liabilities problem and attempts to solve it must therefore be viewed in this wider context.

WORLD LIQUIDITY

Since 1938 the volume of world trade has increased about four or five times. Meanwhile, certain traditional methods of meeting balance of payments difficulties – like drastic domestic deflation or beggar-my-neighbour trade policies – have become very much less acceptable. For both of these reasons the level of international *reserves* which most countries have thought 'safe' has very substantially risen over the last twenty-five years.

This increased demand for liquidity has only been very partially met by an increase of 50% in the stock of gold used for international payments and an outflow from the United States redistributing it more evenly among the leading trading nations. Much more important has been the greater reliance which has been placed on the use of certain *national* currencies for financing international transactions. We have already noted that United Kingdom sterling liabilities have increased seven-fold since 1938. An even greater expansion, both absolutely and proportionately, has taken place in United States short-term liabilities. The point bears repeating that, however embarrassing these debts may be to the countries concerned, they are a vital element in the present mechanism of international payments.

Using national currencies for international payments has a number of disadvantages – both for the countries which do so and for those whose currencies happen to be used. Holders, for example, of dollars or pounds (the chief 'key currencies') court the danger that part of their reserves will be wiped out as a result of alterations in the exchange rate. Realization that this is so, on the other hand, throws an often unwanted responsibility on the centre countries supplying the additional reserves to *maintain* existing exchange rates; at the same time, unfortunately, this is made a much more difficult task because of the greater pressures to which they are exposed by speculative interswitching of holdings from one currency to another.

Quite apart from these drawbacks, it seems doubtful whether the expedient of using national currencies for international payments can anyway be much extended. At the present time, world trade is growing at over 6% a year – well in excess of the annual 2% addition to the monetary stock or gold. If the present ratio of reserves to trade is to be maintained (and this is the least that can be required since there are very few countries which would consider even their present level of reserves to be adequate), what is to fill the gap? British short-term liabilities already greatly exceed liquid assets and, although the United States assets/liabilities position remains much more favourable than that of Britain, further liquidity creation will be limited by lack of confidence, both internally and externally. Any attempt by the U.S. authorities to allow their liabilities to increase still further is likely to be self-defeating in that it will cause renewed doubt about the stability of the dollar. Nor can we be very optimistic about currencies other than the pound and dollar being more extensively used. A proliferation of domestic currencies on the international scene would merely serve to increase speculative movements of funds between them; it could, in the end, even lead to a breakdown of the world monetary system on the lines of 1931.

Since the centre countries not unnaturally view even the present extent of their liabilities as much as a problem to be solved as a contribution towards facilitating the growth of world trade, perhaps the time has come to restore gold to some of its former international glory. Why has the world monetary gold stock been increasing so slowly? It is largely due to the fact that its price has

Economic Policies

been held stable since before the war by the willingness of the
U.S. Treasury to buy and sell unlimited quantities at a fixed price.
An obvious candidate solution to the world liquidity problem is
therefore an increase in the price of gold. This would simultaneously raise the present value of reserves held in the form of
gold, and stimulate both gold output and the proportion of that
output used for monetary purposes. There are, however, serious
snags involved in this approach. The benefit of the initial increase
in liquidity would be distributed according to existing gold
holdings, those countries most in need of larger reserves being the
ones who would gain relatively least. The present mal-distribution
of international reserves would thus be crystallized – particularly
as there would be an inherent discrimination against those
countries which presently hold their reserves primarily in the form
of foreign exchange (which, in particular, happen to be the less-
developed economies most pressed for reserves). Moreover, the
danger would exist that, when the price of gold had once been
altered after innumerable declarations that such a course would
never be taken, it would be difficult to avoid speculation against
further changes in its price – which might, in fact, prove necessary
to ensure that the amount of metal dug from holes in the ground
was just appropriate to avoid a deflationary drag on the development of world trade.

The fact is that neither national currencies *nor* gold are really
satisfactory means of financing international transactions. The
tremendous expansion of the major economies which has occurred since the nineteenth century would undoubtedly have been
inhibited if their domestic monetary systems had continued to
be rigidly tied to gold, and if regional currencies had continued
to circulate. This deflationary pressure was only avoided, as we
described in Chapter 2, by breaking the link with gold through
the development of fractional reserve banking which allowed
expansion of the means of payment at a rate which the authorities
considered necessary for the development of the economy. It
is being increasingly recognized that if world trade is not to be
restrained by serious liquidity shortage similar principles must be
applied at an international level.

International Monetary Reform

We have already said something about the working of the International Monetary Fund. Its contribution towards meeting the rising demand for world liquidity has been considerable, particularly during the last decade; increases in quotas, the supplementary Paris Club agreement to provide a secondary line of reserve, and the development of lending arrangements between central banks have all helped at least to postpone the impact of inadequate international reserves. All these are, however, only methods of increasing the velocity of a constant stock of liquidity, and do nothing to ensure that reserves increase automatically to the level dictated by trade and confidence. The usefulness of the I.M.F. is limited, in particular, by the fact that its quotas can be increased only after complicated re-negotiation, and that a large part of its currency holdings are anyway in a form not likely to be much, if ever, demanded.

The most radical of the suggestions which have been put forward for preventing a world liquidity shortage therefore envisage transforming the I.M.F. into a genuine international bank with the power actually to create liquidity. Since it could not create gold or national currencies, the implication of this proposal is the introduction of a new unit for international payments. Keynes, in the early forties, suggested that it might be known as *bancor*, which would exist only as book entries at the I.M.F. If, for example, Britain had a balance of payments deficit with the United States to the tune of £100 million, the U.S. account with the I.M.F. would be credited with a similar amount of bancor and the U.K. account debited correspondingly (each national currency being related to bancor as at present it is to gold).

Centralization of international payments in a clearing union of this kind and the introduction of a purely international unit of account would in itself help to reduce the need for reserves by moderating some of the pressures on them which arise from speculation about the exchange rate of key currencies or the price of gold; countries would also have to worry less about the *form* in which payments have to be made. But the basic problem would remain of whether the total of bancor accounts represented a stock of world liquidity sufficient to avoid the necessity for premature deflationary measures by deficit countries, which might unnecessarily slow down the rate at which trade was increasing.

In this respect a country's international reserves may be thought of as comprising two elements. Firstly, there is a 'bedrock' level – a stock for meeting unforeseen contingencies – and all possible measures will be taken to prevent them falling below this; and secondly, there are relatively 'free' reserves to be used as a buffer against normal swings in the balance of payments. If the level of reserves remains constant while trade increases, free reserves may become inadequate to meet the now larger but still 'normal' drains upon them. As a result, the extent of 'temporary' balance of payments deficits which can be allowed without interference with the development of the domestic economy is reduced; remedial deflationary action must be taken sooner. Similar effects follow if there is a rise in the bedrock level of reserves which is thought necessary; since the 'adequacy' of reserves is essentially a subjective assessment, fear of a major disruption of the international payments system, or realization that a general liquidity shortage actually exists or might arise in the future, may itself engender a demand for higher levels of reserves *now*.

Radical reformers of the world monetary system argue that these pressures could be overcome by giving the I.M.F. the power to make additions to the stock of international reserves sufficient to meet the demands arising from increasing trade or 'confidence crises'. Internal economic development was only possible because the banking system learned how to create 'unbacked' deposits to supplement limited supplies of currencies. As we emphasized in Chapter 2, this process did not itself create new *wealth*. But, by making existing wealth more liquid, it helped to mobilize resources into a form which could facilitate further growth. In exactly the same way one method of preventing the growth of world trade from being inhibited by inadequacy of reserves would be to give the I.M.F. similar powers. At the present time the I.M.F. merely enables a fixed stock of gold and currencies to be used more effectively; if, for example, Britain buys dollars from the Fund, the supply of dollars available for other members is correspondingly reduced. It is argued that what is now required is that the Fund should have the right to *create* additional bancor deposits.

Proponents of fundamental reforms themselves differ about how this should be done. An astonishing multiplicity of possible schemes have now been put forward by individual economists and groups of experts. For the uninitiated it is difficult enough to distinguish between them, let alone choose. All that we have done here is to illustrate some general principles of reform. But what degree of centralization of reserves would be sufficient, desirable, or practicable? How could the I.M.F. best be transformed into a liquidity-creator – by its taking over holdings of key currencies in exchange for bancor accounts, or by an initial distribution of credit to the particularly pressed underdeveloped countries? Would the extent of credit creation be at the discretion of the Fund, or would it be limited by a pre-arranged formula to the rate at which world trade expanded?

Despite its obvious attractions, the idea of basically over-hauling the world monetary system is still regarded with considerable suspicion by bankers and governments. This is partly due to a fear that creation of additional international reserves would stimulate inflationary tendencies throughout the world; it also stems from a reluctance to contemplate a loss of autonomy on the scale which would be implied by the operations of a radically reformed Fund. On the other hand, a policy of doing nothing will probably have even less acceptable consequences, and even this very brief analysis of world monetary problems may serve to illustrate the danger of thinking that the British (and, *a fortiori*, the American) balance of payments difficulties can be solved in isolation. It must be recognized that unilateral attempts by the centre countries to achieve greater strength by devaluation, deflation, or international withdrawal may themselves hasten the appearance of a severe liquidity crisis which has so far only been avoided by piecemeal and decidedly second-best expedients.

CONCLUSION

THE aim of this book has been to give some general impression of how the economy works rather than to offer a systematic critique of economic theories or policies. Conclusions may therefore seem somewhat out of place. However, it may be useful to end by drawing together certain threads of argument which have appeared at various points in the analysis.

There are plenty of reasons for thinking that the recent performance of the British economy could be bettered, and no shortage of suggestions about how it could be done. On the other hand, the system has probably never worked better than it has been doing in the recent past. The national income is growing, spasmodically and too slowly for many people, but nevertheless at a rate which was not emulated even during the Industrial Revolution. At the same time we have succeeded in stabilizing the economy to a substantial degree. Full employment or near-full employment has now been sustained for a longer period than ever before; unemployment continues on a local basis, but even here there are signs that we are learning how to deal with the problem. There has been less success in establishing price stability, and the balance of payments is still a matter for frequent concern – although even the measure of stability which we do have has been won only by a massive adjustment of the economy from its pre-war structure.

One thing with which I hope non-economists would agree is that at least part of the credit for this impressive achievement must go to economists. A popular criticism of economic theory is that it is up in the clouds, assuming away all reality and therefore having no practical relevance. 'It's all theory, you know. A month in my factory and you'd know more economics than you'll learn in a hundred years from books . . .' is a jibe which a lot of people who have endured an elementary course on economics would probably endorse. And there is a certain amount of justification in this view. Economists far too seldom cast their theories in a form which enables them to be tested in the real world. But the fact remains that a good deal of recent economic

240

thinking has now filtered through to policy-makers and provided them with a basis for dealing with our economic problems.

The point is that we can rely too much on common sense and practical experience to provide the answers. Common sense suggests, as it did in the thirties, that a firm faced with falling demand can retrieve its position by cutting wage-costs. Economic theory shows that a policy of this kind, if generally applied during a trade depression, will merely cause total demand in the economy to fall as incomes are consequently reduced. Common sense might lead us to believe that the government should behave just like any other well-regulated household, carefully balancing its income and expenditure; economics reveals that the result of such prudence will almost always be fluctuations in the level of activity in the economy. Refusing to import from a low-wage country seems to a businessman the obvious retaliation against unfair competition, and to a common-sensical altruist the best way of ensuring that higher wages are paid in the future; a study of economics, on the other hand, shows that the whole basis of international trade and the gains which can be derived from it lie in the diverse qualities and quantities of labour, capital, and natural resources with which different countries are endowed. Not to buy from poor countries merely adds to their problems and forces the wage level still lower.

However, the purpose here is not to eulogize economics. There is a danger that those who have a little economic knowledge (and, sometimes, those who have quite a lot) may slip into thinking of economic considerations as paramount. Although economics is undoubtedly a useful study, it is important to be clear about the limitations of economic analysis.

The first of these arises from the fact that our understanding of economic systems remains very far from complete. As we pointed out in Part III, for example, much of the policy problem of how to achieve simultaneously full employment, stability of prices and balances of payments, and economic growth stems from the fact that we do not really know what the precise relationship is between the processes necessary for achieving these different goals. Partly, it must be admitted, this is because economists sometimes get spellbound by the intricate elegance of their theories and forget that their main function is to produce hypotheses which can be tested empirically. Thus, although there are plenty of theories about how economic growth is affected by full employment and different degrees of unemployment, we still do not *know*.

A second possible shortcoming of economics is one which is very apparent to non-economists – the inability of economic experts to agree and give unequivocal answers to straightforward questions. Ask any five economists how we should deal with a balance of payments deficit, and you will get five different answers – at least. That this is not wholly due to technical differences of opinion is shown by the fact that if you ask *one* economist the same question, you will still probably get five answers – at least. In fact, economists agree more often than is popularly supposed and this apparent indecisiveness is because most economic problems have *alternative* policy solutions between which choice cannot be made on purely economic grounds.

After all, if you go to the A.A. and ask them for a route from London to Manchester, you will not complain if they offer a selection. Nor, if you then demand to know which is the *best* route, will you be surprised when they hesitate – because, of course, the best route depends on what you have in mind. Are you interested in speed, avoiding the traffic, seeing the country-side, or what? Similarly, the economist can seem singularly un-helpful when in fact he is just trying to be scientifically objective. There is much that he can legitimately say about the conse-quences and relative efficacy of import controls, altering the exchange rate, or domestic deflation as alternative techniques for dealing with balance of payments problems. What he *cannot* say (at least as a conclusion of his economic analysis – although he may personally have strong views on the matter) is which of them is *right*. Which policy *ought* to be adopted is something which cannot be decided just by reference to facts. The decision has to be taken within the framework of our system of political and moral values.

The scope of the economist is rather similar to that of a top-ranking civil servant. In theory at least, the Minister at the head of a government department lays down the broad principles according to which policy matters are to be decided. It is then up to his Permanent Secretary and staff to show him *how* those principles can be translated into detailed action and what will be the consequences of doing so. Likewise, the economist, given the ends which it is hoped to achieve, can offer advice about whether and how it is possible to do so. In practice, of course, the fact that civil servants and economists are also human beings, with perhaps strong political and moral principles of their own, means that their advice is not always completely objective; and their technical expertise may make them particularly influential in modifying generally accepted value premises. Economic analysis, by illuminating the implications of value principles (and sometimes, perhaps, even showing their inconsistency), may make us change our minds about what ought to be done. But it is important to see that conclusions about what we *should* do cannot be derived purely from the technical analysis which it is the function of economics to provide.

However, much economic jargon has highly persuasive overtones which can confuse us into thinking that economic considerations are all-important. Quite technical conclusions of economic analysis can sound very like demands for action. An economist may look at the provision of education and public health services primarily as ways in which the efficiency of the working force may be improved. But, if he manages to show that the economic benefits from any given level of expenditure on these things are less than the economic costs incurred, this does not tell us that we should therefore cut back spending on such services. We may also think of education and a high standard of public health as good in themselves – justified whether or not they *pay* in terms of increased output.

Thus, 'uneconomic', as we have noted on a number of occasions, has come to have a condemnatory connotation. But this is justified only if we are *solely* concerned with getting maximum output from the limited resources at our disposal. If we are also interested in fairness, humanity, security, and so on, then to distinguish between economic and uneconomic measures and conditions becomes the starting-point rather than the be-all-and-end-all of policy decisions.

Conclusion

The State and the Economy

In every chapter of this book we have had occasion to refer to the role of the State. Whether we have been talking of the financial system, international trade, industry, agriculture, retailing, or labour there has been something to say about the part played by the authorities. The most direct form of intervention is, of course, when the government itself acts as producer, buyer, or seller of goods and services – as in the nationalized industries or in the provision of social services. Secondly, the State can introduce specific measures designed to control particular sectors of the economy – for example, restrictive practices legislation or agricultural price guarantees. And thirdly, the authorities may aim, by monetary, fiscal, and direct controls, to exercise a *general* regulation of the economy along the lines which we discussed in Part III.

A traditional difference between political parties in this country has been in their conceptions of how to make the economic system function most effectively. One party has emphasized the need for vigorously competitive free enterprise while the other has stressed the importance of the role of a large public sector. What I hope may have emerged in the course of our analysis is the extent to which these contrasting attitudes have become blurred and modified by our increased understanding of economic mechanisms, and, even more, by our acceptance of certain goals. Together, these add up to the need for a much higher *minimum* of State economic activity than many people seem to realize.

In the first place, if the virtue of free enterprise is that it instils a competitive spirit into the economy, then we have to accept that the necessary framework is unlikely, in an advanced economy, to be created by a policy of *laissez-faire*. Private enterprise cannot nowadays be equated with competition, because, as Sir Robert Shone has recently put it, 'the players in the economic game are powerful enough to adjust the goal-posts or move the touch-line.' The trouble with competition is that those who compete aim ultimately at eliminating competition. The businesses which are most competitive in the first place may manage to kill competition by forcing their rivals to the wall, absorbing them, or reducing them to a number at which collusion becomes

244

feasible. Competition thus contains the seeds of its own destruction. Maintenance of competition requires that the State intervenes – either to ensure that the players play according to the competitive rules or to provide a competitive stimulus itself.

On top of this, as Keynes foresaw in 1936, the

central controls necessary to ensure full employment will, of course, involve a large extension of the traditional functions of government.

We all more or less agree now that those who are able and willing to work should be given the opportunity of doing so. It is doubtful, however, whether the extent to which this implies deliberate government manipulation of the economy is commonly appreciated. With regard to full employment, we have shown that there is no reason at all to expect an unregulated economy to deliver the goods. If spending and production plans are to add up to compatible totals, action from the authorities is essential – either to influence the private sector of the economy in the right directions or to make good its deficiencies by compensatory policies. Once we will the end of the full employment (and particularly when we also stipulate stability of prices and stability in the balance of payments) then we also have to will the means – a system of fiscal, monetary, and sometimes direct controls of the economy by the State.

There is a third field in which government participation in the economy has increased, is increasing, and is likely to continue to increase. Governments now accept more and more responsibility for providing not just a social infra-structure but a super-structure as well. This is the sort of distinction which we drew in the first chapter. Government expenditure before the war and much of the increase which took place just after the war was devoted to providing services which, it was felt, many people would be insufficiently responsible or too poor or inadequately educated to provide for themselves. Putting aside enough each week to meet the costs of medical treatment or schooling, for example, were matters which it was decided could not safely be left to private foresight. In more recent years, however, a large part of the resources which have been shifted from the private to the public sector have been used to serve a rather different purpose. Both political parties are today committed to rapidly

Conclusion

rising expenditure programmes designed radically to improve and extend a variety of social amenities. Public investment is to be poured into the construction of roads, the replanning of towns and cities, the building of new hospitals, and the provision of educational and cultural facilities – all on a much larger scale than in the past. The important thing to note here is that relatively little of this spending of public money is justified in terms of relieving immediate distress. It is mostly, as we expressed it earlier, less an antidote to poverty than a concomitant of affluence. It is aimed at avoiding the imbalance of 'private affluence and public squalor' – of people becoming more and more materially opulent in a social environment remaining narrow, uncongenial, and overcongested – an imbalance which arises because of the failure of a private enterprise system to consider social as well as private costs and benefits, and to take into account non-economic ends.

Altogether then, demands for a genuinely competitive framework for economic activity, for economic stability, and for the provision of a wide range of services and facilities which might be neglected by commercial enterprise add up to a substantial sphere in which State intervention is required. The need for government economic activity stems from the fact that we have accepted certain goals which economic analysis helps to suggest are unlikely to be attained in an unregulated economy. Grumbling about the extent to which the State 'interferes' in our everyday lives therefore only makes sense if we think that the ends of economic policy – freedom of consumer choice, full employment, reasonable stability of prices, achievement of a 'fair' distribution of income, and so on – are not worth the price which has to be paid in terms of restraints on individual liberty to do precisely what we please regardless of the social consequences. If, on the other hand, these ends of social policy are fairly generally accepted, then much of the *laissez-faire* versus State intervention controversy is a relic of the past with no real place in the political arena of today.

However, the future expansion of public spending which is envisaged by both political parties implies that the State should secure control over a much larger volume of resources than it does now. And both intend that this should be accomplished not by shifting existing wealth from the private to the public sector but by increasing total national wealth and earmarking a part of the growth increment for public use. In this respect, the old controversy remains very much a live issue. Can growth, at a fast and sustained enough rate to enable us to get things done, be achieved by just encouragement, stimulation, and inducements from the authorities, or does it require a much more radical extension of the part played by government in the economy? And if it turns out to be the case that even more management of the economy is the only way of ensuring rapid economic development how much are we prepared to accept in order to enjoy its fruits? These are issues which we considered in Chapter 10, and we concluded that economists do not have any clear-cut advice to offer on how to get the economy moving steadily on an upward path. When it comes to the political aspects of the issue they are, of course, even less qualified to adjudicate.

BIBLIOGRAPHICAL NOTE

THESE brief suggestions for further reading only include books and pamphlets which can be obtained fairly easily and which are likely to interest people without formal training in economics.

Covering similar ground to the present book but with a rather different approach is Gertrude Williams's *The Economics of Everyday Life* (Penguin Books, 2nd edn 1964) which has now been thoroughly revised to take into account recent changes in the economy. Other general analyses in the Pelican series are *The Stagnant Society* by Michael Shanks (Penguin Books, 1961) and Andrew Shonfield's *British Economic Policy Since the War* (Penguin Books, 2nd edn 1959); Shanks suggests that the performance of the economy has been crucially limited by outdated social attitudes while Shonfield stresses overcommitment in the international sphere as the main factor retarding the domestic rate of growth. Other diagnoses are put forward in *Sunshades in October* by N. Macrae (Allen & Unwin, 1963), *The British Economy* by Sir Roy Harrod (McGraw-Hill, 1963), and *The Treasury under the Tories 1951–1964* by Samuel Brittan (Secker & Warburg and Penguin Books, 1964); all of these are intended for the general reader as well as economists.

One of the best short accounts of monetary economics is A. C. L. Day's *The Economics of Money* (Home University Library, Oxford University Press, 1959); also available now is a new edition of Paul Einzig's *How Money is Managed* (Penguin Books, 1954; 2nd edn published under the title *Monetary Policy: Ends and Means*, 1964). *The City* by Paul Ferris (Gollancz, 1960; Penguin Books, 1962) is a thoroughly entertaining description of the financial Establishment, while those with a taste for the technical details of the monetary system might graduate to *The British Banking Mechanism* by W. Manning Dacey (Hutchinson, rev. edn 1958) or even the *Radcliffe Report* itself. On international monetary mechanisms, see B. Tew's *International Monetary Cooperation 1945–60* (Hutchinson, rev. edn 1960) and *Gold and the Dollar Crisis* by R. Triffin (Yale: Oxford University Press, 1960). Professor Triffin is one of the leading proponents of international monetary reform; his irreverent and often hilarious style makes his book readable by the non-specialist.

British Industry by J. H. Dunning and C. J. Thomas (Hutchinson, 1960) is comprehensive, concise and easily understood; it is particularly good on the impact of successive technological revolutions. The problems of nationalized industries are treated, with a nice balance between economic and non-economic considerations, in the Fabian Society symposium *The Lessons of Public Enterprise* (edited by Michael Shanks, Cape, 1963) and in an excellent short introduction by Leonard Tivey, *Nationalisation in British Industry* (Jonathan Cape, 1966). *The Economics of Subsidising Agriculture* by Gavin McCrone (Allen & Unwin, 1962) exposes the arguments for supporting farmers to critical economic analysis, while those interested in labour economics could look at E. Wigham's *What's Wrong with the Unions?* (Penguin Books, 1961) and *The Social Foundations of Wage Policy* by Barbara Wootton (Allen & Unwin, 1963). Trends and current issues in retailing are reviewed in *Competition for Consumers* by Christina Fulop (published for the I.E.A. by André Deutsch, 1964); the two sides of the resale price maintenance case are put by B. S. Yamey, *Resale Price Maintenance and Shoppers' Choice* (Barrie & Rockcliff, 1960) and *Fair Trade* by P. W. S. Andrews and F. A. Friday (Macmillan, 1960).

Some books on general economic policy have already been mentioned. Those who want a fuller understanding of what determines the level of employment and income in an economy should refer to Joan Robinson's *Introduction to the Theory of Employment* (Macmillan, 1937). On general economic theory, *Introduction to the World Economy* by A. J. Brown (Allen & Unwin, 1959) and *The Essentials of Economics* by D. C. Hague and A. W. Stonier (Longmans, 1955) are two of the introductory textbooks which the general reader will not find indigestible.

INDEX

251

Index

Index